APPROACHING THE HOLOCAUST

Parkes-Wiener Series on Jewish Studies

Series Editors: David Cesarani and Tony Kushner
ISSN 1368-5449

The field of Jewish Studies is one of the youngest, but fastest-growing and most exciting areas of scholarship in the academic world today. Named after James Parkes and Alfred Wiener, this series aims to publish new research in the field and student materials for use in the seminar room, to disseminate the latest work of established scholars and to re-issue classic studies that are currently out of print.

The selection of publications reflects the international character and diversity of Jewish Studies; it ranges over Jewish history from Abraham to modern Zionism, and Jewish culture from Moses to post-modernism. The series also reflects the inter-disciplinary approach inherent in Jewish Studies and at the cutting edge of contemporary scholarship, and provides an outlet for innovative work on the interface between Judaism and ethnicity, popular culture, gender, class, space and memory.

Other Books in the Series

Holocaust Literature: Schulz, Levi, Spiegelman and the Memory of the Offence
Gillian Banner

Remembering Cable Street: Fascism and Anti-Fascism in British Society
Edited by Tony Kushner and Nadia Valman

Sir Sidney Hamburger and Manchester Jewry: Religion, City and Community
Bill Williams

Anglo-Jewry in Changing Times: Studies in Diversity 1840–1914
Israel Finestein

Double Jeopardy: Gender and the Holocaust
Judith Tydor Baumel

Cultures of Ambivalence and Contempt: Studies in Jewish-Non-Jewish Relations
Edited by Siân Jones, Tony Kushner and Sarah Pearce

Alfred Wiener and the Making of the Wiener Library
Ben Barkow

The Berlin Haskalah and German Religious Thought: Orphans of Knowledge
David Sorkin

Myths in Israeli Culture: Captives of a Dream
Nurith Gertz

The Jewish Immigrant in England 1870–1914, Third Edition
Lloyd P. Gartner

State and Society in Roman Galilee, A.D. 132–212, Second Edition
Martin Goodman

Disraeli's Jewishness
Edited by Todd M. Endelman

Claude Montefiore: His Life and Thought
Daniel R. Langton

APPROACHING THE HOLOCAUST

Texts and Contexts

ROBERT ROZETT
Yad Vashem, Jerusalem

VALLENTINE MITCHELL
LONDON • PORTLAND, OR

First published in 2005 in Great Britain by
VALLENTINE MITCHELL & CO. LTD
Suite 314, Premier House,
112–114 Station Road, Edgware, Middlesex HA8 7BJ, UK

and in the United States of America by
VALLENTINE MITCHELL
c/o ISBS,
920 NE 58th Avenue, Suite 300, Portland, OR 97213-3786, USA

www.vmbooks.com

British Library Cataloguing in Publication Data
have been applied for

Library of Congress Cataloging in Publication Data
have been applied for

ISBN 0 85303 581 4 (cloth)
ISBN 0 85303 582 2 (paper)

Printed in Great Britain by
MPG Books Ltd, Bodmin, Cornwall

Dedicated to my grandmother Irma Rozett, née Marosi. She survived Auschwitz, Trautenau and Bergen-Belsen, to reach America after the war and help raise me.
May her memory be blessed.

Contents

Acknowledgements   ix

Introduction   1

1. Towards a Critical Reading of Books and Articles
on the Holocaust   11

2. The Place of the Holocaust in Popular Histories
of the Twentieth Century   31

3. Historical Atlases and the Holocaust   57

4. Reflections on Jewish Leadership during
the Holocaust   71

5. Learning from Personal Accounts of the Holocaust   93

6. Using and Abusing History: The Holocaust,
the Press and the Middle East   125

7. The Inscription: A Case Study in Historical
Evidence, Memory and Commemoration   159

Select Bibliography   172

Index   177

Acknowledgements

There are many people who contributed to the writing of this book of essays. Without support from the people I work with at Yad Vashem, this book never would have seen the light of day. Avner Shalev, Chairman of the Directorate, and Yishai Amrami, Director-General, have encouraged me to engage in research and writing. The staff of the Yad Vashem Library have shown much forbearance toward their boss, who at times has been more preoccupied with scholarship than with the running of the library. In particular I owe thanks to the manager of the library offices, Rachel Cohen, who has done wonders in creating space for me to write. The staff of the library-archive reading room, headed by Nadia Kahan, have been helpful in ways to great to enumerate. My good friends Dr David Silberklang, editor of *Yad Vashem Studies*, and Dr Yaacov Lozowick, Director of the Archive, have always been reliable sounding boards for my ideas. In particular, the essay about historical atlases benefited greatly from the excellent editorial skills of Dr Silberklang and his staff. Professor Dan Michman, Chief Historian at Yad Vashem, provided essential help deciphering the Hebrew abbreviations in the cryptic inscription that lies at the core of the essay exploring it. The impetus for clarifying the inscription's meaning and context came from our spokesperson Iris Rosenberg. Many of the ideas that find expression in this book first germinated under the guidance of Professors Yehuda Bauer and Israel Gutman, my teachers and colleagues. While lecturing at the International School for Holocaust Studies these ideas were polished, and I thank the school's staff for providing me with such opportunities.

The essay about personal accounts grew out of a request by the managing editors of *Studies in Contemporary Jewry*, Laurie Fialkoff and Hannah Levinsky-Koevary, to review a medium sized pile of Holocaust memoirs. Their professionalism and good humor are a boon to all who write for them.

My close friend Professor David Cesarani deserves special thanks. When I first told him I hoped to publish a book of essays, he encouraged me heartily. Through him I reached Frank Cass and Vallentine Mitchell. Both Sally Green and Sian Mills, my editors at Vallentine Mitchell, undoubtedly improved the manuscript significantly. I am deeply indebted to Frank Cass for publishing the book.

Finally, without the support and love of my wife and children, I would not have the wherewithal to do any writing at all.

I would like to remind my readers that the criticism of various sources found in this volume is just that, criticism of the sources. It is not meant to be a criticism of the person behind the sources; if I have overstepped the bounds of such criticism, I ask pardon from those I have offended. Of course all the errors found in the following pages are mine alone.

Robert Rozett
Jerusalem, 1 September 2004

Introduction

In the early twenty-first century discussion about the Holocaust continues to be widespread in venues ranging from universities to the media, to courts of law. One would think that when the word 'Holocaust' is uttered, its meaning would be clear to both the speaker and the listener. But if one follows how the word is used, it soon becomes apparent that not everybody means the same thing when they talk about the Holocaust. One of the best illustrations of this is the frequent use of two very different figures for the number of victims of the Holocaust: six million and 11 million. Those who use the former figure are talking about murdered Jews, whereas those who use the latter include many other victims of the Nazi regime. In order to understand according to which definition, or set of definitions, the Holocaust is being discussed, one must clarify the following basic questions:

- What events come under the heading 'Holocaust'?
- What is the time frame in which the Holocaust occurred?
- Who is a victim of the Holocaust?
- Who is a Holocaust survivor?

Clearly the Nazi regime and its partners perpetrated numerous crimes that fall under the rubric of crimes against humanity, and the victims of these crimes belong to many and sometimes intersecting groups. In addition to the Jews, there were the Romany (often referred to by the derogatory term 'gypsies'), Slavs (people who lived in countries in which Slavic languages are spoken), Soviet prisoners of war, communists, Jehovah's Witnesses and homosexuals. In fact, the first group murdered by the Nazis in a systematic way were citizens of the Third Reich, considered Aryans by Nazi racial standards. These unfortunates, although of the 'right racial stuff' according to Nazi ideas, suffered from mental or physical disabilities, or chronic illness. So the Nazis murdered them as 'life unworthy of life'. Should all of victims of Nazism, some designated as inferior because of the supposed racial characteristics, others victimized because of their behaviour and yet others because of their physical disabilities, be put under one heading – the Holocaust?

During the Second World War, it was planned that all Jews who fell into the hands of the Nazis and those countries formally allied with Nazi Germany would eventually be murdered. The Nazi leadership adopted this sweeping policy, which came to be known as 'the Final Solution', most probably in autumn 1941, several months after the mass systematic murder of Jews in the newly occupied areas of the Soviet Union had begun.[1]

The Romany experience under the Nazis most closely parallels that of the Jews. The testimonies of Romany survivors often sound nearly identical to those of Jewish survivors. Yet, despite the experiences of the individual victims, one must recognize that Nazi policies toward the Romanies and the Jews differed on two very central points. First, the Romanies were victimized not because they were considered a racial problem, as were the Jews; but because they were considered a social problem. Second, and more significant, the Nazis never planned to kill every single member of the Romany people. The Nazis sought to murder those Romanies they considered most dangerous, as was the case with most of the other groups they decimated. In other words, the Nazis and their cohorts subjected the Romanies to selected mass murder. For example, in the Soviet territories taken by the Germans, wandering tribes of Romanies were killed in a mass and systematic fashion, and those who had settled down were not. In the Reich itself, however, those who lived the traditional nomadic lifestyle were left alone by and large, and those who had settled down generally were persecuted. None of this, of course, detracts from the suffering of the Romanies as individuals or as a people. Nor does it detract from the responsibility of the Nazis for their crimes against the Romanies.

The so-called Slavs were treated in different ways by the Nazi regime. Some Slavs, such as the Croatians, Slovaks and some Ukrainian nationalists, were partners of the Nazis. Others, such as the Poles, were frequently treated ruthlessly. According to *Generalplan Ost*, one of the main documents written by Nazi racial engineers about their plans for the residents of eastern Europe, essentially three things were to be done to the Slavs. Those who constituted a threat to the Nazis, meaning they were leaders of resistance or potential leaders of resistance, were to be murdered. This included many intellectuals, politicians and priests. Those children who were considered to have Nordic-Aryan looks – that is, who were blond and blue-eyed – were to be integrated into the German population. The rest of the Slavs were to be used as a slave-like workforce.[2] Soviet prisoners of war, many of whom were Slavs and all of whom had fought for the Soviet government – detested above all others by the Nazis – were also treated ruthlessly. Most were imprisoned in what can only be described as murderous conditions in camps that intentionally lacked the most basic facilities to preserve life, such as adequate food, water, shelter, hygiene and medical care. Most prisoners succumbed to these miserable conditions. However, some Soviet prisoners of war, those whom the Nazis regarded as anti-communists, were allowed to escape these camps by joining German military formations.[3]

Jehovah's Witnesses and homosexuals were also persecuted by the Nazi regime and were often imprisoned in concentration camps, as were other 'social dissidents' such as jazz lovers.[4] Many perished in Nazi camps, but there was no policy of outright murder of members of these groups. Selective mass murder was also practised against people the Nazis considered to be of their own racial stock, the Nordic Aryans. These were the mentally retarded, the physically disabled and the chronically ill, who were killed in what came to be known euphemistically as the Euthanasia Programme, or, in the Nazi code of the time, the T4 operation (named after the head offices of the Euthanasia Programme in the Reich Chancellery on Tiergartenstrasse 4). Beginning in autumn 1939, this continued officially until late summer 1941, when, owing to public outcry, the killings were halted. Even after the official end of the operation, similar killings continued to take place in the areas of Europe occupied by the Nazis. It is estimated that some 200,000 people were murdered as part of the T4 operation.[5] With the advent of the Final Solution, the Nazi policy toward the Jews became one of indiscriminate murder of all Jews simply because they were Jews by the Nazi definition. It is clear that the Nazis' treatment of Jews differed significantly from their policies toward other groups. Because of this difference, to my mind it makes sense to provide a specific term for the Nazi attempt to murder all the Jews. The word 'Holocaust', first used in this very particular context, remains the most common term for denoting the Nazi attempt to annihilate the Jews.[6]

If we accept that the word 'Holocaust' denotes the Nazi attempt to murder the Jews that fell under their and their partners' control, some basic issues of definition still remain unresolved. Perhaps chief among them is: what is the time frame of the Holocaust? Every historical event has antecedents and repercussions, which is to say that no event just arrives on the scene out of nowhere, without roots in prior events and without continuing to cause after–effects. For this reason it is not always a simple matter to set the boundaries of a given chapter in history. Nevertheless, it is easier to set the boundaries of some events than of others.

It is generally accepted that the Second World War began on 1 September 1939 with the German invasion of Poland. Nevertheless, it could be argued that this date is not accurate. Perhaps the war became a world war only after Britain and France declared war on Germany on 3 September 1939? Perhaps it became a world war only after the

Germans invaded western Europe in spring 1940, or after the German invasion of the Soviet Union in June 1941, or with the Japanese attack on Pearl Harbor in December 1941? Perhaps it began when the Japanese invaded Manchuria in 1931–32?

The end of the Second World War in Europe is generally celebrated on 8 May, VE Day. But one could argue that the war ended on 7 May the day the Germans actually surrendered, or on 9 May because when the surrender came into effect, it was already 9 May in eastern Europe.[7] Despite this fuzziness at the margins, it is generally acknowledged that the Second World War was fought in Europe between September 1939 and May 1945, and ended in the Pacific in August 1945. Other events such as the Holocaust, however, are not as easily placed within a clear time frame.

It could be argued that the Holocaust itself began with the advent of the Final Solution. Until recently, because of the lack of documentation, it was nearly impossible to date when the Nazi leadership decided to extend the murder to all the Jews. However, with the discovery of Heinrich Himmler's appointments diary in archives in the former Soviet Union and other relevant documents, we now know that autumn 1941 was a pivotal date. We know that by December Hitler had clearly decided on including all Jews under Nazi control in the Final Solution. At that time he announced to his intimate circle that the murder of the Jews, which had begun with the invasion of the Soviet Union in June, would be extended to include the last group of Jews that up to that point had not yet been slated for murder – those in the Reich itself.[8] So it could be argued that the Holocaust began in autumn 1941.

It could just as reasonably be argued, however, that it began with the advent of the systematic mass murder of Jews by the special units of the SS, the *Einsatzgruppen*, other police and military formations and local civilians in the Soviet Union. This wave of murder, first of Jewish men and soon thereafter of women and children, began with the invasion of 22 June 1941. But the Jews of the newly conquered areas of the Soviet Union were not the first to be subjected to Nazi mass murder.

Albeit it on a smaller scale, from the moment the Germans entered Poland in September 1939, thousands of Jews were murdered simply because they were Jews. Dieter Pohl has written that despite the lack of evidence of an order from Berlin, some 7,000 Polish Jews were killed in Poland during the last quarter of 1939, which indicates the crossing of the threshold from persecution to murder, even if the murder was yet to be systematic.[9] The establishment of ghettos, starting in the same autumn of 1939, also led to Jews being placed in a situation that led to many deaths. We know from the work of the *Oneg Shabbat* underground, which was dedicated to documenting events in the Warsaw Ghetto, that about 20 per cent of the over 440,000 ghetto inhabitants died from the terrible living conditions before they were deported from there to the extermination camps. We know that the very first German policy regarding the ghettos was to leave them alone, so Jews would starve to death. This only changed when the fear of epidemics led to a policy for a while of self-sustaining ghettos.[10] So it would also be plausible to date the start of the Holocaust with the German invasion of Poland in autumn 1939, since from that point onward masses of Jews died or were murdered outright as a result of Nazi policies, and simply for the reason that they were Jews.

Some of the literature on the subject considers the pogrom against the Jews of Greater Germany, *Kristallnacht*, to be the start of the Holocaust. The supporters of this viewpoint argue that the night of 9–10 November 1938 was a watershed because it was when Jews were first arrested in large numbers simply because they were Jews. They were incarcerated in concentration camps and scores were killed.[11]

Of course the Holocaust happened, at all, because the Nazis came to power. This was the most basic condition for the evolving persecution of the Jews, which eventually became murderous, during the years that Hitler was in power. So it could also be argued that one must really begin the period of the Holocaust with the Nazi ascent to power in January 1933.

In some ways it seems merely an academic exercise to try clearly to delineate when the Holocaust began. But the setting of a more rigorous time frame is important for other issues. One cannot really discuss who are the victims of the Holocaust without determining when it began. Of course, as has been already touched upon, this is not the only issue involved in trying to determine who is or is not a victim of the Holocaust. Let us examine several scenarios about how Jews met their deaths during the period in which the Nazis were in power, in order to see more clearly the complexity of the issue of who is a victim of the Holocaust.

No one but a denier of the Holocaust would argue with the idea that Jews who were murdered by the *Einsatzgruppen* and their partners in the Soviet Union were victims of the Holocaust. Nor would they dispute that Jews who were murdered in one of the six extermination camps perished in the Holocaust. But how should we consider a Jew who was deported to a slave-labour camp from one of the Polish ghettos in 1940, before the advent of systematic mass murder or the Final Solution, and was killed by a savage guard or perished because of the combination of back-breaking labour, poor nutrition and brutal treatment? Is this person a victim of the Holocaust? If we say the Holocaust began with the advent of systematic mass murder, then the answer would be no. But if we consider the start of the Holocaust to be the day the Nazis invaded Poland or the outbreak of the *Kristallnacht* pogrom, the answer could be yes.

What about a Jew who died from malnutrition and disease in the Warsaw ghetto before the deportations to the extermination camps? Is he or she a victim of the Holocaust? In this instance, as in the case of the forced labourer mentioned above, the person died because of Nazi anti-Jewish policies and could be considered a victim of the Holocaust.

What about a Jew who fled from Nazi-occupied Poland to the Soviet sector in autumn 1939, and from there fled the advancing German forces in summer 1941 into the Soviet interior, where he died of disease? Is that person a victim of the Holocaust or a victim of unfortunate circumstances in the wartime Soviet state? How do we regard a Jew who fled from the Nazis to Soviet territory, was arrested by the NKVD and put in a gulag and died there? Is this person a victim of the Holocaust or a victim of Stalinism, which was more directly responsible for her death?

Now let us turn to some scenarios from pre-war Germany. How should we consider a Jewish student, active in communist circles, who was arrested by the Nazis during the first weeks of their regime and taken to a Gestapo cellar where he was shot? One could argue that here the victim suffered his fate less because he was a Jew and more because of his political affiliation with the hated communists. Moreover, he died well before the Nazis had adopted a policy of brutal, deadly treatment of Jews. But what about the scores of Jews who were killed during the violent outburst on 9 November, *Kristallnacht*? They died in a riot aimed specifically against the Jews, and they died as a result of the racially motivated Nazi policy of persecution of Jews. Even though in November 1938 a policy of systematic mass murder of Jews had not been adopted or even seriously discussed, it could be argued that those who died on *Kristallnacht* or in the concentration camps, where they were imprisoned during the riot, were among the first victims of the Holocaust.[12]

The death of Jews during the Nazi period was not always the result of deeds performed by the Germans. About 100,000 Jewish men were drafted into slave-labour units attached to the Hungarian army, and the majority of them were sent to the front. Tens of thousands of these men never returned home. Some were killed or driven to their deaths by their Jew-hating Hungarian officers. Others fell in the course of the fighting. Still others surrendered to the Soviet forces, hoping to be allowed to fight with them against the Nazis and their partners. Instead, they became Soviet prisoners of war, and some died in the Soviet prisoner-of-war camps. Are the Hungarian forced labourers who were killed in the course of fighting or who died as prisoners of war victims of the Holocaust? On the one hand, they were not direct victims of the Nazi policy of murder or the explicit actions of Germans. On the other hand, they found themselves in the situation they were in because Hungary, an ally of Germany, adopted many aspects of Nazi racial ideology and discrimination, and it was this basic circumstance that ultimately led to their deaths.[13]

Another question related to the issue of who is a victim of the Holocaust is the very complicated, delicate and politically charged question of who is considered a Jew. There are of course many answers to this question, depending primarily on one's religious, political or ideological orientation. Orthodox Jewish religious law is very clear on the issue. A Jew is either the child of a Jewish mother, or one who has been converted to Judaism in accordance to a prescribed programme of study and ritual. Reform Jews say that anyone who has a Jewish parent or has converted according to their procedures is a Jew. The Nazis, of course, had their own definition (which was adhered to more or less by their partners) saying that a person with at least three Jewish grandparents (meaning they had belonged to the Jewish community) was a full Jew, and those with one or two grandparents were considered part-Jews. It could and did happen that a person born into a Christian family, who did not consider himself a Jew, was persecuted by the Nazis or their partners as a full or part-Jew, and was murdered by them because they considered him a Jew. The problem here is especially difficult for statistical analysis of the Holocaust. Most of the pre-war statistics about the Jewish population concern those people who considered themselves Jews and not people who were Jewish by the Nazi racial definition. In some places (such as Hungary in 1941) there are also statistics that relate to a racial definition. But it is very possible that people murdered by the Nazis as Jews do not show up in the statistical studies, because they are not included in the pre-Holocaust statistics.

These questions of definition not only bear upon issues about victims of the Holocaust, but are also important for discussion about survivors of the Holocaust. It is clear that a Jew who managed to survive one of the extermination camps, even if he was only in it for a short time before being transferred to a labour camp, may be said to have survived the Holocaust. This is equally true for the few individuals who were actually shot at by the Nazis and their partners in the mass murder drives in eastern Europe, but somehow were not killed and crawled out of the bloody death pits. It would also be hard to argue that someone who managed to hide during these murder *Aktionen*, hid at the time when Jews were being deported to the extermination camps or managed to flee on the verge of a murder or deportation *Aktion* should not be called a Holocaust survivor; even if they never actually witnessed the killings or saw the inside of a Nazi extermination camp. But what about a Jew who was never sent to an extermination camp, but 'only' to a labour camp? Is such a person a Holocaust survivor? Given the brutal, murderous conditions in these camps, with their usually high death rates, and given the fact that Jews found themselves in these camps almost always simply because they were Jews and moreover, were usually accorded the worst treatment, those who survived could most certainly be said to have survived the Holocaust.

But what about Jews who fled Germany after the Nazis gained power and before the violence of *Kristallnacht*? Are they Holocaust survivors? Their lives were almost never (or only very rarely) in immediate danger, although they became subject to increasingly painful discrimination. Certainly if they had not left Germany their fate would have been that of the Jews from the rest of Europe who came under Nazi influence during the war years, and their chances of survival would have been slim. Certainly, many German Jews who managed to flee Hitler's Germany as long as it was possible, until autumn 1941, today consider themselves Holocaust survivors. But in some of the writing about the Holocaust, only those who actually experienced the camps are considered Holocaust survivors.

A similar question may be asked about a Jew who managed to remain one step ahead of the Nazis. Several hundred thousand Polish Jews fled to Soviet territory in autumn 1939 and then to the Soviet interior in summer 1941, some of them never experiencing even one day under the Nazi regime. Are they Holocaust survivors?

These issues of definition have ramifications beyond those of purely academic discussion. They can, and already have, influenced issues of compensation. They also are of importance to institutions that gather documentation and build libraries, since they may influence the boundaries of such collections. They have ramifications for creating educational material, for teaching the subject in schools and on the creation of museum exhibits.

The essays in this book, like the discussion just presented, are aimed at making us think more critically about the Holocaust in particular, and history in general. This is often the overt or underlying theme of the lectures I frequently give at Yad Vashem, the Holocaust Martyrs' and Heroes' Remembrance Authority in Jerusalem. So it should come as no surprise to the reader that some of the essays in this collection began their lives as lectures, whereas others became part of my repertoire of lectures after they were written down. Most of the essays in this collection are being published here for the first time. But the essay on historical atlases was originally published in *Yad Vashem Studies*, and the essay on first-hand accounts of the Holocaust and their use by historians was published in a shorter form in *Studies in Contemporary Jewry*.

The essay entitled 'Towards a Critical Reading of Books and Articles on the Holocaust' is meant to help readers understand salient issues about which they should be aware when reading about the Holocaust. It is intended to help readers put out their antennae and think critically as they go along. The essays about historical atlases, personal accounts of the Holocaust, the place of the Holocaust in one-volume histories of the twentieth century and the use of the Holocaust and its terms of reference in the press regarding the Israeli–Palestinian conflict all delve deeper into issues of critical reading, our understanding of published texts that concern the Holocaust and how we use the Holocaust.

The remaining two essays are somewhat different in focus. 'The Inscription' offers a case study of the detective work involved in trying to interpret a cryptic note concerning an event from the Holocaust and place it in its historical context. The essay also discusses texts, especially the problems inherent in some of the published sources we rely upon for our understanding of events. The essay on Jewish leadership does not deal with historical sources, but seeks to show the critical role of context for understanding important issues in history. Even before approaching the thorny subject of the behaviour of Jewish leaders in the Holocaust, one must be aware of numerous factors that affected those leaders and their decisions.

Sometimes, as students of history, we are able to uncover a complete or a nearly complete picture of events – a picture that we also deem to be reliable. Sometimes we have only sundry fragments with which to try to compose a coherent picture. At times, because of the nature of events and the distance between them and ourselves – either the distance of time or the psychological distance created by our inability to put ourselves in the place of the protagonists, or both – we are like a person trying to assemble and interpret a jigsaw puzzle with many missing parts in a dense fog. This obscurity is often the reality with which we must contend when studying the Holocaust.

It is often easier and more comforting to give in to the problem of obscurity, and simply view history in black and white without its vibrant colours. But like those events to which we are witness, past events also occurred in full colour. Approaching history in all of its hues, despite the often incomplete and out-of-focus picture we are able to construct, demands that we use our faculties to the fullest. We must struggle with our inclination to generalize, and try to remain aware of the complexity of human behaviour – to the colour around us. To my mind, this is the only way to approach history, especially the history of a seminal and multifaceted event like the Holocaust, which continues to touch us all.

NOTES

1. For an excellent summary of the development of the Final Solution see C. R. Browning, *Nazi Policy, Jewish Workers, German Killers* (Cambridge: Cambridge University Press, 2000).
2. Y. Bauer, 'Jews, Gypsies and Slavs: Policies of the Third Reich', *Unesco Yearbook of Peace and Conflict Studies 1985: The Second World War* (New York: Greenwood Press, 1987), pp. 73–99.
3. For a fuller discussion of the Nazi treatment of Soviet prisoners of war see C. Streit, *Keine Kameraden: Die Wehrmacht und die Sowjetischen Kriegsgefangenen 1941–1945* (Stuttgart: Deutsche Verlags-Anstalt, 1978).
4. For a fascinating discussion of jazz in the Third Reich see M. Kater, *Different Drummers, Jazz in the Culture of Nazi Germany* (New York: Oxford University Press, 1992), pp. 157–62
5. I. Gutman (ed.), *The Encyclopedia of the Holocaust* (New York: Macmillan, 1990), pp. 451–4.
6. J. Petrie, 'The Secular Word HOLOCAUST: Scholarly Myths, History and 20th Century Meanings', *Journal of Genocide*, 2, 2, March (2000), pp. 31–63.
7. In the former communist bloc and Israel, VE Day is celebrated on 9 May.
8. C. Gerlach, 'The Wansee Conference, The Fate of Germans, Jews and Hitler's Decision in Principle to Exterminate All European Jews', *The Journal of Modern History*, 70, 4, (1998), pp. 759–812. H. Himmler, *Der Dienstkalender Heinrich Himmlers 1941/42* (Hamburg: Christians, 1999) p. 289.
9. D. Pohl, 'The Murder of the Jews in the General Government', in U. Herbert (ed.), *National Socialist Extermination Policies, Contemporary German Perspectives and Controversies*, (Oxford: Berghahn Books, 2000), pp. 83–103.
10. Browning, *Nazi Policy*, pp. 58–88.
11. A. Read, *Kristallnacht, Unleashing the Holocaust* (London: Michael Joseph, 1989).
12. According to the Hall of Names at Yad Vashem, ews murdered during *Kristallnacht*, Jews killed by the Gestapo before the war and Jews killed in the early concentration camps are counted among the victims of the Holocaust. So are Jews who died in forced labour camps or in the ghettos during the war, but before the advent of the Final Solution.
13. For a short yet lucid account of Hungarian forced labourers see R. Braham, *The Hungarian Labor Service System, 1939–1945* (Boulder, CO: East European Quarterly, 1977).

1
Towards a Critical Reading
of Books and Articles
on the Holocaust

Soon after the Nazis rose to power, books and articles began to be published that sought to describe various aspects of the new order, many of which focused on the increasingly barbaric treatment of innocent civilians.[1] After the end of the Second World War, contemporary accounts started to give way to the first historical works, memoirs and fiction about the Nazi period, and the persecution and attempt ultimately to destroy the Jews of Europe. In the last 50 years, tens of thousands of books and articles have appeared about the Holocaust and subjects akin to it. The Yad Vashem Library, which probably houses the largest collection on the Holocaust and related subjects, alone contains roughly 93,000 titles of books and article off-prints, as well as thousands of additional articles contained in periodicals. This vast literature, which currently increases at a rate of about 3,500 new titles per year, includes historical monographs, memoirs, contemporary eyewitness accounts, journalistic accounts, fiction, poetry, albums and reference material.[2] Almost every written language is represented in this great assemblage and the quality of the published material ranges from scholarship that is exemplary to presentations that are at best highly problematic. It should be borne in mind that no publication is perfect; and just as we assess many things in our world for their merits and faults, so must we assess the material that we read. Sometimes we notice flaws that so overshadow worthwhile material that we turn away. At other times, despite a few unsound points, we formulate a generally positive opinion of something or are able to extract points of merit from it. Undoubtedly, even the very best books and articles have shortcomings which may be and often should be pointed out.

Navigating this sea of information is a formidable task for scholars. It is even more vexing for teachers, students and others who are interested in learning about the events that have left such deep scars on the body of Western civilization. No single person could possibly read all of the available material and every reader must make choices concerning how to invest valuable time. Bibliographical tools exist that may help readers but, like the publications that they list, their quality varies greatly and they are far from complete.[3] Because of the uneven quality of the literature on the Holocaust, it is quite possible for readers to come away from their reading with incorrect information and gross misconceptions. Until a frequently updated on-line annotated bibliography of the subject is created, if such a creation is possible, understanding certain problems and issues that have come to the surface in this broad array of publications may help readers find their way and reach the best material available. The following is meant to be neither a concise bibliography nor a historiographical essay about the Holocaust. It is an attempt to illuminate certain issues about which one should be aware while reading historical publications concerning the Holocaust.

Regarding books that approach the Holocaust primarily from the discipline of history, it is possible to classify the issues about which readers should be aware into the following categories:

- issues stemming from the documentation used by scholars;
- issues of an historiographical nature;
- issues virtually intrinsic in personal accounts;
- tunnel vision;
- overtly subjective or non-historical writing perceived as historical writing; and
- problems essentially inherent in reference works.

ISSUES STEMMING FROM DOCUMENTATION

Written history is based on sources. Readers of history need to keep this in mind as they read and should make an effort to evaluate the sources that are cited by authors. Of course, not every reader is equipped to evaluate the sources on the level of an expert in a given field. But every reader can note whether an author is using primary sources or secondary sources, or some combination thereof. For example, when a reader notices that an author has used only secondary sources, it should be clear to him or her that the book is a work of historiography, not basic research. The reader might then ask if the author has made that point clear in his other writing, or is the historiographical essay presented (either overtly or by omission) as primary source research?

Some of the best-known, most widely read and most significant books on the Holocaust suffer from problems concerning the archival sources on which they are based. Sometimes authors were not able to obtain certain primary source materials, or at the time of their writing specific documents were still unknown. In other cases authors were not aware of relevant archival resources or, for unexplained reasons, simply ignored germane material. To help put this in perspective, consider the fact that at Yad Vashem, primarily because of the granting of wider access to archives in the former communist countries, over two million new pages of documentation have been added to the collection yearly since 1998.

Because the Holocaust was perpetrated throughout most of Europe, the wide range of languages used in various source materials also constitutes a problem for some researchers. Again by way of illustration, over 50 languages are represented in the Yad Vashem Library and Archives.

One of the first seminal books about the Holocaust is Raul Hilberg's *The Destruction of the European Jews*, originally published in 1961 and revised and republished in 1985 and 2003.[4] Hilberg's analysis of the German machinery of murder is considered masterful. Today, some 37 years after its original publication, it remains a book that every scholar and student should consult. The sterling qualities of his study notwithstanding, Hilberg's book is considered by many scholars to be faulty. Many have attacked Hilberg for his analysis of Jewish leadership in the Holocaust and of Jewish response in general. Hilberg posits that Jews were so steeped in a mindset of accommodating acts which affected them throughout their history, that during the Holocaust they were unable to take a pro-active stand. In the appendix on sources in the revised edition of Hilberg's book and in the notes themselves there are more references to Jewish sources than in the earlier edition; nevertheless, Hilberg's emphasis on German archival material and his approach to the Holocaust through German history are clearly evident not only from his narrative and analysis, but also from his sources.[5] Yet many writers point out that Hilberg apparently has ignored a large body of literature and documentation that shows a very wide range of active responses by Jewish leaders.[6]

The issue of sources is also important for reading *Ordinary Men: Reserve Police Battalion 101 and the Final Solution* by Christopher Browning,[7] one of the most thought-provoking books to be published in recent years. Browning discusses how a group of men, who essentially were not diehard adherents of Nazi ideology, became murderers. In particular, Browning posits that the men in Battalion 101 by and large were not imbued with the Nazi style of racial anti-Semitism, but became killers owing chiefly to other factors. Critics of Browning's book point out that his conclusions are problematic, in part because his main archival source is the protocols of interrogations prepared for the trial of several members of the unit. All oral testimony and other types of personal accounts are problematic, since they are the retelling of events after they have been filtered through the memory of the witness. Those who use such sources try to gather as many testimonies as possible about the event under investigation in order to achieve consistency and to minimize other problems such as mixing in hearsay or second-hand evidence with eyewitness testimony. In addition to the more common problems posed by oral testimony, the testimonies of perpetrators for a trial, it may be argued, are exceedingly subjective for obvious reasons, and therefore are not a reliable source for understanding the motivations of the killers.[8] For his part, Browning has argued that the large mass of detailed and often converging testimony at this particular trial compensates for this problem.[9]

It is not only the question of on which sources a book is based but also the question of how they are noted in the text that may be of importance to readers. The late, prolific scholar of Jewish thought and culture, Raphael Patai, has written one of the most informative books yet published about the history of Hungarian Jewry: *The Jews of Hungary: History, Culture, Psychology*.[10] His is a panoramic sweep, from the earliest record of Jewish presence in Hungary during the Roman period, through the middle and early modern age, into the period of emancipation, modern anti-Semitism and the Holocaust. Written clearly, with great erudition and referring to many documents, the book has one major flaw, representative of a whole class of books. Other than a bibliography given on a per-chapter basis, it has not one single specific source note. As informative as the book is, it cannot really be cited by other scholars nor be given the same weight as academic historical studies with clear reference notes. Books lacking clear source citations range greatly in their value, from well-written and well-conceived historical accounts such as Patai's, to journalistic or even sensationalist narratives. Many such books are apparently meant to be 'popular history'; that is, they were published to reach a broader reading public than academic historical studies. Yet leaving out source citations to enhance their appeal is precisely what makes them problematic for use by scholars, teachers and students.[11]

ISSUES OF HISTORIOGRAPHY: OLDER SCHOLARSHIP VERSUS NEWER SCHOLARSHIP

It may be said for the subject of the history of the Holocaust, as for many other subjects, that newer works build upon earlier publications, newly accessible documentary material and perspectives gained by the passage of time. This does not mean that earlier studies have no value or that newly published works are automatically superior to their

precursors. Indeed, many early books remain the best books on a particular topic. Israel Gutman's *The Jews of Warsaw, 1939–1943: Ghetto,
Underground, Revolt* is a case in point.[12] Many scholars still consider it
the definitive study of the Warsaw Ghetto, even though the book was
published in Hebrew in 1977 and English in 1982. Nevertheless, there
are numerous examples of early books that have been superseded by
newer studies. Perhaps the most well-known instance is William
Shirer's *The Rise and Fall of the Third Reich*[13], which has been supplanted
by a plethora of books and articles. A recent comprehensive bibliography on the Third Reich compiled by Michael Ruck lists well over
twenty thousand monographs and articles, the large majority of which
were written after Shirer's account. In the last ten years alone, many
important monographs have appeared in English that cover all or significant parts of the territory covered by Shirer. Outstanding among
them are the works of Michael Burleigh, Henry Friedlander, Norbert
Frei, Sebastian Haffner, Ian Kershaw and Detlev Peukert.[14]

The earliest writings about the Germans and the Final Solution were
often monochromatic and blunt in their presentation. Material that was
published in the wake of the Nuremberg trial – such as *The Black Book:
The Nazi Crime Against the Jewish People* – accuses the entire German
people in the name of the Jewish people for perpetrating the
Holocaust.[15] Leon Poliakov, writing in one of the first attempts to present a comprehensive history of the Holocaust, *Harvest of Hate*, places
the immediate blame for the Holocaust on the entire German nation
and overall blame on Western civilization, at the head of which stood
German society. In his introduction Poliakov writes:

> Such blood-letting is without precedent in European history; the
> Nazi enterprise was unique in its very principle. But to treat this
> subject is also to treat a part of the history of contemporary
> Germany, for in the actual event the Jews were chiefly passive vic-
> tims; the active role, that of the protagonist in the tragedy, fell to
> the German people as a group, acting under the stimulus of the
> leaders of their choice.[16]

In his book *The Germans and the Final Solution*, published in 1992,
David Bankier presents a still accusatory, but much more complex and
polished argument, largely based on sources that neither the Black
Book Committee nor Poliakov used.[17] As the debate following the publication of *Hitler's Willing Executioners* by Daniel Jonah Goldhagen
shows, the discussion about the relationship between a posited special
German national character, a unique German form of antisemitism and
the perpetration of the Holocaust is far from over. Among other things,
from the Goldhagen debate we learn that the passage of time and

availability of new documentation do not necessarily supersede older, once popular arguments, which merely have been lying dormant.[18]

The first studies about the responses of the Allies to the murder, such as *While Six Million Died* by Arthur Morse, assumed a journalistic and frankly accusatory tone.[19] Morse's tone has given way to much more sophisticated books, such as David Wyman's *The Abandonment of the Jews*, which is still accusatory but reflects methodical scholarship and more documentation.[20] Even more sophisticated in scholarship and tone is Tony Kushner's monograph *The Holocaust and the Liberal Imagination*.[21]

In his summation of the work of the War Refugee Board, the agency created in 1944 by Franklin D. Roosevelt to facilitate rescue, Morse terms it and its activities '... a small gesture of atonement by a nation whose apathy and inaction were exploited by Adolf Hitler'.[22] Here Morse states that American inertia was a result of indifference and ultimately served the Nazi murder machine. Writing 26x years after Morse, Tony Kushner, in comparing American and British responses, sees the creation and activities of the War Refugee Board as a significant official act of concern by the United States government and not merely a gesture. Britain, he maintains, did less, but the reasons for this he stresses are not those of Morse. Britain's relative failure 'was not ... due to the politics of indifference or even that of "antisemitism" – it was the politics of liberal ambivalence'.[23] Expressing a much more nuanced idea than Morse's, Kushner posits that the very nature of liberalism considerably contributed to British inaction.

COMPREHENSIVE HISTORIES

Especially since not everyone is able or inclined to read extensively about the Holocaust, concise comprehensive histories, those written in one or two volumes by a single author, have a very important place in the pantheon of works on the subject. They may provide important overviews and allow for the discussion of over-arching themes. However, such publications suffer from the inherent problems present in any attempt to package in concise form a wide and deep subject. Unlike monographs on more specific subjects, they cannot really delve into the myriad sub-themes and sub-chapters that the Holocaust raises; almost by definition they present relatively superficial or telegraphic information. Robert Wistrich's short history of the period, *Hitler and the Holocaust*, is a case in point. In an attempt to be concise, it places subjects under chapter headings that make little sense.[24] To try to compensate for these kinds of problems, of course, more information may be presented, which in turn runs the risk of making the book either burdensome to read because of its density or hard to follow because of its complexity. As the volume of available archival material has so greatly increased, such works also must be based to a large degree on second-ary rather than primary sources, simply because no single historian could possibly analyse all the necessary available primary source material to write such a book. The use of secondary sources could hardly be considered a flaw. However, excellent second-ary sources do not yet exist for all chapters of the Holocaust (the destruction of Greek Jewry is one such lacuna). Therefore, authors writing concise comprehensive histories must sometimes rely on sources of inferior quality, incomplete sources or their own primary source research for those chapters.

Leni Yahil's *The Holocaust, The Fate of European Jewry, 1932–1945*[25] is among the more recent efforts to present the history of the Holocaust in one thick volume (two in the Hebrew version). Her treatise relies on documentary material, and many monographs and articles written through the 1980s. As a reflection of that scholarship and the historical perspective gained by the passage of time, it displaces earlier popular comprehensive works, among them those written by Lucy Dawidowicz, Nora Levin, Leon Poliakov and Gerald Reitlinger. The picture Yahil presents is not only more comprehensive than the earlier works, but the portrait she is able to paint of events is both subtler and more refined than that of her predecessors. Moreover, because of advances in scholarship, she is able to address issues – such as Jewish responses to the unfolding events or the availability of information about the Holocaust – more fully than those previous writers. But with the recent appearance of the first volume of Saul Friedlander's deftly woven study on the Holocaust, *Nazi Germany and the Jews*,[26] which cov-ers the period from Hitler's rise to power until the outbreak of the Second World War, Yahil's study has also begun to seem somewhat dated. Friedlander has employed a very special method in his presen-tation, interlacing the history of the period from many vantage points, ranging from particular details culled from Nazi documentation to accounts by individual survivors. His chosen method offers the possi-bility of transmitting the complexity of the web of events to the reader. However, because he must select the most specific details presented from the tremendous mountain of those available, Friedlander courts the risk of inadvertently implying that certain events or chapters are more important than others and thus offering a slightly skewed version of the history.

PERSONAL ACCOUNTS

The published personal accounts of the Holocaust survivors comprise one of the most significant sources for information about the Nazi era. Approximately 6,000 such books have appeared in print.[27] Sometimes these memoirs are the only published sources for certain events or places. Scholars, teachers, students and others with an interest in the subject are often drawn to these works, which tell the story of an individual with whom it is easier to identify than with analytical history books. Among the most famous publications about the Holocaust are memoirs by eloquent writers including Elie Wiesel, Primo Levi and Saul Friedlander.[28] For their immediacy and ability to get across to the reader the horrors experienced by their authors, published memoirs vie only with diaries and recorded oral testimony. It is also important to note that published memoirs are essentially different from both diaries and oral testimony. The latter are assumed to be unadulterated eyewitness reports of events that the survivor experienced (although as has been already mentioned this is not always the case), whereas the former are usually self-edited and almost always edited professionally prior to publication. As Elie Wiesel states in his memoir, *All Rivers Run to the Sea*:

> I must warn you that certain events will be omitted, especially those episodes that might embarrass friends and, of course, those that might damage the Jewish people. Call it prudence or cowardice, whatever you like. No witness is capable of recounting everything from start to finish anyway. God alone knows the whole story.[29]

Wiesel not only illustrates the point stated above, but also reminds the reader that all types of personal accounts of events are problematic and may be quite subjective.

By reading memoirs alone, very important aspects of the Holocaust may remain unclear and readers may even come away with misconceptions. Memoirs often provide important illustrations of historical events and issues, but alone, they cannot be a source for constructing most concepts. In the same way that they use other forms of testimony, historians, using published memoirs in conjunction with additional types of documentation, may weave together a coherent picture of hitherto unknown events or processes.[30] For example, by reading only memoirs of Jews in Poland, one might assume that all Jews everywhere first were crowded into ghettos before they were sent to be murdered in Nazi camps, but of course this was not the case. Except for some Dutch Jews, the Jews of western Europe were not concentrated together in

ghettos or one section of a city. And the Jews of those parts of the former Soviet Union that were taken by German forces in the summer of
1941 were generally subject to mass murder actions before ghettos
were established.

Survivors who have written of their experiences are experts concerning their own experiences, and it is their personal accounts of
events that they witnessed that have such tremendous value for the
reader. Unfortunately, some survivors try to extend their memoirs into
historical narratives, which does justice neither to their experiences nor
to historical writing. In such cases it is not always clear to the reader
what the writer is saying as witness and what he or she is saying as an
historian. Moreover, much of the historical writing that is intermixed in
memoirs is amateurish at best, with the survivors falling into one or
many of the pitfalls that good historians try to avoid. Only a handful of
survivors, who have become professional historians, have proven their
capability to be both historians and witnesses, and they usually take
great care to delineate between their two voices. Among the survivors
and refugees from Nazism who have become important historians are
Yitzhak Arad, Yehuda Bauer, Randolph Braham, Shalom Cholavski,
Saul Friedlander, Israel Gutman, Raul Hilberg and Dov Levin.[31]

Since the end of the Second World War, over 1,100 books have been
published by emigrés and survivors of various communities, or by
non-Jews interested in the history of the Jews who once lived among
them. These books have become known as *Yizkor* (memorial) books. As
in the case of memoirs, it may be said that the strongest point of the
Yizkor books is the personal accounts they often contain, about both
pre-war Jewish life and the destruction of the Jewish communities.
Many also contain moving photographs of now destroyed scenes and
murdered people, as well as lists of the Jews from the community who
perished in the Holocaust. Some of the books were edited by trained
historians, but most were edited by members of the community and
their work reflects their earnest commitment to their task.
Nevertheless, many of the historical essays in the *Yizkor* books must be
read with a critical eye, their unique value notwithstanding. For
English language readers, there is an additional problem: most of the
Yizkor books are in Hebrew, Yiddish or the language of the place about
which they were written.

TUNNEL VISION

Some authors seem so focused on proving their thesis that they never
look to the right or left of their material, and they may be said to be suffering from tunnel vision. Because of this, they often miss important

points of comparison; and had they noted these points, their argument would have been adjusted accordingly. Two clear examples of tunnel vision are the previously mentioned book by Goldhagen, *Hitler's Willing Executioners,* and William Rubenstein's book *The Myth of Rescue: Why the Democracies Could Not Have Saved More Jews from the Nazis.*[32]

Regarding his discussion of German antisemitism, Goldhagen is so hell-bent on showing its inherent and unique lethal nature that he hardly discusses antisemitism in other countries. He totally misses the point illustrated so trenchantly by the late George Mosse: Mosse used to explain that if two men were discussing the future of the Jews in the late 1930s and the first said: 'You know they are going to murder the Jews,' the second probably would have answered: 'Yes, those Frenchmen are capable of anything.' That is to say, virulent and potentially extremely violent forms of antisemitism did not exist only in Germany after the First World War.

Rubenstein, for his part, seeks to prove that the Allies could have done absolutely nothing to rescue the Jews of Europe. In making such a sweeping argument, he makes bombastic statements about those who sought to facilitate rescue and about their plans. Regarding proposals made in 1943 and 1944 by the British-based National Committee for Rescue from Nazi Terror, he writes:

> For the most part, however, these draft proposals were every bit as useless and misguided as their American counterparts. Manifestly, they centrally conceived of the task of 'rescue' as the reception of refugees rather than the liberation of captives of the Nazis. In 1943–4, the British government, with the best will in the world, had precisely as much ability to liberate the Nazis remaining Jewish captives as they had to influence events on Mars.[33]

Rubenstein may be right that the main issue during the war years was how to free Jews from Hitler's grasp. Nonetheless it is a ridiculous oversimplification to say that proposing havens for Jews was both 'useless' and 'misguided'. Freeing Jews from the Nazis and bringing them to safe havens were tightly bound together. For example, the Danish Jews could never have been rescued if Sweden had not been willing to provide a safe haven. As to Britain's ability to extricate Jews from Nazi-dominated territory, Rubenstein makes no mention of the fact that the British and the Nazis reached an exchange agreement that led to the release of Jews who reached Palestine in November 1942. Although this agreement did not lead to mass rescue, it did happen; and therefore Britain could influence the fate of Jews more than it could 'events on Mars'.

OVERTLY SUBJECTIVE OR NON-HISTORICAL WRITING PERCEIVED AS HISTORICAL WRITING

Some of the writing about the Holocaust, which may lead readers to draw far-reaching conclusions, is riddled with factual errors and unfounded interpretations. A common denominator among these books is that they are essentially journalistic in their approach and do not reflect rigorous historical scholarship, yet they are often perceived by the reading public as scholarly historical accounts. Among the best-known books that may be placed in this category are *Eichmann in Jerusalem* by Hannah Arendt (1963) and *Perfidy* by Ben Hecht (1961).[34] Both works reflect the early struggles of intellectuals to understand how it was possible for the Holocaust to happen and the tendency of the time to put more of the blame for the catastrophe on the victims than the perpetrators. Both concern riveting trial proceedings that were held in Israel.

Soon after Hannah Arendt's book *Eichmann in Jerusalem* appeared in print, intellectuals began debating it. Arendt draws a theory based on her interpretation of the proceedings of the Eichmann trial, which holds that the defendant and Nazi criminals as a group were rather conventional and not as exceptional as one might expect. She also lambasts the Jewish leadership in Nazi-dominated Europe, which she categorizes as co-operationist and meek. Because Arendt is one of the most popular thinkers of the second half of the twentieth century, her words carried great weight with many people and her book was widely read. Perhaps more than any other before it, her book furthered the myth of Jewish passivity during the Holocaust and provided ammunition to those who sought to relieve the perpetrators of the Holocaust of individual responsibility.

Her critics were many and often very vocal. In the words of the most thorough and painstaking of them, Jacob Robinson: 'She has misread many of the documents and books referred to in her text and bibliography. She has not equipped herself with the necessary background for an understanding and analysis of the trial.'[35] According to Walter Laqueur, her narrative and conclusions, some of which might be true and others of which have no real basis, were undoubtedly shaped by her world-view. Hannah Arendt was an anti-Zionist, steeped in European intellectualism, and she held in high esteem intellectuals who were also activists. Hannah Arendt, however, was not an historian who wrote an objective account of events. Her account, which was put forth as historical, could more accurately be said to have jumped track from the path of historical analysis into the realm of aesthetics.[36] In the words of Yaacov Lozowick, who wrote about Eichmann's department, 'the facts that stare one in the face, it seems to me, indicate the opposite of Arendt's thesis'. She did not understand the context in which Eichmann gave his testimony (at a trial at which his life was at stake), nor that he was anything but a cog in a wheel. Lozowick shows, based on documents generated by Eichmann's office, that Eichmann and his associates knew exactly what they were doing, and were deeply immersed in Nazi antisemitic, racial ideology.[37]

Perfidy, by author and playwright Ben Hecht, is one of the most tendentious works ever to be written about the Holocaust (excepting those whose authors deny the Holocaust). In it, Hecht accuses a leading Hungarian Zionist, Rezso (Israel) Kasztner, and the Zionist establishment of selling out the Jews of Hungary for their own personal security and gain. His theme clearly reflects many of the arguments put forth by the attorney Shmuel Tamir in the so-called Kasztner trial in Israel in the mid-1950s.[38] It also apparently reflects his personal politics, which were supportive of the opposition party in Israel at the time.[39] Using arguments presented against Kasztner at the trial, Hecht misquotes and misinterprets much of what Kasztner and the Budapest Relief and Rescue Committee did in their attempt to rescue Jews in Hungary. Like many of his peers, Hecht seems to be looking for a scapegoat to explain the murder of over 550,000 Hungarian Jews during the last year of the Second World War.[40] Subsequent research, to a great extent based on written documentation about the Budapest Relief and Rescue Committee found primarily in the Yad Vashem Archives, the Central Zionist Archives, the Israel State Archives and Beit Lohamai Hagetaot, has shown just how biased his book is.[41]

PROBLEMS ESSENTIALLY INHERENT IN REFERENCE WORKS

Given the flood of data available to us on all subjects, reference works, whether they are printed or in digital format, are particularly important. They are the place to which we turn for quick and, we hope, clear and reliable information. Students use them for preparing reports or for background reading. Teachers need reference works to help deepen their knowledge about subjects related to those they are teaching, or to refresh their knowledge on the subject they are about to present in class. Scholars use them regularly to double-check small details: dates, spellings, etc. Yet reference works by their very nature inevitably contain factual errors, misinterpretations and unreliable information – even the best among them.

The *Encyclopedia of the Holocaust*,[42] which after its publication was generally lauded as an excellent reference work, is a case in point.[43] The editorial staff, of which this author was a part, received letters from readers correcting various details following its publication. As are most reference works, *The Encyclopedia of the Holocaust* is based on the studies of scholars and reflects research that already has been carried out. Thus some important subjects are missing from its pages, such as an entry on Turkey during the Holocaust years and comprehensive entries on Orthodox Jewry or children. Scholarly studies had not yet been published on these topics at the time that the encyclopedia was being produced.

Another problem that is common in works such as the *Encyclopedia of the Holocaust* is that of proportion. The length of a given article does not always correspond to the subject's importance for the history of the period. For example, the entry on Adolf Hitler is the same length as the entry on the Mufti of Jerusalem, Hajj Amin Al-Husseini, even though the roles they played in the persecution of the Jews are clearly of vastly different significance.

The recently published *Historical Atlas of the Holocaust*[44] by the United States Holocaust Memorial Museum exemplifies an array of problems found in reference works aimed at the general reading public. The introduction does not state either the boundaries of the period being presented or how the order of the maps was chosen, leaving the reader bereft of a clear understanding of the structure of the atlas. An examination of the placement of the maps highlights the complexity in translating historical processes and events into a series of maps; for example, the Warsaw Uprising comes before maps that discuss the 'Final Solution'. Because of the many times borders have changed during the course of history, choosing the spelling for place names and employing clear and systematic parameters for the choices also pose a problem for those who create historical atlases. In the *Historical Atlas of the Holocaust* it is not always clear why a particular spelling was chosen.

Condensing information in the text that accompanies the maps in historical atlases also opens up a door to inaccuracies and superficial presentations. In the *Historical Atlas of the Holocaust* a great deal of history is presented in a very telegraphic way and, unfortunately, some statements are made in an absolute fashion when it would have been better to have qualified them. In the text that accompanies the map of rescue in Budapest, it states that 'Raoul Wallenberg led one of the most extensive and successful rescue efforts during the Holocaust'.[45] Although no historian would dispute that Wallenberg was among the most famous and influential diplomats working to rescue the Jews of Hungary, it is an exaggeration to say that he led the rescue attempts. The Papal Nuncio, Angelo Rotta, officially stood at the head of the team of diplomats who protested against the treatment of the Jews to the Hungarian government. The earliest rescue attempts were made weeks before Wallenberg even reached Budapest. The Swiss representative Charles Lutz distributed far more protective documents than

Wallenberg. Jewish rescuers worked most closely with Lutz and the representative of the International Red Cross, Friedrich Born. Last, George Mantello, a diplomat representing El Salvador in Switzerland, worked ardently for the welfare of Hungarian Jews.[46] Still, despite all of these problems, the *Historical Atlas of the Holocaust* has become a commonly used reference tool throughout the English-speaking world.

Large teams of scholars have produced most of the better-known reference works about the Holocaust, the Nazi period and the Second World War. Some 200 scholars contributed entries to *The Encyclopedia of the Holocaust*; the entries in *The Encyclopedia of the Third Reich* were written by nearly 40 well-known scholars; and *The Oxford Companion to the Second World War* lists some 140 contributors.[47] Works have also been published by individuals or by small teams of authors. Among the more popular publications of this nature are Edelheit and Edelheit's *A History of the Holocaust: A Handbook and Dictionary*; Gilbert's *Atlas of the Holocaust*; Ready's *World War Two, Nation By Nation*; Wheal, Pope and Taylor's *The Meridian Encyclopedia of the Second World War*; and Wistrich's *Who's Who in Nazi Germany.*[48]

Unlike reference works to which scholars the world over have contributed (works that seek to present the most up-to-date and best scholarly information on a given topic as written by a recognized expert), individuals or small teams creating broad reference works must face the extraordinarily difficult task of collating, digesting and concisely presenting enormous amounts of information in lieu of a broad team of experts. It is not surprising, therefore, that such works have many endemic problems, some prevalent in most reference works and others more common in this class of publications.

In the Edelheits' *History of the Holocaust* some of the shortcomings also seen in works created by many authors, such as lack of proportion, exist and are compounded by individual bias, which is not tempered by a larger team. For example, in the Edelheits' book the entry on the Hebrew Committee for National Liberation is longer than any other entry about Jewish organizations in the United States. This body, however, which was backed by the New Zionists (Revisionists), was of no greater importance during the period than other organizations, among them the American Jewish Joint Distribution Committee and the American Jewish Congress.[49] Perhaps more than anything else, the source citations at the back of the Edelheits' book illustrate the problems posed by a small team creating a comprehensive reference work. No one person or small team can be aware of all the best published sources for the Holocaust, and perhaps because of this their source citations are both incomplete and inconsistent. The list of memoirs omits the works of Primo Levi, Saul Friedlander and others, but includes the unpublished memoirs of Hershel Edelheit. The list of journal articles, although containing some important sources, is neither comprehensive (a daunting task) nor clear regarding what was included, what was not and why.[50]

EXAMINING THE HOLOCAUST USING OTHER DISCIPLINES

Although the focus of this essay is historical writing about the Holocaust, it is important at least to hint at the most salient problem concerning the many works written from the perspective of other academic disciplines and to note some of the more important authors. Perhaps because of the highly charged nature of the subject of the Holocaust, and perhaps because it touches so many people so deeply, a great many authors of varying backgrounds and abilities have written about it. Some have displayed a sounder understanding of events and processes than others. The Holocaust is a phenomenon that occurred in history, so first and foremost the historical events under discussion must be presented as accurately as possible in any scholarly work. It is not always self-evident that inaccuracies in the presentation of events can easily lead to misinterpretations and the formulation of theories that are dubious.

One of the best-known theories to grow out of questionable historical information and analysis was set down by Bruno Bettelheim, a psychologist and psychoanalyst.[51] Bettelheim, himself a former inmate of the Dachau camp, wrote that among inmates in the Nazi camps who had been incarcerated for a long period a last stage of regression ensued whereby some reached such a high level of identification with their wardens that they mimicked their behaviour. Bettleheim's recital of events, his analysis and his theory have been examined by many researchers of the period. What at first was essentially uncritical acceptance of his theories by many has given way to a much more critical evaluation of them. Both researchers and camp survivors have vociferously challenged the argument that such behaviour was commonplace or that a specific stage of regression may be posited from isolated occurrences.[52]

Nevertheless, when the analysis of events using the tools of a variety of academic disciplines is securely anchored in history, the results can be of great value. The list of valuable, if not necessarily perfect, studies from other disciplines is long. A small sample of noteworthy publications includes *Accounting For Genocide* by Helen Fein, who applied statistical methods to a country-by-country analysis of the murder of the Jews.[53] Robert Jay Lifton, using his insight as a psychiatrist, wrote a very illuminating study of Nazi physicians during the Holocaust.[54] The sociologist Wolfgang Sofsky's graphic account of life in the Nazi concentration camps is as troubling as it is instructive.[55] Works from the perspectives of philosophy, theology and religious thought include those by prominent authors such as Eliezer Berkovits, Arthur Cohen, Emile Fackenheim, Steven Katz, Richard Rubenstein and Eliezer Schweid.[56] From the field of literary criticism and analysis, one must at least mention the publications of Sidra Ezrahi, Lawrence Langer, Alvin Rosenfeld, David Roskies and James Young.[57]

CONCLUSION

Just as the authors working with historical material must take care to be as true as possible to the historical record, so must readers strive to use all of their critical faculties to discern quality scholarship and writing. What has been set forth in this essay are some of the issues about which readers should try to be aware. Assuredly there are other issues that may be discussed, and many more examples and deeper ramifications for those that have been mentioned. Being aware of the issues discussed here does not guarantee that a reader will not pick up wrong factual information or arrive at unfounded conclusions about the Holocaust and the events that surrounded it, but awareness should help minimize such occurrences. Undoubtedly, a critical reading of the bibliography of the Holocaust is necessary, as it is in all subjects, and the art of reading critically improves with use.

NOTES

1. A sample of books published in 1933 and 1934 includes H. A. Heinz, *Germany's Hitler*, (London: Hurst and Blackett, 1934); Roy Pascal, *The Nazi Dictatorship* (London: Routledge, 1934); H. Powys, *The German Revolution* (London: Routledge, 1934); B. T. Reynolds, *The Saar and the Franco-German Problem* (London: E. Arnold, 1934); P. Van Passen (ed.), *Nazism: An Assault on Civilization* (New York: H. Smith and R. Haas, 1934); J. W. Wise, *Swastika: The Nazi Terror* (New York: H. Smith, 1933).
2. This figure represents the average number of new publications obtained by the Yad Vashem Library during the last three years.
3. Among the better-known and more widely used general bibliographies are S. S. Cohen (ed.), *Antisemitism: An Annotated Bibliography*, 3 vols (New York: Garland, 1987–94) [this bibliography also is available on-line through the Hebrew University of Jerusalem]; A. J. Edelheit and H. Edelheit, *A History of the Holocaust: A Handbook and Dictionary* (Darmstadt: Wissenschaftliche Buchgesellschaft, 2000); M. Ruck (ed.), *Bibliographie zum Nationalsozialismus. Vollstaendig, Ueberarbeitete und Wesentlich Erweiterte Ausgabe* (Boulder, CO: Westview Press, 1994); M. Piekarz, *The Holocaust and Its Aftermath: Hebrew Books Published in the Years 1933–1972*, 2 vols. (Jerusalem: Yad Vashem, 1974 [in Hebrew]); D. Szonyi, *The Holocaust: An Annotated Bibliography and Resource Guide* (New York: Ktav, 1985).
4. R. Hilberg, *The Destruction of the European Jews, Revised and Definitive Edition* (New York: Holmes and Meier, 1985). The original book was published by Quadrangle Books, 1961 and a third edition was published by Yale University Press, 2003.
5. Hilberg, *Destruction* (1985), pp. 1223–31.

6. I. Gutman, 'Jewish Resistance – Questions and Assessments', in I. Gutman and G. Greif (eds.), *The Historiography of the Holocaust Period: Proceedings of the Fifth Yad Vashem International Conference* (Jerusalem: Yad Vashem, 1988), pp. 641–78; A. Weiss, 'The Historiographical Controversy Concerning the Character and Functions of the Judenrat in Jewish Resistance – Questions and Assessments,' in Gutman and Grief, *Historiography*, pp. 679–96.

7. C. R. Browning, *Ordinary Men: Reserve Police Battalion 101 and the Final Solution* (New York: HarperCollins, 1992).

8. D. J. Goldhagen, 'The Evil of Banality', *The New Republic* (double issue, 13 and 20 July, 1992), pp. 49–52; F. Littel 'Review of Ordinary Men', *Holocaust and Genocide Studies*, 7, 1, Spring (1993), pp. 121–4.

9. Round-table discussion at Yad Vashem with Professor Christopher Browning, 1993. Among the participants were Dr Yitzhak Arad, Professor Steven Aschheim, Professor David Bankier, Professor Yisrael Gutman, Dr Shmuel Krakowski, Dr Yaacov Lozowick and Dr Robert Rozett.

10. R. Patai, *The Jews of Hungary: History, Culture, Psychology* (Detroit: Wayne State University Press, 1996).

11. There are numerous books that are written as history books and, although they may contain a bibliography and relate to sources, they include neither footnotes nor endnotes. A small sample includes T. Bower, *Klaus Barbie, Butcher of Lyons* (London: Michael Joseph, 1984); C. Genese, *The Holocaust: Who Are Guilty?* (Sussex: The Book Guild, 1988); D. Kranzler and E. Gevirtz, *Profiles of Holocaust Rescue: To Save A World* (New York: CIS, 1991); A. Latour, *The Jewish Resistance in France* (New York: Holocaust Library, 1981); J. E. Persico, *Piercing the Reich: The Penetration of Nazi Germany by American Secret Agents during World War II* (New York: Viking Press, 1979).

12. I. Gutman, *The Jews of Warsaw, 1939–1943: Ghetto, Underground, Revolt* (Bloomington, IN: University of Indiana Press, 1982).

13. W. L. Shirer, *The Rise and Fall of the Third Reich: A History of Nazi Germany* (London: Secker and Warburg, 1960).

14. M. Burleigh, *The Racial State: Germany 1933–1945* (Cambridge: Cambridge University Press, 1991); N. Frei, *National Socialist Rule in Germany: The Führer State, 1933–1945* (Oxford: Blackwell, 1993); H. Friedlander, *The Origins of the Nazi Genocide from Euthanasia to the Final Solution* (Chapel Hill, NC: University of North Carolina Press, 1995); S. Haffner, *Germany's Self Destruction: From Bismarck to Hitler* (London: Simon and Schuster, 1989); I. Kershaw, *Hitler, 1889–1936: Hubris* (London: Allen Lane, 1998) and *Hitler, 1936–1945, Nemesis* (London: Allen Lane, 2000); D. Peukert, *Inside Nazi Germany: Conformity, Opposition and Racism in Everyday Life* (New Haven, CT: Yale University Press, 1987).

15. *The Black Book: The Nazi Crime Against the Jewish People* (New York: Duell, Sloan and Pearce, 1946), p. 3. This book was written under the auspices of the World Jewish Congress, the Jewish Anti-Fascist Committee, the Jewish National Council of Palestine and the American Committee of Jewish Writers, Artists and Scientists.

16. L. Poliakov, *Harvest of Hate* (London: Best Seller Library, 1954), p. 13.

17. D. Bankier, *The Germans and the Final Solution: Public Opinion Under Nazism* (Oxford: Blackwell, 1992).

18. D. J. Goldhagen, *Hitler's Willing Executioners: Ordinary Germans and the Holocaust* (New York: Alfred A. Knopf, 1996).

19. A. Morse, *While Six Million Died: A Chronicle of American Apathy* (New York: Random House, 1968).

20. D. Wyman, *The Abandonment of the Jews: America and the Holocaust* (New York: Pantheon Books, 1984).

21. T. Kushner, *The Holocaust and the Liberal Imagination: A Social and Cultural History* (Oxford: Blackwell, 1994).

22. Morse, *While Six Million Died*, p. 383.

23. Kushner, *The Holocaust and the Liberal Imagination*, p. 201.

24. R. Wistrich, *Hitler and the Holocaust* (New York: Modern Library, 2001). Wistrich places the Jewish response in a very strange context.

25. L. Yahil, *The Holocaust: The Fate of European Jewry, 1932–1945* (New York: Oxford University Press, 1990). The original Hebrew edition was published under the Hebrew title *Ha Shoah, Goral Yehudei Europa, 1932–1945*, 2 vols (Jerusalem: Yad Vashem, 1987).

26. S. Friedlander, *Nazi Germany and the Jews* (New York: HarperCollins, 1997).

27. The Yad Vashem Library collection contains nearly six thousand books that have been classified as memoirs by Jews, but this number includes quite a few publications that have appeared in more than one language.

28. Of course the list of memoirs is long and, even among lesser-known works, many may be called eloquent. The following are perhaps the best-known memoirs to have been published: S. Friedlander, *When Memory Comes* (New York: Farrar, Straus, Giroux, 1979); P. Levi, *Survival in Auschwitz: The Nazi Assault on Humanity* (New York: Collier Books, 1971); E. Wiesel, *Night* (New York: Hill and Wang, 1960), *All Rivers Run to the Sea: Memoirs* (New York: Knopf, 1995) and *And the Sea is Never Full, 1969* (New York: Knopf, 1999).

29. Wiesel, *All Rivers*, p. 17.

30. A book such as Y. Zuckerman, *A Surplus of Memory: Chronicle of the Warsaw Ghetto Uprising*, (Berkeley: University of California Press, 1993), has a great deal of information about the Jewish response in Warsaw. But even the information presented in a memoir by a figure like Zuckerman (who, as the deputy commander of the Jewish underground in Warsaw, was in the vortex of events that accompanied the destruction of Warsaw Jewry and the advent of the uprising) needs to be critically compared with other accounts, historical narratives and analysis of the events he discusses. From a completely different angle, the same may be said about the autobiographical books of Albert Speer and his role in the higher levels of the Nazi bureaucracy. Speer originally gained prominence in Nazi Germany as Hitler's architect and later as his armaments minister. Because of his unusually close relations with Hitler, Speer has much to say about the inner workings of the Third Reich, some of it problematic. See A. Speer, *Inside the Third Reich* (New York: Macmillan, 1970) and *The Slave State, Heinrich Himmler's Master Plan for SS Supremacy* (London: Weidenfeld and Nicolson, 1981), and compare it to G. Sereny, *Albert Speer: His Battle With Truth* (New York: Macmillan, 1995) and to J. Fest, *Speer: The Final Verdict* (New York: Harcourt, 2001).

31. Some of the writings of Friedlander, Gutman and Hilberg have been mentioned. Among the most important books by Arad, Braham, Cholawski and Levin that have appeared in English are Y. Arad, *Ghetto in Flames: the Struggle and Destruction of the Jews in Vilna during the Holocaust* (Jerusalem: Yad Vashem, 1980) (later publication – New York: Holocaust Library, 1982) and *Belzec, Sobibor, Treblinka: The Operation Reinhard Death Camps* (Bloomington, IN: University of Indiana Press, 1987); R. Braham, *The Politics of Genocide: The Holocaust in Hungary, Revised and Enlarged Edition*, 2 vols (New York: Rosenthal Institute for Holocaust Studies Graduate Center, the City University of New York, 1994) (originally published by Columbia University Press, 1981); S. Cholavski, *Soldiers from the Ghetto* (San Diego, CA: A. S. Barnes, 1980); D. Levin, *Fighting Back: Lithuanian Jewry's Armed Resistance to the Nazis* (New York: Holmes and Meier, 1985) and *Baltic Jews under the Soviets, 1940–1946*, (Jerusalem: The Hebrew University, 1994).

32. W. D. Rubenstein, *The Myth of Rescue, Why the Democracies Could Not Have Saved More Jews from the Nazis*, (London: Routledge, 1997).

34. H. Arendt, *Eichmann in Jerusalem: A Report on the Banality of Evil* (New York: The Viking Press, 1963); B. Hecht, *Perfidy* (New York: J. Messner, 1961).

35. J. Robinson, *And the Crooked Shall Be Made Straight: The Eichmann Trial, the Jewish Catastrophe and Hannah Arendt's Narrative* (New York: Macmillan, 1965), p. vii.

36. W. Laqueur, 'Hannah Arendt in Jerusalem: The Controversy Revisited', in L. H. Legters (ed.), *Western Society After the Holocaust* (Boulder, CO: Westview Press, 1983), pp. 107–20.

37. Y. Lozowick, *Hitler's Evil Bureaucrats: The Nazi Security Police and the Banality of Evil* (London: Continuum, 2002), p. 9.

38. Kasztner was the co-chairman of the Hungarian Zionist movement in Hungary. During 1944 and 1945 he engaged in negotiations with representatives of the SS to rescue Jews. In the Israeli press of the 1950s he was accused of complicity in the murder of Hungarian Jewry. He sued for libel. At the end of the trial the presiding judge declared that Kasztner had 'sold his soul to the devil'. A subsequent judge found in Kasztner's favour, but in the meantime Kasztner was assassinated in Tel Aviv by fanatics who believed him a Nazi collaborator. The best book about the Kasztner trial has appeared only in Hebrew: Y. Weitz, *Ha-Ish She-Nirtsach Paamaim, Hayav, Mishpato, u-Moto shel Yisrael Kasztner* [The Man Who Was Murdered Twice, The Life, Trial and Death of Israel Kastner] (Jerusalem: Keter, 1995).

39. Ben Hecht was associated with the Bergson Group, which was headed by Hillel Kook

(also known as Peter Bergson), a member of the Irgun underground, which opposed the British in Mandatory Palestine. Later, Hecht was associated with the New Zionist movement's party, Herut, headed by Menacham Begin, which was the largest opposition party at the time of the Kasztner trial and in the years following it.

40. The Budapest Relief and Rescue Committee, headed by Kasztner and the Zionist leader Otto Komoly, was recognized as an official arm of the Jewish Agency in January 1943.

41. For more information in English about Kasztner's activities in Hungary see Y. Bauer, *Jews for Sale: Nazi–Jewish Negotiations, 1933–1945* (New Haven, CT: Yale University Press, 1994); R. Rozett, 'The Relationship Between Rescue and Revolt, Jewish Rescue and Revolt in Slovakia and Hungary during the Holocaust', PhD dissertation (Jerusalem: The Hebrew University, 1987).

42. I. Gutman (ed.), *The Encyclopedia of the Holocaust* (New York: Macmillan, 1990).

43. Richard Libowitz, 'Review: Encyclopedia of the Holocaust', *Holocaust and Genocide Studies*, 6, 2 (1991), pp. 201–6.

44. United States Holocaust Memorial Museum, *Historical Atlas of the Holocaust* (New York: Macmillan, 1996).

45. USHMM, *Atlas*, p. 197.

46. A. Cohen, *The Hehalutz Resistance in Hungary, 1942–1944* (Boulder, CO: Social Science Monographs, 1986), pp. 128–50; R. Rozett, 'Rescue and Revolt', pp. 244–87.

47. I. C. B. Dear (ed.), *The Oxford Companion to the Second World War* (Oxford: Oxford University Press, 1995); C. Zenter and F. Beduerftig (eds), *The Encyclopedia of the Third Reich* (New York: Macmillan, 1991).

48. Edelheit and Edelheit, *A History of the Holocaust*; Martin Gilbert, *Atlas of the Holocaust* (New York: William Morrow, 1993); J. L. Ready, *World War Two, Nation By Nation* (London: Arms and Armour Press, 1995); E. Wheal, S. Pope and J. Taylor, *The Meridian Encyclopedia of the Second World War* (New York: Meridian, 1992); R. Wistrich, *Who's Who in Nazi Germany* (London: Weidenfeld and Nicolson, 1982);.

49. Edelheit and Edelheit, *A History of the Holocaust*, pp. 360–3.

50. Ibid., pp. 461–78.

51. Bettelheim's most widely known accounts about camp inmates are to be found in his books B. Bettelheim, *The Informed Heart, Autonomy in a Mass Age* (Glencoe: The Free Press of Glencoe, 1960) and *Surviving and Other Essays* (New York: Knopf, 1979).

52. C. Fleck and A. Mueller, 'Bruno Bettelheim and the Concentration Camps', *Journal of the History of the Behavioral Sciences*, 33, 1 (1997), pp. 1–37.

53. H. Fein, *Accounting for Genocide: National Responses and Jewish Victimization* (New York: The Free Press, 1979).

54. R. J. Lifton, *Nazi Doctors: Medical Killing and the Pyschology of Genocide* (New York: Basic Books, 1986).

55. W. Sofsky, *The Order of Terror: The Concentration Camp* (Princeton, NJ: Princeton University Press, 1997).

56. The subject of philosophical, theological and religious responses to the Holocaust is vast. The following are among the foremost authors on this subject from a Jewish perspective: E. Berkovits, *Faith After the Holocaust* (New York: Ktav, 1973) and *With God in Hell: Judaism in the Ghettos and the Death Camps* (New York: Sanhedrin Press, 1979); A. A. Cohen, *The Tremendum: A Theological Interpretation of the Holocaust* (New York: Crossroad, 1981); E. Fackenheim,*God's Presence in History: Jewish Affirmations and Philosophical Reflections* (New York: New York University Press, 1970) and *To Mend the World: Foundations of Post-Holocaust Jewish Thought*, (Bloomington, IN: Indiana University Press, 1994); S. Katz, *Post-Holocaust Dialogues: Critical Studies in Modern Jewish Thought* (New York: New York University Press, 1985); R. Rubenstein, *After Auschwitz: Radical Theology and Contemporary Judaism* (New York: Bobbs-Merril, 1966); E. Schweid, *Wrestling Until Day-break: Searching for Meaning in the Thinking of the Holocaust* (Lanham, MD: University Press of America, 1994).

57. One of the main avenues for exploring the Holocaust is through literature and the analysis of that literature. The following authors are at the forefront of this discipline: S. Dekoven Ezrahi, *By Words Alone: The Holocaust in Literature* (Chicago, IL: University of Chicago Press, 1980); L. Langer, *The Holocaust and the Literary Imagination*, (New Haven: Yale University Press, 1975) and *Versions of Survival: The Holocaust and the Human Spirit*, (Albany: State University of New York Press, 1982), *Holocaust Testimonies: The Ruins of*

Memory (New Haven, CT: Yale University Press, 1991); A. Rosenfeld, *A Double Dying: Reflections on Holocaust Literature* (Bloomington, IN: Indiana University Press, 1980); D. Roskies, *Against the Apocalypse: Responses to Catastrophe in Modern Jewish Culture* (Cambridge, MA: Harvard University Press, 1984); J. Young, *Writing and Re-Writing the Holocaust: Narrative and the Consequences of Interpretation* (Bloomington, IN: Indiana University Press, 1990) and *The Texture of Memory: Holocaust Memorials and Their Meaning* (New Haven, CT: Yale University Press, 1993).

2
The Place of the Holocaust in Popular Histories of the Twentieth Century

Towards the end of the twentieth century a number of single-volume books were produced in English by reputable publishing houses and scholars that sought to present the most salient aspects of the history of the twentieth century.[1] At the same time a great deal of attention was being given, and still is being given, to the Holocaust and related issues in a great variety of forums. At the end of the twentieth century an international task force for furthering education about the Holocaust was set up on the initiative of the then Prime Minister of Sweden, Göran Persson; it continues to encourage educational activities. Thousands of books and scholarly articles about the Holocaust and related subjects are published each year. Films with the Holocaust as their subject or background have been worldwide box-office hits in recent years. Any keen observer of the media can attest that over the last few years a significant amount of space has been given to reporting and discussing issues such as dormant bank accounts in Switzerland that belonged to victims of the Holocaust; insurance payments to the heirs of Holocaust victims that have never been made; the reparation, compensation and indemnification of Jews and others who were forced to perform forced labour for Nazi Germany; various attempts to bring to trial war criminals from the Holocaust years; the commemoration of the Holocaust victims; the denial of the Holocaust and a variety of other subjects. Since the onset of the second Intifada with its accompanying violence, all sides frequently invoke references to the Holocaust to justify themselves or bludgeon the other side. Thus the question arises: do these single-volume books, which seek to discuss the most prominent features of twentieth-century history, reflect what is perceived to be a high popular interest in the Holocaust and related issues? How central is the Holocaust to the history of the twentieth century, according to such publications?

To answer these questions it is helpful to break them down into several parts. How much space is allotted to the subject, both absolutely and in proportion to other important subjects in these books? What is actually being said? What cardinal points are missing from the discussion? From what perspective is the Holocaust being addressed? And how well does the information in these books reflect cutting-edge scholarship about the Holocaust?

The books I have chosen to analyse here differ from each other in their approach and focus. Individual authors wrote three of them, whereas two consist of essays by a variety of scholars. The lengths of the books range from just under 500 pages to just over 1,000 pages. The level of writing, however, is fairly consistent; with quite a limited target audience – from the interested layman to the university student. Most of the books provide a bibliography for suggested further reading, but not all of them do so. None of them provides precise source citations; this is the convention in works written for academic purposes but not for reference books and popular histories.

No single-volume history about the world in a given century can really provide a comprehensive summary, and each author and editor is clearly aware of this inherent problem. In the opening pages each explains his foci and discusses the criteria by which the presentation and discussion of topics were limited. For example, J. M. Roberts, in *Twentieth Century: The History of the World, 1901 to the Present*, articulates these restrictions clearly in his foreword:

> Inevitably, the hardest decisions have been over the question of what to leave out. The book is intended to be a history of the world in a given period, yet not only can it not be factually complete, it must leave out some history altogether. It does not pretend to provide complete or even cover, any more than a guidebook pretends to give information about every part of the region it describes in uniform or equal measure ... I am afraid, many communities whose history has had to be set aside here, not as beneath the consideration of history (every human creation or phenomenon has its own history that demands and is worthy of proper study) but because their story neither illuminates nor contributes to the general themes of this particular book ...[2]

In the *Columbia History of the Twentieth Century* the editor, Richard W. Bulliet, not only rationalizes what was included, but also explains how the slant of the book, which centres on fundamental change and infrastructures, determined what would be addressed. Moreover, Bulliet declares that there is no consensus about what exactly constitutes mainstream history, but the most important issues, he asserts, revolve around innovation and transformation. He writes:

This book's thematic or infrastructural approach takes as a premise the idea that the master narratives of all groups rest to some degree on foundations of historical development outside the arena of political drama, war, and revolution, and that all groups have been affected, to greater or lesser degrees by the currents of change described in each chapter... The question was asked: In what areas of life have twentieth-century developments been so remarkable or revolutionary as to distinguish this century from any preceding era in human history?[3]

Clive Ponting's approach to the history of the twentieth century is through a prism very different to Bulliet's. In the introduction to his book *The Twentieth Century: A World History*, he unequivocally sets forth his perspective on the century under discussion:

The book's major theme is the struggle between progress and barbarism. For many Europeans and Americans the twentieth century was a narrative of almost unbroken progress ... All of these European developments were seen as pointing the way for the rest of humanity ... Within twenty years [after the start of the century] these illusions lay shattered.[4]

Michael Howard and W. Roger Louis, editors of *The Oxford History of the Twentieth Century*, hold neither infrastructure changes nor a specific theme to be representative of the twentieth century. They consider one event to have been the defining point of the century:

The Second World War was thus the pivotal event of the century, and this volume treats it as such. The nations of Europe no longer had the power, even if they had the will, to sustain their empires, and such legitimacy as they retained was destroyed by the nationalist movements which the war had encouraged. The collapse of the colonial empires left two ideologically hostile and militarily victorious 'super powers' to compete for world dominance.[5]

Curiously, this introduction by Howard and Louis seems to skirt around the Holocaust. Although they squarely place the Second World War at the nucleus of events, they say nothing about the centrality of the Holocaust to that war. In fact, the Holocaust is only mentioned in two of the introductions. Ponting, in *The twentieth Century, A World History*, elaborates on the disillusionment with progress ushered in by the First World War, and portrays the Holocaust as a significant part of the continued crushing of delusions. He writes:

Worse was to follow. The rise of fascism, Nazism and the repressive state in the Soviet Union were only forerunners of the most dreadful war of the century, in which probably 85 million people died between 1939 and 1945. Six million of them died in the greatest crime of the century – the death camps and the Jewish holocaust [*sic*][6]

Bulliet, in *The Columbia History of the Twentieth Century*, mentions the Holocaust as an example of a single element in one of the many national narratives that have emerged in the twentieth century. About these narratives he writes:

And so it goes for every group that, in quest of, or from a desire to maintain, a sense of community identity, has knit its own master narrative from the yarns of the past, the bits of historical event and individual biography that everyone truly interested in that community's past must surely know.[7]

He seems to suggest that the Holocaust, as a part of such a narrative, is not really a subject for mainstream history, but a sort of 'yarn from the past', a parochial folk legend. In Bulliet's view, 'the names Theodore Herzl, Chaim Weismann, Vladimir Jabotinsky, Louis Brandeis, and David Ben Gurion evoke for American Jews a master narrative of anti-Semitism [*sic*] and the Holocaust, achievement of statehood for Israel, and the struggle for survival against Arab enemies'.[8] His analysis of this narrative is itself a bit peculiar. Why would the names Herzl, Weismann, Jabotinsky, Brandeis and Ben Gurion be part of a 'master narrative' only for American Jews? Do they not mean as much for Jews in Israel, Europe or anywhere else in the world? Moreover, if the Holocaust is part of this narrative, why does he not include people who are much more closely associated with the events, such as Adam Czerniakow, Mordechai Anielewicz, Anne Frank, Abba Kovner or Hannah Szenes? Undoubtedly, these are names that everyone familiar with the Holocaust has heard. Bulliet's placement of the Holocaust and even the short list of people he associates with it imply that it is far from a pivotal event for him, and his knowledge about it appears to be not very deep.

As an indication of how much information is being presented on the subject of the Holocaust and, in turn, as an indication of how central a theme it is for the authors and editors in this sample of books, it is instructive to see how many pages in the index of each book are cited under the heading 'Holocaust' (or, in the case of one work, under the heading 'Jews – Nazi Holocaust'). In addition, what percentage of the entire book does this index item represent? It is important to understand that the number of pages in which any index term appears does not correspond directly to the amount of space devoted to the subject when under the guise of alternate terminology. To a certain extent, the reliability of such a measurement is closely linked to how thorough and well conceived a given index is and how well the indexer has linked various related terms. This is especially important in the case of the word 'Holocaust', since many terms are used for it or in relation to it. Among these are the words 'Shoah', 'Genocide', 'Ethnic Cleansing', 'Anti-Semitism', 'Nazism', and 'the Third Reich', to name just a few. Moreover, not all indexers approach their work in the same manner. Some indexers cite all related terms under the main heading and use 'see' references, whereas others provide separate citations. Thus different terms may well overlap in their page citations, and it is not always an easy task to try to sort things out. Ultimately, merely looking at each separate term and counting up the amount of page citations actually may muddle the issue more than it clarifies it. Nonetheless, despite these inherent limitations, since all of the indices under discussion here include the term 'Holocaust', the statistical comparison of the specific word does give some clue about the subject's importance in each of the books.

As may be seen from the following statistics, comparatively little weight is given directly to the term Holocaust and discussion about it in four out of the five books. The smallest quantity of pages for which the term 'Holocaust' is cited in the index appears in *The Oxford History of the Twentieth Century*, with only one page, representing 0.218 per cent of the entire book. The largest number of pages on which the term may be found is in *The Twentieth Century: A World History*, with 24 pages, representing 4.1 per cent of the entire book. The other publications all list 'Holocaust' as appearing on far short of 1 per cent of their total pages. In absolute terms, these figures suggest that in 80 per cent of the books the direct discussion of the Holocaust is of relatively little importance to the discussion of the history of the twentieth century.

As the authors and editors themselves noted, there are many subjects competing for their attention. Undoubtedly one of the most important is the Cold War, which appears in all of the books. Comparing the term 'Holocaust' to the term 'Cold War' makes a statement about how the authors and editors viewed the relative importance of the two events. *The Columbia History of the Twentieth Century* has 54 page citations for the Cold War and three page citations for the Holocaust: 8.32 per cent versus 0.462 per cent of the entire book. The *Oxford History* contains 32 page citations for the Cold War as opposed to one for the Holocaust: 6.98 per cent versus 0.218 per cent of the total. *Twentieth Century: The History of the World, 1901 to the Present* contains 43 page citations for the Cold War versus five pages for the Holocaust: 4.75 per cent versus 0.55 per cent. *A History of the World in the Twentieth Century* presents 38 page citations with the term 'Cold War' as opposed to seven pages with the word Holocaust: 3.79 per cent versus 0.698 per cent. Only *The Twentieth Century: A World History* devotes significantly more space to the Holocaust than to the Cold War, with 24 page citations as opposed to 14: 4.1 per cent versus 2.397 per cent. These figures suggest that for 80 per cent of the books the Holocaust is a subject of significantly lesser importance than the Cold War. It is not even half as important, but only one-fifth and as little as one-thirty-fifth as important as the Cold War in the eyes of most of the authors and editors – far as the indices attest.

Some of the other terms one may expect to see in books that discuss the history of the twentieth century are not present in all of the books' indices. In Bulliet's, Howard and Louis's, and Roberts's books, the terms 'Auschwitz', 'Death Camps' and 'Extermination Camps' are not to be found in the indices. 'Genocide', however, is mentioned in all three. Both J. A. S. Grenville's and Ponting's indices include the words 'Auschwitz', 'Death Camps' and 'Genocide'. None of the indices contains the term 'Extermination Camp', except Ponting's, which uses the term 'Auschwitz Extermination Camp'. So it appears that for at least three out of five of the authors and editors, the 'Age of Auschwitz' is not a very appropriate description for the twentieth century or even the 1940s.[9]

Although it is certainly not an absolute measure of relative importance of subject matter, it is definitely thought-provoking to make the following comparison. In *The Columbia History of the Twentieth Century*, as we have seen, the term 'Holocaust' is cited in the index with three scattered pages. The term 'Comic Books' is cited on two consecutive pages and the text discusses comic books' cultural importance. Based on this comparison, it would seem that for Bulliet and his team the cultural significance of comic books does not fall very far short of that of the social significance of the murder of the Jews during the Second World War.

Of course such measurements and exercises are not necessarily the best indications about how the authors and editors view the Holocaust, and they must be used cautiously and in conjunction with other kinds of analysis. Undoubtedly, the words contained in the books must be read carefully for both their narrative and their analytic presentations to arrive at an understanding about how a given topic is treated. Equally important is what is not said, at least in so far as the context of the presentation may leave the reader hanging in mid-air, thinking, where is the rest? The perspective of the author also provides insights about the treatment of the subject.

Several of the articles in *The Columbia History of the Twentieth Century*, by dint of their titles, appear to touch on the Holocaust and related subjects, but for the most part, the authors give the Holocaust short shrift. One of the contributors, Zachary Karabell, devotes 21 pages to a discussion of the changes in religion engendered by events of the twentieth century. His only mention of the Holocaust is concerning the impact of the destruction of the Jews on Zionism. He asserts that the Holocaust made most Jews throughout the world supporters of Zionism.[10] Of course, the historical record regarding the impact of the Holocaust on Zionism is actually very complex and replete with nuances that Karabell's simple statement does not begin to suggest.

Karabell says absolutely nothing about how Jews have wrestled with the impact of the Holocaust on Judaism. The writings of Eliezer Berkovits, Arthur Cohen, Emile Fackenheim, Richard Rubenstein, Joseph Soloveitchik and many others who have struggled with this subject, are not mentioned by the author. Regarding Christianity, he discusses Vatican II, but is silent about the relationship of the Holocaust to it and the decision to stop blaming the Jews for the death of Jesus. Nor does he discuss the impact of the Holocaust on 2,000 years of Church-sponsored Jew hatred, and the many attempts made by Christians throughout the world to re-examine Christianity in light of the murder of the Jews.

In his chapter 'Ethnicity and Racism' J. Paul Martin alludes to the Holocaust only once in his 19-page essay. He writes:

> This century has been marked by the high profiles of the killing of Jews by Nazi Germany, the legalized racism practiced by South African apartheid, and the recent 'ethnic cleansing' in the former Yugoslavia, leaving us, as the century ends, with an acute aware- ness of the many festering ethnic tensions across the globe …[11]

The author discusses race and national politics over the course of six and a half pages, but says nothing about Nazi Germany. He asserts that 'among the many countries in the world where race has played a major political role, none competes with the United States and South Africa in the international visibility of their respective experiences'.[12] One would think he might have hedged his declaration somewhat, given the fact that Nazi Germany was founded upon principles of race; in the name of racial ideology the Nazis murdered six million Jews and engaged in vast attempts to racially re-engineer much of Europe. In addition, scores of thousands of books and articles have been published about the Nazis and their crimes: the deeds of the Nazis are certainly a child of the twentieth century and have left their mark on it. Reading Martin's statement, one is left with the feeling that either he knows so little about the Nazis and their times that he did not realize that the subject should be included in his presentation or, for mysterious, mistaken or tendentious reasons, he decided that Nazism and the Holocaust have little to do with ethnicity and racism in the twentieth century.

In his 30-page article on nationalism in the twentieth century in the same book, James Mayall mentions fascism and the Nazis, not really delineating clearly between the two. He writes:

> Fascism was the pathological heir of that strand of European romanticism which rejected the universalism of both the French Enlightenment and British classical political economy. After Germany's humiliating defeat in the 1918 war, as after the Napoleonic invasions a century earlier, they responded in Berlin's phrase, 'like the bent twig of the poet Schiller's theory, by lashing back and refusing to accept their alleged inferiority.' What interested the National Socialists (Nazis) was what had interested the romantics before them: not what they shared with the rest of humanity, but what distinguished them and placed them on a higher plane ...[13]

He points out quite accurately in another paragraph that there was a connection between nationalism and socialism in the Third Reich.[14] He makes no mention, however, of the conflux of nationalism and racism. There is not a word about the concept of Nazi or *Volkische* nationalism as tribalism. Nor is there an explanation about the *Volksgemeinschaft*, the utopian national unit the Nazis sought to build, and the relationship between this desire and their efforts to purify their national entity by murdering the Jews.

In the 13-page article entitled 'War', by Robert O'Connell, the author might be alluding to the Holocaust when he writes about mass slaughter:

> Much is made of rival warlords and ancient tribal and ethnic hatreds, but just below the surface lurks the age-old need or desire to eliminate excess people. The killing here is typically labeled as senseless; but it is not without purposes. It is simply that the logic behind it is too brutal for most to admit its existence ...

In his essay there is no outright discussion of the Holocaust or genocide as a part of war or allusion to it other than this paragraph, and no mention of the unprecedented mass murder of civilians by the Nazi regime and its partners. Neither does O'Connell explore the role of ideology in the mass murder of civilians in wartime. If he meant to include the Holocaust (even obliquely) in his discussion, perhaps the most problematic feature is that O'Connell apparently says the Holocaust is logical because it is utilitarian. One may argue that, within the distorted Nazi view of the world, the murder of the Jews may have had a purpose and that sometimes logistics and a certain logic affected specific murder operations. For example, Christian Gerlach has written about the relationship between availability of food supplies and the local timing of murder operations in Belorussia.[15] But to suggest that the Holocaust made some sort of real utilitarian sense in the realm of normative, ethical thinking is unconscionable.

Last, it must be noted that although thousands of books have been written about the Holocaust in English, among them some very well-known one-volume histories, the bibliography of *The Columbia History of the Twentieth Century* contains only one item that relates to the history of the Holocaust in any way: Albert Speer's memoir *Inside the Third Reich*. Perhaps this is the clearest indication about the editor's viewpoint regarding the place of the Holocaust in the history of the twentieth century. The source is not really about the Holocaust and rarely alludes to it directly. Rather, it is a subjective memoir that is suspect for trying to whitewash its author, a major figure in the Nazi regime.

The very weak presence of the Holocaust in its index notwithstanding, *The Oxford History of the Twentieth Century* does not totally gloss over the murder of the Jews and topics related to it. Several of the essays in the book allude to the Holocaust and the central chapter on the Second World War devotes two paragraphs directly to it. Events related to the Holocaust also appear in the chronology at the end of the book. In the six-page opening article, 'The Dawn of the Century', the author (and joint editor of the book) Michael Howard writes about antisemitism. He articulates the idea that Jews became the scapegoats of those who feared the changes already unfolding at the turn of the century. Not only the ruling classes, but landowners, petty bourgeois and small shopkeepers all saw Jews as the moneyed class to whom they were growing increasingly in debt. Many regarded the Jews as aliens in their midst.[16] Certainly Howard's short explanation is plausible, but it lacks several important dimensions. It lacks a presentation of the underpinnings of more traditional Church-rooted Jew hatred for modern antisemitism: traditional religious hatred of the Jews was still strong at the turn of the century. It lacks discussion of the newer phenomenon of political antisemitism, which developed alongside the emancipation of the Jews during the course of the nineteenth century. And it also lacks the element of racial antisemitism, which at the turn of the century was poised to become a major phenomenon.

In his chapter 'The European Colonial Empires' W. Roger Louis, the other editor, touches on the Holocaust in passing. In the context of

Germany's loss of colonies in 1919, he writes:

> It remains debatable how the social engineering of the Third Reich might have affected black Africa and whether or not the Holocaust might have taken a slightly different direction with places such as East Africa available as a 'dumping ground' for Jews and Gypsies.[17]

He never even hints at the idea that with extensive plans for settling Germans in various parts of Europe, the Nazis were essentially a colonial power.

Howard writes more extensively about the Holocaust in the 13-page chapter 'Europe in the Age of Two World Wars'. Discussing the occupation of Poland, he alludes to Nazi racial ideology, writing: 'The Germans sealed the Jews into their ghettos and treated the rest of the population as Untermenschen, "sub-people".'[18] He does not, however, discuss the pre-war period in Nazi Germany, with its evolution from a policy of isolating Jews, to promoting emigration, to a policy of coerced emigration through the use of terror.

After Howard describes the invasion of the Soviet Union, he discusses the murder of the Jews. He writes:

> But there was another, parallel step that had to be taken if Hitler was to fulfil all his goals. In his programme, the racial purity of the Third Reich was as important as its economic balance. He had tried before the war to solve the problem of the Jews by hounding them out of the country, but Germany's conquests left them nowhere to go. They could not be maintained indefinitely in concentration camps at home. Logic dictated, therefore, that they should be physically exterminated, and the process of extermination was given equal priority with the conduct of the war. From the beginning of 1942 the police forces of Occupied Europe were set to round up all the Jews, regardless of class, age, or sex, and send them to Germany whence they were transported to camps in a remote corner of Poland, to be either worked to death or killed in gas chambers, their bodies then being destroyed in large crematoria. The logistical expertise, industrial resources and scientific brilliance of the technologically most advanced society of the twentieth century ensured that, by the time the war ended, some six million people had been disposed of in this fashion. From this ghastly self-inflicted wound, European civilization has never fully recovered.

> The exterminators followed in the wake of the German armies as they penetrated deep into Soviet territory in the latter half of 1941. Entire communities of Jews were rounded up and shot as

they were found – and not only Jews. Hitler had made it clear to his military commanders that this was not to be a war like others fought between European powers, but one of colonial conquest and racial extermination. Political commissars were to be shot on sight; all civil resistance was to be met with savage reprisals; prisoners of war were to be worked to death or left to starve. By the end of 1941 over a million of these had been taken, as German arms sliced through the bewildered and disorganized Soviet resistance, surrounding Leningrad in a siege in which a third of the population died, overrunning the Ukraine and the Donetz Basin and reaching, the first days of December, the outskirts of Moscow.[19]

This presentation of the murder makes some important points, directly and indirectly. It places the murder of the Jews in its proper time frame, noting it began in the second half of 1941 and became more fully organized and implemented the following year. It demonstrates that anti-Jewish policy evolved into murder and it situates the murder in the context of the Nazi drive for racial purity. This narrative duly notes the technological aspect of the murder, the role played by the *Einsatzgruppen* and other formations in the Soviet territory (without mentioning them outright) and it offers the generally accepted figure of six million murdered Jews. The author errs in saying Jews were sent to Germany and then to a remote corner of Poland. Most of the Jews who were sent to their deaths in Poland were never sent by way of Germany as a temporary way-station, and the extermination camps were not all located in isolated places. Auschwitz-Birkenau was located on the edge of Oswiecim, an important provincial rail-hub in Poland, and Majdanek was on the outskirts of a major city, Lublin. Howard is correct of course in saying that not only Jews were murdered; however, he does not explain why there is such a significant difference between Jewish victims and other victims of the Nazi murder apparatus. As to his assertion that the Nazis moved from discrimination to murder, because their conquests left no havens for the Jews, it might have been worthwhile had the author consulted a map to see just how many possible havens were still available even at the height of Nazi power.

As the main description of the Holocaust in *The Oxford History of the Twentieth Century*, it is bewildering why there is nothing said about any other aspect of the history of the Holocaust, except the murder. There is nothing about the response of the world to the murder, nothing about the behaviour of the local gentile populations and, most pointedly, nothing at all about Jewish response to the persecution and murder, or about Jewish life in the shadow of death. In this recounting, the Jews are only present as objects and make not even the briefest appearance as subjects.

In addition to the text, there are several photographs with captions that relate to the Holocaust. Two photographs appearing on the same page show the Nuremberg trial and an 'illegal immigration' ship arriving in Haifa harbour after the war. There is also a photograph showing the railroad tracks at Auschwitz-Birkenau. The caption for this photo reads: 'The gates of hell. The approach to the extermination camp at Auschwitz-Birkenau, where approximately four million people were killed in the Nazi "Final Solution" to the "Jewish problem" in Europe.'[20] It is appalling that the editors use the figure four million for the number of victims of Auschwitz-Birkenau. This was the figure quoted by the communist regime in Poland, and it was shown well before the mid-1990s, in readily available sources, such as *The Encyclopedia of the Holocaust* and *Auschwitz, Anatomy of a Death Camp*, to be inflated by a factor of three or four.[21] This anachronistic caption suggests a lack of familiarity with reliable and up-to-date sources as does the bibliography for the chapter on the Second World War. For further reading that in some way touches on the Holocaust, the editors suggest only three works: Hitler's *Mein Kampf*; Norman Rich's *Hitler's War Aims* (1974) and Gerhard Weinberg's *A World at Arms: A Global History of World War II* (1994). One can only wonder why none of the well-known one-volume histories of the Holocaust or major reference works were included, not to mention some of the most highly regarded monographs.

J. M. Roberts's book *Twentieth Century: The History of the World, 1901 to the Present* contains no bibliographic sources, implying it is more for the lay reader than the serious student or scholar. Roberts explains the focus of his book in the following words:

> Some of the greatest historical themes of our century emerge because decisive historical action has in this century moved from the stage of European history to a wider stage, to, indeed, world history in the true sense ... Within my formal and arbitrary dating, I have tried above all to trace that world history, what is general, what pulls the story together.[22]

Two of his chapters deal quite clearly with the events that include the Holocaust: 'The Path to World War', (pp. 378–409) and 'The Second World War' (pp. 410–32). Several other chapters contain paragraphs about the Holocaust and its ramifications. Roberts writes a great deal about politics, but he also writes about ideology. Jews are definitely here as part of the story of Europe in the twentieth century, but there is no chapter or sub-chapter entitled 'The Holocaust'. Roberts presents a more normative division of historical events than does *The Columbia History of the Twentieth Century* and he writes about the Holocaust in greater detail than does *The Oxford History of the Twentieth Century*.

Over the course of six pages in the chapter 'The Paths to World War' Roberts outlines the Nazi rise to power, the attempt to consolidate their power and the effort to make over Germany in their image. As part of this description of events, he notes the importance of both German anti-Semitism and Nazi anti-Semitism, but he says nothing about the relationship of both to racism.[23] Under the sub-heading, 'Ideology's Contamination of International Affairs' he presents a paragraph about Nazi persecution of the Jews in the 1930s. He declares quite accurately that the persecution of the Jews rested on the background of 'Nazi racist ideology'. But he does not give a clear explanation of that ideology, nor even note its main points.

As part of a description about European politics from 1936 to 1939, Roberts notes the shocking nature of the *Kristallnacht* riots. Emphasizing the world's astonishment about the ongoing persecution of the Jews, he offers the rather pat judgement that from Hitler's speeches and writings the world should have known he would target the Jews.[24] It may be true that in the 1930s Hitler clearly marked the Jews as a chief target, but exactly what he planned to do with them was unclear, apparently even to him.

An important element in Roberts's presentation about the Holocaust is the large map he offers entitled 'Hitler's Europe, 1938–1945'. The map includes stars of David inscribed with the number of victims per country and it is taken from Mark Mazower's important book *Dark Continent*.[25] The figures presented in the map are near the generally accepted estimate of six million Jewish victims, and they seem to reflect the study by Wolfgang Benz from the mid-1990s.[26] Since the map contains no explanation, it may remain unclear to more informed readers why these numbers were chosen and which borders they actually reflect. In a later chapter on post-Cold War realities, Roberts returns to the demographic and subsequent cultural repercussions of the Holocaust, making a reasonable presentation of the subject. He writes:

> Other historical ethnic confrontations had been ended or reshaped years before, by the Second World War. Above all the fate of European Jewry had been determined. The Holocaust had brought to an end the story of Eastern Europe as the center of world Jewry. In 1901 three-quarters of the world's Jews had lived there, mostly in the Russian empire. In those once Yiddish-speaking areas, only a little more than 10 per cent of Jews now live, nearly half of the rest now live in English-speaking countries, and some 30 per cent of them in Israel … In Eastern Europe communist parties anxious to exploit traditional popular anti-Semitism (not least in the Soviet Union) encouraged emigration

by some harrying and by judicial persecution. In some countries the outcome was a virtual elimination of the Jewish population as a significant demographic element. Poland was an outstanding example; the 200,000 Polish Jews surviving in 1945 had soon found themselves again victims of traditional pogrom and harassment. Sometimes they were murdered, but most had emigrated when able to do so. By 1990 those who remained numbered a mere 6,000. This left nearly a million Jews still in the CIS republics (mainly in Russia and the Ukraine), as representatives of the centuries-old eastern European Jewish community. The heart of that community, though, had gone. Paradoxically, France in recent years has been alone among European countries in actually experiencing a significant rise in her own Jewish population as immigrants from Islamic North Africa raised its numbers to about half a million.[27]

Roberts's most in-depth discussion and assessment of the Holocaust is contained in the following three rather problematic paragraphs:

There was a deep irony in that Germany had for so long been one of the most progressive countries in Europe, the embodiment of much that was best in culture. Germany was a major contributor to the civilization, which had gone round and, indeed, had made, the modern world. That she should fall prey to *collective derangement* [my italics] on the scale implied by the Holocaust (to say nothing of other atrocities) suggested something rotten at the root of civilization itself. The crimes of Nazism had been carried out not in a fit of barbaric intoxication with conquest, but in a systematic, scientific, controlled, bureaucratic (though inefficient) way about which there was little that was irrational except the appalling end that it sought and the *lunatic* [my italics] mythologies which fed it …

Glib comparisons are, of course, useless and perhaps dangerous. When we say that Nazi behavior in Europe and the Holocaust were 'worse' than earlier atrocities, and that therefore the men who carried them out were 'worse' than the villains of the past, we speak truly, but must be clear about what that means. It is not just a matter of the scale and intensity of the brutality and destructiveness made possible by the capacities of industrial societies. Great atrocities have taken place in the past whose precise extent we can never measure, and the subjective and relative impact of which we cannot imagine, because the mental and cultural context is so hard to understand. Doubtless, too, innumerable acts of appalling cruelty have been lost in oblivion …

The overall record of the Nazis, nonetheless, strikes us still as uniquely dreadful because its perpetrators had no excuse for not knowing better. The torturers and exterminators were born of cultures that had centuries of moral reflexion and argument behind them, all the progressive thought of the last three centuries of European civilization, all slowly refined, humanized teaching of Christianity. They had no excuse of ignorance or tradition. They had deliberately turned their back on the good.

There is a line that can be drawn between the evil and perverted Hitler and bombastic, bullying but less corrupted Mussolini, between the doctrinal, *lunatic* [my italics] cruelty of the SS and often revengeful, embittered but still rationally defensible planners of the Allied strategic bombing offensive. However it felt to be its victim, there is a distinction to be drawn between Nazi tyranny and the fanatical, devoted ruthlessness of the Japanese, or even between Nazism and the brutal defensiveness expressed in Stalin's near-paranoia with possible opposition. It was above all in Germany that the twentieth century revealed itself as an age when men in power in a civilized country deliberately chose to turn their backs on civilization.[28]

Unquestionably Roberts considers the Holocaust to be of great importance to the history of Europe in the twentieth century. He regards it as a retrogressive event that calls into question the very foundations of Western civilization. In his view the Holocaust was an inexcusable negation of progressive Christian teaching and morality. Unfortunately, however, although he warns against glib explanations, Roberts attributes the Holocaust to a most simplistic cause: the collective 'derangement' of the German people and 'lunatic SS'. In the earliest attempts to understand the Holocaust, similar explanations were frequently offered. But in the more serious scholarship of the past 20 years much more sophisticated explanations have been put forth by scholars from many fields of inquiry. For a long time now, no serious student of the period would explain the Nazi murder of the Jews only on the background of mass insanity.[29]

Another key problem with Roberts's presentation is his explanation of the uniqueness of the Holocaust. He is on the mark in writing that the issue of uniqueness goes well beyond the industrialized killing of the Jews, its scale and brutality. His line of reasoning – that the Nazis should have known better because of the advanced stage of Western civilization, of which they were a part, and that they intentionally turned their backs on that civilization – is certainly worthy of consideration. But Roberts misses a main point about the uniqueness of the Holocaust: the Nazis sought to wipe the Jews and their memory off the face of the planet because they considered their biological existence a danger to Germany and all humankind; the mass and system- atic murder of the Jews was considered by the Nazis distasteful, but necessary for the health of the world. The utterly ruthless implementa- tion by the Nazis of their ideology is cardinal to what makes the Holocaust an unprecedented event in history.

J. A. S. Grenville's *A History of the World in the Twentieth Century*, which was republished in the year 2000, is essentially a reworking and enlargement of the original version, which was published in 1980 and updated several times. It is divided into 18 sections, with 94 chapters. Several chapters in Section III ('The Great War, Revolution and the Search for Stability') and, almost in their entirety, sections IV (The Continuing World Crisis, 1929–1939') and V ('The Second World War') relate to the Holocaust. These three sections comprise over 230 pages – about 23 per cent of the entire book.

In a number of ways the latest edition of the book reflects its evolu- tion. Most of the bibliography for the chapters relevant to the Holocaust dates from the 1970s and early 1980s. A few newer books were added that echo the scholarship of the first half of the 1990s, but no publication cited is newer than 1996. Among the most recent publi- cations mentioned that touch on the Holocaust are the works of Daniel J. Goldhagen, *Hitler's Willing Executioners* (1996) and David Cesarani, *The Final Solution* (1994).[30] In the last section of Grenville's work, several chapters evidently have been updated to include information about the wars that raged in the territory of Yugoslavia after the fall of the communist regime, and the events of the 1990s.

An astute reader can see the actual process of updating in some of the text. In one of the chief paragraphs on the Final Solution, Grenville writes:

> The question is often asked: why did Hitler try to force the Jews out of Germany even after the war began? Does this mean he would have preferred this solution to murdering them later? We do not know exactly what was in Hitler's mind but it is safe to conclude that humanitarian considerations did not come into his calculations on so central a question as his hatred of the Jews. He certainly was sensitive to German public feeling and presumably concluded that the German people were not ready to back his rule with increasing enthusiasm if he simply massacred all Jews, men, women and children within Germany.[31]

This paragraph seems not to relate at all to the scholarship of the 1990s that explores German public opinion and the Final Solution. Later on, however, Grenville makes that point that many Germans knew about the murder, precisely reflecting that scholarship.[32] Perhaps better editing of the revised edition might have rooted out such inconsistencies.

The first time he broaches the subjects of the Nazis and the Holocaust, Grenville underscores the racial aspect of the Nazi regime and its crimes, and rightly points out that racism was not a Nazi creation. Moreover, he ascribes a certain naivety to the world, which only was shattered when Allied forces entered the camps and viewed the results of Nazi barbarism. He writes:

> In German-occupied Europe some 10 million people, including some 2 million children were deliberately murdered. Hitler's Reich was a reversion into barbarism. Racism as such was nothing new, nor was it confined to Germany. These doctrines attracted groups of supporters in most of Europe, including France and Britain, in South America and the United States. But it was in Germany that the resources of a modern industrial state enabled criminal leaders to murder and enslave millions. Until the concentration camps revealed their victims the world was inclined to believe that a country once in the forefront of Western Culture, the Germany of Goethe, could not so regress. This faith in civilization was misplaced ...[33]

The statistical information in this paragraph highlights one of the most common problems in reference books about the Holocaust and Second World War. Many numbers are bandied about and, as in this case, often it is not clear what their source is or exactly whom they include. Without clear definitions the numbers are not merely unclear, they are virtually meaningless. Does the figure ten million include the most commonly accepted figure of roughly six million Jewish victims (actually much later on in the book Grenville offers a table with Wolfgang Benz's figures, which total about 5.4 million Jews), and then roughly four million others? If so, who are the four million others? Does the number two million children include the most commonly cited figure of 1.5 million Jewish children (which may actually be a low estimate of the number of Jews under the age of 18 who were murdered by the Nazis[34]), and half a million other children? Who exactly are these other children? Does ten million only include people directly and intentionally murdered by the Nazis and their partners? Or does it also include innocent people who died during the fighting or because of the harsh conditions of occupation? If the latter is true, the figure must be much higher than ten million.

Somewhat later in the book, Grenville addresses some of those who are generally termed 'other victims' of the Holocaust. He writes:

> But, as with the murder of the Jews, Hitler decided that the exter-

mination of 'lives not worthy of life' would have to wait for the
cover of war. Racial discrimination after 1935 was also suffered by
the 22,000 gypsies living in Germany. They too, men, women,
children and babies, together with tens of thousands of Polish and
European gypsies, were designated for extermination.[35]

He does not make a sharp distinction between Nazi policies towards
Jews and their other victims. Here it sounds as if all Romanies, like all
Jews, were destined for murder. Actually, Nazi policies about the
Romanies were somewhat muddled. They sought to murder all
the Romanies whom they considered dangerous, but in different
places in Europe they considered dissimilar groups of Romanies dangerous. In some places they killed wandering bands of Romanies and
left the sedentary ones alone, whereas in other places they did exactly
the opposite.[36]

Grenville accurately notes that some Slavs were allies of Hitler; and
he conjectures that had Poland made an alliance with Hitler before the
war, three million Polish non-Jews would most likely not have died.[37]
This seems to be a rather superficial analysis that casts blame on the Poles
for not aligning themselves with Hitler as, say, the Slovaks and Croatians
did. It does not take into account Polish attempts to refrain from anger-
ing Germany in the 1930s, nor does it recognize Hitler's desire to obtain
Polish territory regardless of anything Poland might do.[38]

Exploring Nazi foreign policy in another context, Grenville suc-
cinctly and lucidly connects the threads of Nazi racial ideology, their
desire to obtain more land, their attempt to reorganize Europe and
their persecution of the Jews. He writes:

> Much confusion of interpretation is avoided if one essential point
> is grasped: Hitler never lost sight of his goal – wars of conquest
> that would smash Soviet Russia, and subordinate France and the
> smaller states of the continent of Europe to the domination of a
> new Germany. This new order would be based on the concept of
> race. 'Races' like the Jews were so poisonous that there was liter-
> ally no place for them in this new Europe. Other races would be
> handled ruthlessly: the Slavs would not be permitted any national
> existence and could only hope for a servile status under the Aryan
> masters. Logically this biological foreign policy could not be
> confined to Europe alone. From the mastery of the European
> continent, the global conflict would ensue.[39]

Throughout the chapter 'The Outbreak of War in Europe,
1937–1939' (pp. 232–51), there is much reliable information about the
continuing evolution of Nazi anti-Jewish measures. Grenville under-

scores the move from isolation to forced emigration, represented by the *Kristallnacht* pogrom. Later in the book, Grenville discusses the evolution of the Final Solution in some detail. He writes:

> Until Germany attacked the Soviet Union in June 1941, there seemed to be a small chance of a Western peace. Jews in Germany and conquered Europe were still allowed to live. Hitler liked to keep options open: alternative solutions to isolate the Jews and drive them out of Europe altogether were considered, such as the plan to banish them to Madagascar. That from the start he had no moral inhibition against mass murder, if that should prove the best course, cannot be doubted. During the summer and autumn of 1941, millions of 'Bolshevik Jews', the mortal enemy in his eyes, were added to the millions of European Jews already under German control, and mass emigration or expulsion overseas was no longer a possibility. Nor, with so much non-Jewish slave labour falling into German hands, Hitler calculated, would Jewish slave labour be needed. The option of mass murder as the final solution now became the most desired and practical course.[40]

On the whole, this is a clear presentation, if not completely up to date. It misses an important point about the relationship of the periphery to the centre in the creation of anti-Jewish policies. Scholarship about this was available before the latest edition of his book was published.[41] Despite this fault, Grenville's account does make what may be considered one of the most cardinal points about the course of Nazi anti-Jewish policies: the Final Solution evolved over time. On subsequent pages, he discusses the different stages in the policy in more detail, summarizing the chief aspects of persecution and murder in each of the countries under Nazi domination. He also notes the rescue of the Jews of Denmark, the rescue of many Jews by Italian troops and various others, who later were honoured by Yad Vashem as Righteous Among the Nations.

His depiction of Jewish response, however, is severely lacking. In a salient example he writes about German Jewish response to persecution, that

> ... pressure on the helpless small German Jewish population in 1933 – there were about 500,000 racially defined as Jews – drove them into increasing isolation and hardship. Even though they did not emigrate to Palestine or elsewhere fast enough. The majority of German Jews wanted to stay in their homes and in their country, whose cultural heritage, the works of Lessing, Goethe and Beethoven, they cherished. German culture was their

culture. Not in the moments of blackest nightmare could they imagine that in the twentieth century in Western Europe women and children would be murdered in factories of death. They were not, after all, stuck in the Middle Ages.[42]

It is reasonable to propose that most German Jews (at first) wanted to remain in Germany, provided it is explained that this attitude changed over time. One can see the evolution of attitudes towards emigration in many memoirs and in Marion Kaplan's excellent study *Between Dignity and Despair: Jewish Life in Nazi Germany.*[43] Moreover, saying 'they did not emigrate to Palestine or elsewhere fast enough' and 'not in the moments of blackest nightmare could they imagine that in the twentieth century in Western Europe women and children would be murdered in factories of death, seems to imply that in some way German Jews were guilty of not reading the road map clearly. This of course is a retro-active evaluation of events of the 1930s, since the Nazis themselves only set the policy of the Final Solution in the autumn of 1941.

Except for a few words about the Warsaw Ghetto Uprising and the uprisings in several of the camps, nothing is really said about the Jewish responses to Nazi persecution during the war itself, or about how Jews struggled to live under the Nazis. Like the writers of the other histories reviewed up to this point, Grenville looks at events primarily from the angle of the perpetrators, with a little bit added about rescuers. For the most part, he writes about Jews as objects and not subjects. But, in summation, it would be fair to say that Grenville gives the Holocaust a significant place in the history of the twentieth century, even if his treatment of it is not fully up to date and lacks the crucial perspective of the victims.

Clive Ponting, in *The Twentieth Century: A World History*, devotes more space to the Holocaust and related subjects than any of the other authors and editors appraised in this study. This is not surprising, given his view that the main theme in the history of the twentieth century is the tension between progress and barbarism. His book is divided into five parts and 22 chapters. Part Four, 'Domestic History', includes full chapters on fascism (pp. 315–32) and genocide (pp. 502–30). In the chapter on genocide there are ten contiguous pages about the Holocaust.

At the outset of his book, Ponting describes very unambiguously the centrality of the Holocaust. In his introduction he writes:

The rise of fascism, Nazism and the repressive state in the Soviet Union were only forerunners of the most dreadful war of the century, in which probably 85 million people died between 1939 and

1945. Six million of them died in the greatest crime of the century – the death camps and the Jewish holocaust [*sic*]. The two most destructive political movements of the twentieth century – Communism and Nazism – had their origins deep in European history and ways of thinking …[44]

The depth of detail in which he addresses the Holocaust and related events is foreshadowed in an excerpt from the chapter on the situation in Europe at the turn of the twentieth century. It is significant for its main point and for the historian he chooses to quote – Simon Dubnow. Dubnow of course is very well known to students of Jewish history, but much less well recognized in general historiography. The final sentence of the quote gets right to the heart of an important aspect of the Holocaust: sometimes distinguished men who made valuable contributions to society were ruthlessly murdered, not only by the Nazi leadership and their fervent disciples, but by petty followers and collaborators. Ponting writes:

> In central Europe, Simon Dubnow, a Jewish opponent of Zionism wrote: 'We are entering the twentieth century. What does it have in store for humanity and Jewry in particular? To judge by the last few decades, it seems as if humanity might be entering a new Dark Age with horrifying wars and national struggles. But the mind refuses to believe it.' Dubnow went on to become a major contributor to the *Jewish Encyclopedia* and also wrote a ten-volume *History of the Jews*. He was battered to death by a drunken Lithuanian Nazi in Vilnius in 1941.[45]

At several points, Ponting raises not only the centrality of the Holocaust but its singularity. In one of his discussions of the issue, he connects the important motifs of ideology, technology and bureaucracy for the perpetration of the Holocaust. Ponting's presentation is a reasonable rendering of the events and their significance, certainly within the bounds of what is known today and appears in recent historiography. He writes:

> These characteristics of the Holocaust differentiate it from the other twentieth-century genocides. The slaughter of the Armenians by the Turks and the ethnic killings in Rwanda were essentially 'primitive', they could have taken place in any century. The Holocaust was a specifically modern, twentieth-century phenomenon. Its origins were deeply embedded in the European history of anti-Semitism, but were magnified by nineteenth-century concepts of racism and eugenics. It depended upon

industrial 'progress', the development of technology that made possible the gas chambers and the mass crematoria. It also relied on another specifically twentieth-century phenomenon – the growth of bureaucracy. The Holocaust required 'rational', ordered organizations that could identify, process and transport people to the killing centers without themselves being directly involved in the killing process. [46]

Reading Ponting's assessment of the Holocaust as a distinctly twentieth-century phenomenon, one is left to ponder why Bulliet and his team essentially left it out of a volume which supposedly focused on conspicuous twentieth-century phenomena.

In his narrative and analysis of the events leading to the Final Solution, Ponting touches most of the main points. He writes about antisemitism in Weimar Germany, and devotes three pages to the development of Nazi anti-Jewish policies and acts until the outbreak of the war. This includes an explanation of the Nuremberg laws, the policy of Aryanization, the deportation of Jews from Germany to Poland in October 1938 and the *Kristallnacht* pogrom of November 1938. Ponting shows that these policies were directed toward convincing Jews to leave Germany, using escalating force to do so. He writes that after *Kristallnacht*: 'this outburst of violence was not repeated and Nazi policy against the Jews appeared to have reached an impasse. Emigration seemed an unlikely option and the Nazi leadership was undecided about what should be done next.'[47]

With the outbreak of the war, Ponting emphasizes the importance of the addition of some two million Polish Jews to the population under Nazi control and the subsequent search for a better solution to the Jewish problem. He describes the use of Jewish forced labour and the establishment of forced-labour camps for Jews. Ponting not only depicts the creation of ghettos, but also describes the starvation that ran rampant in them, including several lines about the situation in Lodz. He points out that Jewish leaders in the ghettos

> were in an impossible position, since they had no realistic means of resistance. The best policy seemed to be to try to meet some demands in order to postpone any drastic decisions by the Germans and in the hope of saving as many people as possible.[48]

This is basically sound, journeyman writing about the development of Nazi anti-Jewish policies. However, in writing about the Jewish leadership in the ghettos, he jumbles the situation before the murder and after it has begun, since saving people from murder is really an issue during the murder campaigns.

In presenting the advent of mass systematic murder in June 1941, Ponting places it in the context of the Nazis' ideological and racial war against the Soviet Union. Regarding the Final Solution to the Jewish question he writes, quite within the limits of our current historical understanding, that 'Until well into 1941 no firm plans were made.'[49] He narrates the events of autumn 1941 and places the Wansee Conference in its historical context. Regarding Hitler's role in the Final Solution, Ponting writes:

> No document has been found giving Hitler's authorization for this programme. However, such a policy could not have been adopted without his approval and a formal order was neither required nor in conformity with his usual method of working. Clearly Hitler was aware of what was going on and as one of the most fanatical anti-Semites [*sic*] in the Nazi government he ensured that the policy was carried through.[50]

This assessment is also within the boundary of current historical discussion.

In his country-by-country survey of events, Ponting also touches on the response of the so-called 'bystanders', the local population. He puts a bit too much emphasis on the rescue activities of the Italians and Hungarians. But on the whole Ponting's rendition of events is sound.

In comparison to the other authors and editors reviewed here, Ponting's presentation of the Holocaust stands out because he quotes eyewitness testimony although, unfortunately, he does not provide source citations for the passages he uses. As part of his narrative about the murder of Jews in the newly conquered areas of the Soviet Union in 1941, Ponting quotes a brutally frank description by a German officer, Lieutenant Erwin Bingel, about the shooting of Jews by the *Einsatzgruppen* in Uman in September. After having described how the Jews were lined up to be shot, including mothers and their children, Bingel reports:

> Nor were mothers spared the terrible sight of their children being gripped by their little legs and put to death with one stroke of the pistol-butt or club, thereafter to be thrown on the heap of human bodies in the ditch, some of which were not quite dead.[51]

The testimony of Zonka Pollack, who was deported from Czortkow in August 1942, describes the round-up of Jews for deportation and the awful trip to the Belzec extermination camp. Her testimony expresses the initial suffering waiting outdoors in the heat to board the train. It goes on to portray the horror of the trip itself. She describes the first moments on the train:

> The doors of the cars are shut. It is dark and tense, impossible to
> stretch out your arms, absolutely no air to breath. Everyone stran-
> gles and chokes and you feel as if a rope were tied around your
> neck and such a terrible heat, as if a fire had been set under the
> car.[52]

As the use of survivor testimony attests, Ponting treats Jews not as
objects, but as subjects. Through the testimonies, he shows the reader
something of what they suffered and thought. Despite this important
difference, Ponting still says relatively little about Jewish response to
the unfolding catastrophe that enveloped much of world Jewry.
Nevertheless, with its relatively detailed narrative, *The Twentieth
Century: A World History* gives much more weight to the Holocaust
than any of the other titles studied here.[53]

As has been demonstrated, the treatment of the Holocaust varies
greatly in the five books surveyed. Except for Ponting, none of the
authors or editors comes close to placing it at the heart of the history of
the twentieth century, and one of the books, *The Columbia History of the
Twentieth Century*, barely recognizes it as a significant event. Without
seeing the protocols of the editorial meetings held for each of the volumes, one cannot ever really know what the considerations of the
authors and editors were regarding the prominence of the Holocaust in
their works. One can conclude hesitatingly that, based on this sample,
the Holocaust is not generally seen as a watershed event either in
human history or in the history of the twentieth century by scholars
outside the academic fields of Holocaust studies, Jewish history,
German history and perhaps a few other related subjects. Even in the
books that devote more space to it, the presentations about
the Holocaust generally are not up to date, and the well-documented
history from the side of the victims is almost completely missing. It is
plain that there is a strong dissonance between the high profile of the
Holocaust in public consciousness at the end of the twentieth century
and its place in these renditions of the history of the century. The implication is that the Holocaust has not been totally omitted from popular
scholarly accounts of twentieth-century history, but neither is a lucid,
precise, proportional and up-to-date presentation of it considered vital
to the story.

NOTES

1. The following books are addressed in depth in this chapter: R. W. Bulliet (ed.), *The
    Columbia History of the Twentieth Century* (New York: Columbia University Press, 1998);
    J A. S. Grenville, *A History of the World in the Twentieth Century*, enlarged edn (Cambridge,
    MA: The Belknap Press of Harvard University Press, 2000); M. Howard and W. R. Louis

(eds), *The Oxford History of the Twentieth Century* (Oxford: Oxford University Press, 1998); C. Ponting, *The Twentieth Century: A World History* (New York: Henry Holt, 1998); J. M. Roberts, *Twentieth Century: The History of the World, 1901 to the Present* (London: Allen Lane the Penguin Press, 1999).

2. Roberts, *Twentieth Century*, p. xvi.
3. Bulliet, *The Columbia History*, pp. 1–4.
4. Ponting, *The Twentieth Century*, pp. 8–9.
5. Howard and Louis, *The Oxford History*, pp. xxi–xxii.
6. Ponting, *The Twentieth Century*, pp. 8–9. Note Ponting's use of the small 'h' in 'Holocaust'. Generally, because it is considered a specific event, the word 'Holocaust' is capitalized. It is hard to tell if this was done on purpose to make a statement about the specificity of the 'Holocaust', or if was an editorial decision devoid of philosophical ramifications.
7. Bulliet, *The Columbia History*, p. 3.
8. Ibid.
9. The phrase 'The Age of Auschwitz' appears, among other places, in the title of an important book by the late, and leading, Jewish philosopher Emile Fackenheim, *The Jewish Return into History: Reflections in the Age of Auschwitz and a New Jerusalem* (New York: Schocken Books, 1978).
10. Bulliet, *The Columbia History*, p. 93.
11. Ibid., p. 127.
12. Ibid., p. 132.
13. Ibid., pp. 178–9.
14. Ibid., p. 187.
15. C. Gerlach, 'German Economic Interests, Occupation Policy and the Murder of the Jews in Belorussia, 1941/43', in Ulrich Herbert (ed.), *National-Socialist Extermination Policies: Contemporary German Perspectives and Controversies* (Oxford: Berghahn Books, 2000), pp. 210–39.
16. Howard and Louis, *The Oxford History*, p. 8.
17. Ibid., p. 97.
18. Ibid., p. 112.
19. Ibid., p. 114.
20. Ibid., p. 138.
21. I. Gutman (ed.), *The Encyclopedia of the Holocaust* (New York: Macmillan, 1990), pp. 107–19; F. Piper, 'The Number of Victims', in I. Gutman and M. Berenbaum (eds.), *Anatomy of the Auschwitz Death Camp* (Bloomington: Indiana University Press, 1994), pp. 61–80.
22. Roberts, *Twentieth Century*, p. xvii.
23. Ibid., pp. 390–6.
24. Ibid., pp. 401–2.
25. Mark Mazower, *Dark Continent* (London: Allen Lane, 1998).
26. W. Benz (ed.), *Dimension des Voelkermords: Die Zahl der Juedischen Opfer des Nationalsozialismus* (Muenchen: Oldenbourg, 1991).
27. Roberts, *Twentieth Century*, p. 785.
28. Ibid., pp. 430–1.
29. For a few examples of more up-to-date explanations see Y. Bauer, *Rethinking the Holocaust*, (New Haven, CT: Yale University Press, 2000); M. Berenbaum (ed.), *The Holocaust and History: The Known, the Unknown, the Disputed, and the Reexamined* (Bloomington, IN: Indiana University Press, 1998); R. S. Wistrich, *Hitler and the Holocaust* (New York: Modern Library, 2001).
30. D. Cesarani (ed.), *The Final Solution: Origins and Implementations* (London: Routledge, 1994); D. J. Goldhagen, *Hitler's Willing Executioners: Ordinary Germans and the Holocaust* (New York: Knopf, 1996) .
31. Grenville, *A History of the World*, p. 237.
32. Ibid., p. 284; see also David Bankier, *The Germans and the Final Solution: Public Opinion Under Nazism* (Oxford: Blackwell, 1992).
33. Grenville, *A History of the World*, p. 192.
34. The commonly used number of 1.5 million children under the age of 18 seems to be an extrapolation of the number of 1.2 million children under the age of 16 used by M. Dworzecki, *Europa Lelo Yeladim: Tochnit Hanazit Leheres Biologit* [Europe Without Children: The Nazi Program for Biological Destruction] (Jerusalem: Yad Vashem, 1964), p. 58 (in

Hebrew). In his PhD thesis, Hayim Shalom Halevi offers various statistics about Polish Jewry on the eve of their destruction and after. If one projects his numbers it would appear that more than 1.5 million Jews under the age of 18 were murdered. See H. S. Halevi, 'Hashpaat Milhemet Haolam, Hashenia Al Techonot Hademografiot Shel Am Yisrael' [The Influence of the Second World War on the Demographic Characteristics of the People of Israel] (Jerusalem: Hebrew University, 1963), unpublished thesis, p. 63 (in Hebrew).

35. Grenville, *A History of the World*, p. 238.
36. Y. Bauer, 'Jews, Gypsies and Slavs: Policies of the Third Reich', in *Unesco Yearbook of Peace and Conflict Studies: The Second World War* (New York: Greenwood Press, 1987), pp. 73–99.
37. Grenville, *A History of the World*, p. 247.
38. Jerzy Lukowski and Hubert Zawdzki, *A Concise History of Poland* (Cambridge: Cambridge University Press, 2001), pp. 223–5.
39. Grenville, *A History of the World*, p. 214.
40. Ibid., pp. 282–3.
41. For a more up-to-date discussion of the timing of the decision for the Final Solution see C. R. Browning, *Nazi Policy: Jewish Workers, German Killers*, (Cambridge: Cambridge University Press, 2000); U. Herbert (ed.), *National Socialist Extermination Policies: Contemporary German Perspectives and Controversies* (Oxford: Berghahn Books, 2000); Wistrich, *Hitler and the Holocaust*.
42. Grenville, *A History of the World*, pp. 236–7.
43. M. Kaplan, *Between Dignity and Despair: Jewish Life in Nazi Germany* (New York: Oxford University Press, 1998). Two recent examples of personal stories that illustrate the evolution in response among German Jewish families are L. Muhlfelder, *Because I Survived, An Autobiography* (Rockville, MD: Shengold, 2000); M. Roseman, *A Past in Hiding: Memory and Survival in Nazi Germany* (New York: Metropolitan Books, 2001).
44. Ponting, *The Twentieth Century*, pp. 8–9.
45. Ibid., p. 33.
46. Ibid., p. 522.
47. Ibid., p. 515.
48. Ibid., p. 517.
49. Ibid., p. 519.
50. Ibid., p. 520.
51. Ibid, p. 518.
52. Ibid.,p. 525.
53. One of the more baffling aspects of Ponting's book is his treatment of Israel. While he writes very empathetically about Jews in the Holocaust, the sections about Israel are less than charitable. For Ponting, Israel is a colonial society (pp. 241–4). Unlike Ponting, this author sees a vast difference between colonization and Zionism. Colonization is a process in which outsiders who have never lived in a territory take it over. According to Zionism, a people who had lived in the land and were exiled from it return to it. Ponting also stresses Israeli discrimination against the Palestinians (pp. 488–9). He offers no mitigating factors whatsoever for the discrimination – such as the ongoing conflict and security problems. Neither does he mention that alongside measures that discriminate against Palestinians living in the occupied territories, those living within the borders of pre-1967 Israel vote and have representatives in the Knesset. Although it is well within an author's right to have political views and express them in his writing, when writing a supposedly balanced account of an historical period, one should really strive to be a bit more balanced. One need not be uncritically pro-Zionist to explain more objectively the Zionist project – with all its beauty marks and warts – *versus* the Palestinian narrative of their recent history.

3
Historical Atlases
and the Holocaust

For most scholars born in the American Midwest, locating the exact boundaries of a place like the Pripet Marshes, and determining whether they are in Polesia or Volhynia, or in present-day Belarus or Ukraine, may be a daunting task. For such a person, like any person interested in understanding events that happened in a specific location or geographical area, maps obviously are an important tool. Especially when exploring events such as the Holocaust, which happened over a period of several years and over a large physical area, maps that reflect the geography of those events àre often indispensable tools. Since not all students, teachers and researchers of the Holocaust have access to wide-ranging and in-depth map collections, gazetteers or other geographical tools that may help them in their study, published atlases are often the first and perhaps the only sources of readily available geographical information consulted. Because atlases that were in use at the time the events under scrutiny were unfolding are not always on hand, historical atlases are commonly used to fill the need for geographical information concerning past events such as the Holocaust.

It is clear that students, teachers and scholars may have different needs regarding geographical material. It may be assumed that students who are not engaged in primary source research generally have less need for complex physical and political detail in maps. Rather, such students are more likely to require maps that give more information about concepts, processes, social groups and the like, or show changes of territory and borders without minutiae. Teachers may require maps with somewhat more physical and political detail than their students, but on the whole their needs are similar. Scholars, however, may have very different needs. Sometimes they require very explicit topographical maps. For example, knowing the exact distance from the main street of the Tuczyn ghetto to the forest nearby would certainly help a researcher understand why the leadership of that ghetto chose the strategy of flight to the forest to evade deportation. Scholars and researchers sometimes need highly articulated political details, maps that include every settlement in the area being presented, with a clear delineation of regions and districts. They sometimes need maps that show the particulars of infrastructure, such as entire railway systems, bridges etc.

In recent years several historical atlases have been published which are relevant to students, teachers and scholars of the history of the Holocaust. *The Historical Atlas of the Holocaust*, published by the United States Holocaust Memorial Museum, as its title indicates, focuses directly on the subject. *The Penguin Historical Atlas of the Third Reich*, by Richard Overy, also intersects with the events of the Holocaust, as does the atlas edited by Eli Barnavi, *A Historical Atlas of the Jewish People*. Somewhat farther afield, but still potentially relevant, are *The* (London) *Times Atlas of European History: A Concise Historical Atlas of Eastern Europe*, by Dennis P. Hupchick and Harold E. Cox, Assistant Professor and Professor respectively at Wilkes University, Pennsylvania; and *An Atlas of Eastern Europe in the Twentieth Century*, by Richard and Ben Crampton.[1]

In addition to their stated subject of presentation, historical atlases may be roughly divided into two categories, each with its own implications for the types of maps used and presented. One genre of historical atlas seeks to present political or physical maps true to the situation at different junctures in history. For example, such an atlas might present a set of maps that show Poland at different epochs in history: the nation before and after the partitions at the end of the eighteenth century; Poland on the eve of the First World War; the situation following the resurrection of the Polish state after that war; Poland in the wake of the Nazi and Soviet conquests; and Poland as it has existed since the end of the Second World War. In this type of atlas, the maps tend to be standard political and physical maps, some with more details and some with less.

The second kind of historical atlas strives to teach history through maps – that is to say, such atlases present historical concepts, processes and situations in map format. This type of atlas might present the results of regional elections in Germany between 1924 and 1933 in a series of maps to show where the Nazi party increased its voter-base on its road to power.[2] The maps used in these kinds of atlases tend to have less political and physical detail, unless such details are crucial to the presentation of the historical concept or process being illustrated.

Both kinds of atlases obviously have their uses for scholars, teachers and students of the Holocaust and both, as may be surmised from the examples given, have their limitations. Among the atlases under discussion here, *The Times Atlas of European History* and *A Concise*

Historical Atlas of European History may be classified as atlases that present maps at different junctures in history, whereas the other atlases under discussion seek to teach history through maps. All of the atlases discussed here may satisfy some of the needs of students and teachers, but none of them comfortably fulfils the occasionally extraordinary needs of scholars.

All of the historical atlases under scrutiny in this review have accompanying text. Some also contain visual material other than maps, including photographs, charts, tables and reproductions of works of art. The textual problems that may be found in these historical atlases are similar to those evident in other types of published reference material, such as lexicons and encyclopedias. Since they offer concise explanations of often complex events (without footnotes), almost every word used is of consequence. In such writing it is easy to convey the wrong information or message because of a nuance that might be less noticeable in more expansive or more scholarly writing. Also, as with most reference works, factual errors are nearly impossible to root out totally.

Because these historical atlases are being assessed for their value for people who study, teach and research the Holocaust, a salient question that must be addressed is how does each one present the subject of the Holocaust and the Jewish presence in Europe before and after the catastrophic events of the Holocaust era? To this reviewer it seems to be axiomatic that comprehensive reference works dealing with the history of the twentieth century must address the Jewish presence in Europe and the Nazi attempt to erase that presence. Such reference works must strive to present the Holocaust in proportion to other subjects depicted in their pages, and in proportion to the importance of the subject to human history. It almost goes without saying that they must aim at presenting the Holocaust, as all subjects they discuss, in as clear and unbiased a way as possible.

On the face of it, *The Times Atlas* is probably the least useful for scholars, teachers and students of the Holocaust. With over 180 pages dedicated to maps illustrating 3,000 years of European political history, only the last 23 pages concern the twentieth century. Even though the maps used are political maps and some of them, according to the introduction, are meant to show quite detailed information, most show very little. For example, the map illustrating the Nazi–Soviet pact of 1939, which focuses on the countries of Poland, Estonia, Latvia and Lithuania, contains only five rivers, without naming them, and eleven cities. Maps of this type are more useful for gaining impressions than for solving geographical problems, such as which communities in this region actually fell into Nazi hands and which into Soviet hands in the autumn of 1939.[3]

Even on the level of creating impressions, the maps dealing with the war years are problematic in this particular atlas. There are two double-paged maps that show Europe during the Second World War, one showing Nazi conquests in 1940 and another showing Hitler's Europe in 1942. According to the colour scheme, it appears in the first map as if Spain fell 'under Axis occupation', and according to the second map it appears that Spain was 'under Axis administration', because both Spain and the 'German Empire' are the same shade of light brown. Since Spain was a member of the Anti-Comintern pact, this colour scheme may have been adopted deliberately. But in that case, other members of the pact should have been shaded the same tone of brown – among them Italy, Hungary and Slovakia – but were not. When one considers the internal logic of the two maps, it appears that the colouring of Spain is simply a mistake.[4]

The Times Atlas does not contain any maps that present aspects of the Nazi atrocities against the Jews. The only references to the atrocities are in the accompanying text, and they are indirect and by no means compensate for the lack of maps. In the context of 'nominal self-government' of territories under Nazi influence, the text notes that such areas 'were expected to impose Nazi measures, especially against the Jews ...'[5] In a discussion of the Croatian regime, it is stated that savage atrocities against 'Serbs, Jews and other minorities, made the Croatian regime notorious'.[6] Last, as part of the discussion of the effect of the German occupation on the Soviet Union, which is said to have 'left no traces on the ground', it was also asserted that 'Only the "negative" policy of mass extermination of Jews and other groups targeted as enemies by the Nazis was carried out on an enormous scale.'[7]

Despite its cursory and fragmented treatment of the Holocaust, *The Times Atlas* may be of use in unexpected ways to those who deal with the geography of the Holocaust years, because it does contain a wealth of geographic information about Europe through the centuries. Looking through its pages, this reader finally realized why part of the area taken over from Yugoslavia by Hungary during the Second World War is referred to as 'the Banat'. In one of the maps showing Hungary in the early eighteenth century, there is an area called 'the Banat of Temes', or the area governed by the Ban (Viceroy) of Temes, whose main settlement was Temesvar (the fortress or castle of Temes). Thus it is clear that this area has retained its historical association with the Viceroy of Temes by the continued use of the term Banat.[8]

The preface to *A Concise Historical Atlas of Eastern Europe* is quite useful for clarifying why the authors compiled the atlas as they did. According to Hupchick and Cox:

The primary purpose of this atlas is to provide students and interested general readers with a basic and affordable visual aid for grasping the geopolitical situation at selected important moments in the history of Eastern Europe … Only those elements deemed necessary for the general understanding of the topics presented are included. Most rivers and mountain ranges, therefore, either do not appear or do so only relative to their information purpose within any given map.

They also explain that the text does not describe the maps, but gives 'a broad perspective on particular periods or issues represented in the maps'.[9] Finally, they address issues that students of history encounter whenever they deal with geography over the continuum of time: the choice and spelling of place names. In this case, the authors have chosen to spell place names in their contemporary form, according to contemporary borders. To this rule they have made one major exception – names that have a different common usage in English are noted by their English name. The authors also explain their method of transliteration from Cyrillic to Roman characters, another issue that poses problems for the spelling of place names.[10] As a result Cracow (the prevalent English-language spelling) is never referred to as Krakow and Lviv (the current Ukrainian spelling) is never referred to as Lwow (the Polish spelling) or Lvov (the common Russian transliteration). Yet, inexplicably, the name of Constantinople changes to Istanbul as the maps progress from the fifteenth century to the mid-sixteenth century even though, according to *The Columbia Lippincott Gazetteer*, Istanbul was adopted as the official name of the city only in 1930, and Istanbul is both the current and a widely accepted English-language name for the city.[11]

Despite problems of internal consistency, this atlas may be quite useful (more for students and teachers than for scholars) as a reference tool for the geography of eastern Europe, but not for maps concerning the events of the Holocaust itself. The second map presented is a physical map of eastern Europe, which gives a sparse yet clear general picture of the rivers, marshes and mountains of the region, as defined by the authors. Unfortunately, the authors have chosen a rather narrow definition of eastern Europe, defining its eastern border 'as the line formed by the combined western borders of Belarus, Ukraine, and the Russian Federated Republic'.[12] Thus they have excluded these former Soviet republics from the confines of eastern Europe. Although they say that setting such a border may be justified, they do not really explain themselves.[13]

The last ten maps of the book (nos 41–50) are potentially of most interest to those who investigate the history of the Holocaust. These maps range from the outbreak of the First World War to the situation in

Europe in 1950. The series of maps showing Europe between the wars is particularly instructive for understanding which territories were lost by Hungary and gained by Romania, Yugoslavia and Czechoslovakia, and which areas of Transylvania retained a Hungarian majority following the agreements at the end of the First World War. Essentially, three separate maps illustrate aspects of this exchange of territory.[14]

It is clear that the atlas suffers from the problem of proportion, i.e. the number of maps reflecting (or really not reflecting) the importance of the issues being illustrated. Whereas the above-mentioned three maps depict the territory taken from Hungary as a result of the Trianon treaty, only one map illustrates the situation of all of eastern Europe during the Second World War. Moreover, on that single map there is no reference to the fate of the region's Jews, and this was the most populous Jewish region in the world on the eve of the Holocaust. As in *The Times Atlas*, the only reference to Jews is textual and in this case the text is extremely problematic. The murder of the Jews is discussed solely in the context of the fate of Poland during the war. After citing the Nazi conquest of Poland, the authors write:

> The Nazis then set about following a propaganda campaign inside Germany portraying Slavic Poles as somewhat subhuman, which lent perverted credence to the genocidal policies they followed inside conquered Poland during the four years of occupation. *At least 3 million Poles were exterminated during World War II* [emphasis added], and those who escaped that fate were subjected to the most degrading conditions. The Nazis transformed Poland into the chief killing ground in their efforts to rid future Europe of those they considered undesirable, human 'vermin' – Jews, Eastern Slavs, Gypsies, political opponents, among others – through medical experimentation.[15]

If it were not clear from the place of employment of the authors, a university in the United States, one would be hard pressed to believe that this paragraph was not written in a former communist-bloc country in another era. Perhaps the tone of this paragraph, which severely skews the context of the destruction of European Jewry, helps drive home the astonishing fact that in the entire atlas the authors chose not to present even one map which indicates any aspect of Jewish presence in eastern Europe, or the destruction of that extraordinary presence on the soil of eastern Europe. One may only wonder how a respected firm like St. Martin's Press published a reference book with such overt bias, omissions and untenable proportions.

Unlike Hupchick and Cox's atlas, Richard and Ben Crampton's *Atlas of Eastern Europe in the Twentieth Century* presents greater detail over a shorter period, and on the whole it is much more useful for geographical information about Holocaust-related events. The series of inter-war maps and many accompanying charts and tables are very informative. By using black-and-white maps, but with different textures, various sub-areas are clearly presented. The maps that show border changes after the First World War for each of the individual countries show few towns and cities, but they tend to show more physical and geographical details than the other atlases discussed here. The map showing the territorial changes throughout eastern Europe between 1938 and 1941 still suffers somewhat from a lack of cities and geographic features, but gives a good overall impression of the changes in those years.[16]

In further contrast to Hupchick and Cox, the Cramptons squarely place Jews in the geographical, ethnic, cultural and political history of eastern Europe. One of the first maps they present shows the Pale of Settlement, the area to which the czars confined the Jews. The map clearly shows the many districts that comprised the Pale and indicates which districts contained Jewish populations of over 10 per cent.[17] The Jewish population, as well as those of other minorities, is also depicted on the map of ethnic composition in inter-war Poland.[18] Only two maps deal directly with the destruction of the Jews during the Holocaust: one shows the murder by the *Einsatzgruppen* and in the extermination camps and the other shows the percentage of Jewish losses per country. The accompanying text is succinct, touches the main points and appears unbiased.[19]

A Historical Atlas of the Jewish People, compiled under the direction of Eli Barnavi and employing a team of respected scholars, seeks to teach Jewish history through its many aesthetic illustrations and maps. Even though it is called 'a historical atlas', this book contains more text and as many illustrations as it does maps. Indeed Barnavi refers to it as a 'fresco'.[20] It is clearly of more use to teachers and students of the Holocaust than to scholars, and would not disgrace the surface of any coffee table. Many of its maps shed light on aspects of Jewish history which may be linked to events that evolved towards the Holocaust and the Jewish situation at the time of the Holocaust, but the main part of the book that is relevant for those interested in the Holocaust comprises only 18 pages (pp. 226–43: the section beginning with the 'Prelude to the Holocaust' and ending with 'The Struggle for a Jewish State').

Despite its polished appearance and distinguished team of scholarly contributors, this atlas does not escape some of the commonplace problems plaguing reference works in general and historical atlases in particular. The text contains its share of dubious statements, where nuances are very important. In the opening sentence of the section entitled 'The Holocaust: First Act' the author, Dr Idith Zartal, writes:

There is no explicit mention of the systematic physical annihilation of human beings in general, and of the Jews in particular, in official Nazi documents, with the exception of the agreement between Himmler and Thierack (Reich Minister of Justice) dated September 18, 1942 stating that men and women were to be 'worked to death'.[21]

Most scholars would agree that many such documents, such as the *Einsatzgruppen* reports; which have been published in English and are thus readily available, are 'official German documents', and certainly record the systematic physical annihilation of Jews and others.[22]

Another small textual slip-up may be seen in one of the generally informative chronological entries in the atlas: according to the entry from July to October 1944, Raoul Wallenberg saved thousands of Jews by providing them with Swedish documents, food and shelter.[23] Wallenberg certainly rescued thousands through such activities, but most of the actual rescue work was carried out after October 1944 and ended with his arrest by arriving Russian forces in January 1945.

Every scholar and student of the Holocaust is aware of the problems posed by statistics concerning the murder of the Jews. Because of many factors, including frequent border changes in the first half of the twentieth century, large movements of populations, missing relevant statistical information (such as the Jewish population of a certain place on the eve of the war) and incomplete records regarding the fate of individuals and even whole communities, many of the statistics we commonly use are really estimates. Regarding the losses of Romanian Jewry in the Holocaust, this atlas clearly illustrates, if only by accident, the complexity of some of the issues. On the map showing Jewish losses in the Holocaust from 1941 to 1945, the losses for the 800,000 Jews of Romania is set at 350,000. In the text about Romania in the nineteenth and twentieth centuries, it is stated that of 608,000 Jews living under Romanian rule in 1939, 265,000 were killed during the Holocaust. The first problem here is: which Romania is being discussed? Romania with its borders in 1939 or Romania of 1940, after the Second Vienna award, which transferred Northern Transylvania to Hungarian hands? The first set of figures given (800,000 Jews and 350,000 losses) does not reflect the situation from 1941 to 1945, but reflects the population of Romanian Jewry before the transfer of Northern Transylvania to Hungary. The text states outright that the second set of figures (608,000 Jews and 265,000 losses) reflects Romanian Jewry in 1939, but this is incorrect: the figure of 608,000 and the subsequent losses reflect the borders of Romania after the transfer of Northern Transylvania in 1940.[24]

The *Atlas of Modern Jewish History* by Evyatar Friesel[25] in many respects is the standard against which Barnavi's atlas must be measured. Like Barnavi, Friesel illustrates history through the use of maps, and the book contains a great deal of information in the form of text, tables and graphs. It too is a book intended more for students than for scholars. Friesel's atlas is not nearly as glossy as that of Barnavi, but on the whole the maps contain much more physical and political detail and are clearly articulated. None of the maps shows infrastructure such as roads and railway lines, but nearly all of them show major rivers and some suggest mountainous areas. The map of Jewish communities in Poland in 1921 even indicates districts, including Volhynia and Polesia, and contains Jewish communities with populations over 2,000.[26]

Many of the maps are directly relevant to the study of the Holocaust, including those scattered throughout the book that show various countries and cities during the inter-war period, and the eight maps that relate to the Holocaust itself. Perhaps because its focus is on Jewish history from the eighteenth to the end of the twentieth centuries, the information presented in this atlas is often more detailed than that of Barnavi, but some of it is outdated. The text on the section about the Holocaust reflects the way the subject was often taught 20 years ago. In particular, the evolution of the Nazi policies against the Jews is presented in a rather deterministic fashion; and the discussion of the murder by the *Einsatzgruppen* does not mention that other German forces, such as regular soldiers and police units, also took part in the murder. Some of the statistics used are also outdated; the figure for Jews murdered in Auschwitz is given as 1.8 million, whereas today most historians use a lower figure of roughly one million.[27]

In his introduction to *The Penguin Historical Atlas of the Third Reich* the editor and highly regarded scholar Richard Overy writes,

> This atlas is not intended as a geographical guide … The maps and charts have been chosen because they tell the story of this dozen years effectively in atlas form. Issues of race, area and resources were, as we have seen, central to the Nazi view of Germany's future.[28]

Using text, illustrations and charts as much as maps – text on a reading level for college freshmen or above, and maps, charts and other illustrations that are colourful if not always clear – Overy relates a history of the Third Reich. For the most part the atlas is set out like a textbook, and in its 143 pages touches subjects such as the establishment of the Nazi dictatorship, German foreign policy from 1933 to 1939, the course of the war, the German 'new order', 'German society and total war', and the aftermath. Some of the maps are very informative; for example, like the map that illustrates the countries of origin of foreign labourers brought to Germany and the map that presents Nazi plans

for the post-war order in Europe.[29] But the atlas consistently under-
plays the Holocaust, giving it little attention and at times simply ignor-
ing it. Only six of the 97 maps Overy presents address the persecution
of the Jews and their reactions.

Overy presents three maps relating to German Jewry before the
outbreak of the war: Jewish emigration from 1933 to 1938, Zionist training centres in Germany, and the destruction engendered by
Kristallnacht.[30] The map of resistance to the Reich illustrates some ghetto uprisings, albeit not very clearly. The accompanying text mentions
only the Warsaw Ghetto Uprising, and the map does not include the
uprising in Bialystok. Nor does it hint at the establishment of other
major Jewish underground units, flights to the forests, partisan activities or other forms of resistance. The map of the Nazi camp system
includes extermination camps, but classifies Chelmno, the first extermination camp, as a concentration camp.[31] The map showing Jewish
losses is also problematic and in particular, here, too, the figures for
Hungary and Romania are very unclear. Romanian losses are set at
slightly over 269,000 (which does not include Northern Transylvania),
but Hungarian at only 200,000, when the figure should be well over
half a million (especially if it includes the losses for Transylvania not
included in the figure for Romania). Perhaps this mistake is what leads
Overy to give the overall number of Jewish losses as only 5.3 million, a
figure much lower than that agreed upon by most scholars.[32]

Although it is not within the confines of this particular essay, one
must wonder if Overy's and *The Times Atlas*'s curt discussion about the
Holocaust, and Hupchick and Cox's skewed discussion of it, are isolated
cases or symptomatic of how the Holocaust is often still given short
shrift in many reference works. *The Times Atlas*'s treatment of the topic
suggests that the Holocaust was not a very central event in the 3,000
years of European history. In his handling of the destruction of the
Jews, Overy implies that it was neither a central nor a significant feature of the Nazis and their regime. Hupchick and Cox barely consider
the Jews a subject of eastern European history. Each of these positions
seems to this reader to be severely biased and historically inaccurate
and the messages they transmit are, to say the least, unfortunate.

As its name clearly states, the *Historical Atlas of the Holocaust* by the
United States Holocaust Memorial Museum focuses on the destruction
of European Jewry during the Nazi period. This atlas exemplifies an
array of problems found in reference works aimed at the general reading public. Lacking a clear conceptual explanation in either the preface
or the introduction, the authors state only that the grouping of the
maps follows the chronology of the Holocaust. This, however, is only
partly true. For example, the map of the Warsaw Ghetto Uprising of the
spring of 1943 is placed ten pages before the set of maps that show the

murder operations of the Nazis in the occupied portions of the Soviet Union. The uprising occurred nearly two years after those operations had begun.[33] This placement of maps underscores the difficulty in presenting complex and at times overlapping historical processes in chronological order.

The maps in the *Historical Atlas of the Holocaust* are very attractive visually, but have few geographical details and contain some incongruities. For example, on two facing pages, maps of the Baltic countries contain different, albeit legitimate, names for the same Latvian town: one map uses the name Dvinsk and the other Duenaburg.[34]

Like the other atlases under discussion, the *Historical Atlas of the Holocaust* presents a great deal of history in a very telegraphic way and, unfortunately, some of the text is written in an absolute fashion when it would have been better to have been circumspect. A salient example is the discussion of the Nazi persecution of the Gypsies (Romanies). According to the editorial team, 'Roma [Gypsies] were among the groups singled out on racial grounds for persecution by the Nazi regime … '[35] It may be argued, and has been argued by scholars such as Yehuda Bauer, that the persecution of the Romanies occurred primarily because the Nazis considered them to be a-socials and was not because of their racial origins.[36]

One cannot refrain from comparing this atlas to its forerunner by many years, Martin Gilbert's *Atlas of the Holocaust*.[37] Gilbert's atlas, like that of the United States Holocaust Memorial Museum, seeks less to impart geographical information than to teach the history of the Holocaust through maps. The maps, as illustrations of geographical and physical issues, are rather amateurish, seemingly sketched by hand. At times they can be unnerving, as when they cite a region, but give it no borders: for example, map 48 cites Polesia and Volhynia, without delineating between the two.[38] Gilbert's atlas also suffers from problematic statistics, compounded by the lack of clear source citations. He presents hundreds of figures and it would be an immense task to try to verify them all. As an example of these problems: it is not clear why he gives the Jewish pre-murder population of Hungary of 742,800 as quoted at the Wansee Conference, and not the much more widely used 825,000 (which includes about 100,000 Jews who had converted to Christianity).[39] Yet Gilbert's atlas is so full of information, provided from so many angles and in such detail, that it simply dwarfs the United States Holocaust Memorial Museum's publication.

None of the atlases discussed here combines accurate, extensive information about the Holocaust years with clear and detailed maps. Some are better at one aspect than another, but none manages to put it all together. It seems to this reader there is both a conceptual and a medium problem. It is safe to say that the atlases discussed here are not really meant for scholars, but seem to be geared more to students, teachers and the informed reading public. A traditional way of trying to deal with the complexities of showing political, physical and infrastructural features that scholars sometimes need is to use overlays. But binding overlays into a book is not very practical; among other reasons, to be able to use the overlays in any combination, according to the user's need, they would have to remain unbound inserts. A much better way to provide such complex and detailed maps is to use computer technology. Computerized geographical systems exist for tourists or motorists, where one may zoom in on a specific area and obtain great detail.

The United States Holocaust Memorial Museum's atlas exists in CD format, but it does not pretend to be this kind of computerized resource. According to the user's guide that accompanies the CD, '... the Atlas can be regarded as a condensed history of the Holocaust, presenting the geographical aspects of historical events'.[40] One may read between the lines and conclude that this resource is best used in the classroom or the household, and is not really meant to provide detailed geographical information to scholars. So, as in its print counterpart, the maps on the CD generally lack physical details. Unlike the print counterpart, however, the CD allows the user to link from more general maps to more specific maps, and to toggle between maps, text and photographs. For example, one may begin with a map of Poland, and then link to a more detailed map of Warsaw and its environs, and from there to a still more detailed set of maps of the Warsaw ghetto in various stages of its existence; and all the while text and photographs may be consulted. However, the linked sets of maps are of an uneven quality. Some of the maps of ghettos and various uprisings contain street names, whereas others do not. The map that shows the different zones of occupation in Berlin looks like a work of modern art – it has several sections painted in different colours to represent the American, British, Russian and French zones, but gives not a clue as to the streets that were contained in those zones. Although the CD contains linked maps it does not allow for true zooming. That is to say, one cannot begin with a map of Poland, zoom in on Warsaw, zoom in on a section of Warsaw, and then zoom in on a street. Neither is it possible to see the same map of Poland with different overlays, such as roads, railway lines, rivers or any combination thereof.

To view maps in this way, across the broad expanse of territory on which the events of the Holocaust happened and through the continuum of time, the maps would have to be generated by the proper software resting on a very detailed database. Such a database would need to include all the relevant place names and their variants, accompanying physical features in great detail, border changes and of course historical and statistical information relevant to the subject of the Holocaust. This is the tool that scholars need: a tool that they can tailor for themselves, a tool that allows them to see the details that they need at a given moment and which also could be easily adapted for students and teachers alike. Creating such a database and making it accessible would go a long way towards solving most problems that arise with the study of the geography of the Holocaust.

NOTES

This essay was first published in *Yad Vashem Studies*, Vol. 27, 1999.

1. E. Barnavi (ed.), *A Historical Atlas of the Jewish People from the Time of the Patriarchs to the Present* (New York: Alfred A. Knopf, 1992); R. Crampton and B. Crampton, *Atlas of Eastern Europe in the Twentieth Century* (London: Routledge, 1996); D. P. Hupchick and H. E. Cox, *A Concise Historical Atlas of Eastern Europe* (New York: St. Martin's, 1996); R. Overy, *The Penguin Historical Atlas of the Third Reich* (London: Penguin Books, 1996); *The Times Atlas of European History* (London: Times Books, 1994); United States Holocaust Memorial Museum, *Historical Atlas of the Holocaust* (New York: Macmillan, 1996).
2. Overy, *The Penguin Historical Atlas*, pp. 18–21.
3. *The Times Atlas*, pp. 7 and 178–9.
4. Ibid., pp. 176–81.
5. Ibid., p. 180.
6. Ibid., p. 183.
7. Ibid.
8. Ibid., p. 138.
9. Hupchick and Cox, *A Concise Historical Atlas*, p. vii.
10. Ibid.
11. Ibid., maps 22 and 24;. L. E. Seltzer (ed.), *The Columbia Lippincott Gazetteer of the World* (New York: Columbia University, 1952), p. 854.
12. Hupchick and Cox, *A Concise Historical Atlas*, Map 2.
13. Ibid.
14. Ibid., Maps 42–47.
15. Ibid., Map 49.
16. Crampton and Crampton, *Atlas of Eastern Europe*, p. 134.
17. Ibid., p. 13.
18. Ibid., p. 104.
19. Ibid., pp. 138–41.
20. Barnavi, *A Historical Atlas of the Jewish People*, p. iv.
21. Ibid., p. 228.
22. Y. Arad, S. Krakowski and S. Spector (eds), *The Einsatzgruppen Reports* (New York: Holocaust Library, 1989).
23. Barnavi, *A Historical Atlas of the Jewish People*, p. 235.
24. Ibid., pp. 233 and 253.
25. Friesel, *Atlas of Modern Jewish History* (New York: Oxford University Press, 1990).
26. Ibid., p. 93.
27. Ibid., pp. 106-7; F. Piper, 'The Number of Victims,' in Y. Gutman and M. Berenbaum (eds), *Anatomy of the Auschwitz Death Camp* (Washington, DC: United States Holocaust Memorial Museum, 1994), pp. 61–80.
28. Overy, *The Penguin Historical Atlas*, p. 5.
29. Ibid., pp. 88 and 84–5.
30. Ibid., pp. 36–7.
31. Ibid., pp. 90–1.
32. Ibid., p. 93.
33. USHMM, *Historical Atlas*, pp. 7, 41 and 51–3.
34. Ibid., pp. 64–5.
35. Ibid., p. 42.
36. In Nazi jargon a-socials were people of Aryan stock who were unable to conform to the standards of society as set by the Nazis. Y. Bauer, 'Jews, Gypsies and Slavs: Policies of the Third Reich', in *Unesco Yearbook of Peace and Conflict Studies: The Second World War* (New York: Greenwood Press, 1987).

37. M. Gilbert, *Atlas of the Holocaust* (New York: William Morrow, 1993). This is a completely revised and updated edition: the first edition was published in 1982.
38. Gilbert, *Atlas of the Holocaust*, pp. 47, 85.
39. Gilbert, *Atlas of the Holocaust*, p. 85; R. Braham, *The Politics of Genocide, the Holocaust in Hungary*, revised edn (New York: Columbia University Press, 1994), p. 77 (originally published in 1981); I. Gutman (ed.), *The Encyclopedia of the Holocaust* (New York: Macmillan, 1990), p. 1799.
40. J. Weinberg, 'Introduction', in *User's Guide for the CD Rom Version of the Historical Atlas of the Holocaust* (New York: Macmillan, no date).

4
Reflections on Jewish Leadership during the Holocaust

Early writing about the Holocaust often portrays the role of the Jewish leadership in sharply judgemental and disapproving terms. Raul Hilberg, in *The Destruction of the European Jews* (published at the start of the 1960s) and in a subsequent paper delivered at a Yad Vashem conference on Jewish leadership in 1977, characterizes the behaviour of Jewish leaders as being steeped in norms and a consciousness rooted in pre-modern Jewish history. In the medieval and early modern period, according to Hilberg, the situation of the Jews was such in Europe that the best way for Jewish leaders to protect their fellow Jews was through their personal contacts with the authorities. In Hilberg's view, this mentality of intercession based on personal ties contributed greatly to allowing Jewish leaders to become a tool used by the Nazis to further the destruction of the Jews of Europe during the Holocaust.[1]

Not long after Hilberg's book was published, Hannah Arendt wrote a series of articles about the Eichmann trial that were later printed together in the book *Eichmann in Jerusalem: A Report on the Banality of Evil*.[2] Among Arendt's more controversial conclusions is that Jewish leaders were collaborators and, as such, they bore great responsibility for the Holocaust. Neither Hilberg nor Arendt, however, was the first to articulate such ideas in print.

In the mid-1950s a trial rocked the young state of Israel, because similar claims had appeared regarding one of the leaders of Hungarian Jewry during the Holocaust. The publicist Malchiel Grunwald accused Israel (Reszo, Rudolph) Kasztner, a leader of the Hungarian Zionist movement and the Budapest Relief and Rescue Committee, of having collaborated with the Nazis in Budapest in 1944–45. Ostensibly he did this in order to save people close to him, in exchange for allowing the Nazis to destroy Hungarian Jewry. During the highly politicized trial, in which Kasztner accused Grunwald of libel, Kasztner was depicted as self-serving and amoral. The verdict of the lower court found in favour of Grunwald. In the infamous decision of Judge Benjamin Halevy, Kasztner was said to

have 'sold his soul to the devil'. Later a higher court overturned this decision. In the meantime, Kasztner was felled by an assassin's bullet in Tel
Aviv, and a negative image of Jewish leadership during the Holocaust
gained even more ground in the popular mind in Israel.[3]

Such disapproving images were to be found not only in Israel in the
immediate post-war years. In the Netherlands a court of honour barred
the two leaders of the Joodse Raad, the Dutch Jewish Council, Avraham
Ascher and David Cohen from holding any future public office in the
Jewish community. They too were depicted as intentionally having
acted against the best interest of the Dutch Jewish community during
the Holocaust.[4]

Since the 1970s, much has been written that presents a more balanced and variegated picture of Jewish leadership in the Holocaust.
The study *Judenrat*, by Isaiah Trunk, published in English in the early
1970s, was seminal for igniting this change in interpretation.[5] Aaron
Weiss's important research about the attitudes and deeds of the leaders
of Jewish councils also contributed to this change in perception.[6] Later
scholarship, such as that by Yehiam Weitz about the Kasztner trial,
tracked these changes in historiography and public opinion.[7]

If the earlier scholarship about Jewish leadership was rather two-
dimensional, today it can be seen not only as three-dimensional, but as
multifaceted. It is clear that each community, indeed each situation,
must be explored on its own merits. The following is an attempt to
explain the many factors that must be taken into account in order to
begin examining the issue of Jewish leadership during the Holocaust.
Different periods, different places, different personalities, different
authority structures and different community characteristics must all
be taken into account when broaching a study of Jewish leadership in
a given place or across a given spectrum.

One cannot meaningfully discuss any aspect of the history of the
Holocaust without taking into consideration the fact that events
evolved over time. Jewish leaders faced evolving circumstances, as did
everyone else. So we must recognize that a Jewish leader in Germany
in 1933, for example, faced a situation very different from that faced by
his counterpart in Hungary in 1944.

In general, German Jews before the war faced a governmental policy
of discrimination. At first, following the Nazi rise to power in January
1933, anti-Jewish measures focused on isolating the Jews, impoverish-
ing them and making them believe they had no future in Germany, so
that they would leave of their own volition. Later, from 1938 through
to the outbreak of the war, violence and coercion were added to the
recipe, and Jews were essentially extruded from German territory.
Until the autumn of 1941, however, German Jews were not facing a
policy of systematic mass murder directed against them.

In Poland, at the time of the occupation in autumn 1939 and immediately afterward, Jews were not yet facing systematic mass murder either. Many died in the fighting and bombings, and thousands of Jews met their deaths at the hands of the Nazis in erratic acts of violence and terror.[8] Nevertheless, until late 1941 and, more pointedly, 1942, Polish Jews and their leaders primarily faced the twin evils of concentration in ghettos and brutal forced labour. It was only after many months of suffering in the ghettos and labour camps of Poland that they would face the new policy of the Final Solution, the Nazi attempt to murder all the Jews of Europe.

In the German-conquered areas of the Soviet Union, Jews faced mass systematic murder almost from the first moments German forces arrived in late June 1941. It was common practice for the Nazis either to incite a pogrom as soon as they were poised to take over a given community, or to begin the mass shootings that characterized the first wave of murder that hit the occupied Soviet Union, almost directly after they began their occupation. Ghettos were set up either immediately prior to the first murder *Aktion* or, more commonly, closely in its wake. Living in the ghettos for weeks, months and even years, the shadow of murder hung heavily over all the inhabitants.

In the Slovak state, established by the Germans in March 1939, a local version of anti-Jewish persecution struck the community until the spring of 1942. In September 1941 Jews were defined by a Slovak version of the Nuremberg Laws; in the meantime their property was despoiled and their activities were restricted. In March 1942 the Slovak government, working closely with a special German adviser on Jewish issues Dieter Wisliceny, began bankrolling the exile of Slovak Jewry. Thus Slovak Jews were the first community outside Poland to be subjected to the Final Solution in what became its classical form: deportation by train to the killing centres in the east. During this first wave of deportations, which lasted until October 1942, some two-thirds of the nearly 90,000 Jews of Slovakia were sent to their deaths in Poland.[9]

In Hungary, Jews suffered an ordeal similar to that of their Slovak cousins, but with the all-important difference that it began two years later, in March 1944. Like the Slovak Jews, those of Hungary suffered at first primarily from their own government. About 16,000 Jews, most not Hungarian citizens, were deported to Kamanets Poldosk in today's Ukraine by Hungarian forces. There they were subjected to a murder action in August 1941 carried out by the SS. Mass deportations were not repeated again until the Germans occupied Hungary three and a half years later. In the meantime, Hungarian Jewish men were subjected to forced labour as auxiliary units of the Hungarian Army. There were some 40,000 casualties among these Jews in the Hungarian Labour Service System.[10] In Hungary, Jews lived under restrictions but more or less normally until the advent of the German occupation. By March 1944 there was some information available to Hungarian Jewish leaders about the murder in other parts of Europe, and there was also a feeling among many that the government would not allow Hungarian Jewry to be attacked by the Nazis. Despite this belief, in the weeks that followed the occupation Hungarian Jews were subjected to a condensed and therefore very intensive process of persecution, robbery and concentration that culminated in the deportation of over 435,000 Jews during seven weeks.[11] These short descriptions illustrate that in a range of places and at different times, Jews and their leaders confronted the multifaceted events of the Holocaust from diverse points of departure and angles.

Jewish experience not only varied because different Jewish communities collided into the Holocaust at diverse points along the time line of events. Jews also found themselves subjected to a variety of authority structures, either under the Nazis themselves or under the Nazis' partners. This, of course, meant that Jewish leaders were not always facing the same type of regime, with the same characteristics or the same short-term agenda.

In Germany, for example, Jewish leaders dealt with a civilian government and its apparatus, in which the lines between government institutions and Nazi party formations became less and less distinct. A good example of this blurring is to be found in the relationship of the SS and the German police. On the eve of the Nazi rise to power Heinrich Himmler was the head of the SS, a Nazi party organization. His first major government job after Hitler became chancellor was as chief of the Bavarian police. Later he became chief of the entire German police. Himmler gave senior policemen SS ranks and at the same time he appointed SS men to various police positions. Ultimately, the line between the party organization, the SS, and the government organization, the police, became blurred since the same man often belonged to and was obedient to both hierarchies.[12]

The part of Poland designated by the Nazis as the Generalgouvernement was under civilian rule. The SS, however, constantly vied with the civilian administration for control over the Jewish question in Poland, and this dynamic affected how Jewish leaders perceived the authorities there. The Netherlands also had a civilian administration with a strong SS flavour, which included a stratum of senior Dutch civil servants who worked closely with the Germans regarding the implementation of measures. Belgium was subjected to the rule of the German military, which in this case was less enthusiastic than other elements in the German regime about implementing brutal anti-Jewish measures. Moreover, senior Belgian civil servants did their best to refrain from co-operating with the Nazi administration regarding anti-Jewish activities.[13]

Slovakia, from its inception as a separate state in March 1939, could best be termed a client or puppet state. Slovakia had its own government and accompanying bureaucracy, but the influence of Nazi Germany on all aspects of public and private life was great. The government under the Catholic priest, Jozef Tiso, proffered up its own native version of fascist corporatism and co-operated closely with the Nazis on issues regarding Jews. At the end of August 1944, anti-fascists in Slovakia rebelled against the regime, and only in the framework of putting down the uprising did German troops enter Slovak territory and effectively take over the reins of government in order to shore up the faltering Tiso regime.

Hungary, until the German occupation of 1944, was a sovereign state allied to Nazi Germany. As such, the direct influence of Germany on life in Hungary was relatively muted during the first years of the war. However, following several attempts by the Hungarian government to extricate itself from this alliance, German forces occupied Hungary. Concomitantly, the Nazis began to influence directly all aspects of life. One of the clearest repercussions of the German occupation was the beginning of the systematic destruction of Hungarian Jewry, which has been briefly described above.

France provides yet another variation on the theme of the types of authorities the Jews faced – in this case a rather convoluted set of factors within a single country. With the fall of France in June 1940, German forces occupied the northern zone of the country and allowed a French government to be established in the southern zone at Vichy, under Marshal Philippe Pétain. The relationship between the two zones and the Jewish leaders in them was complex. In February 1941, the Commissariat Général aux Questions Juives, primarily under the supervision of the Vichy regime, began to co-ordinate Jewish policy in both zones. In November 1941, the main official body of Jewish leadership, the Union Générale des Israélites de France (UGIF) was established in the northern zone by the German authorities, followed in February 1942 by the creation of a branch in the southern zone. At this time, the Germans stepped up their own efforts to implement the Final Solution in France and began vying with the Commissariat Général for the upper hand regarding the Jews. In November 1942, the Germans occupied most of the southern zone, allowing the Italians to establish themselves in a small strip near the Italian and Swiss borders. In the Italian zone of administration, Jews were treated much more leniently than in the German area. The Italian strip, in turn, was taken over by the Germans in summer 1943, when the Italians unsuccessfully tried to oust Mussolini and his regime. So Jewish leaders in France faced a shifting situation in which divergent forces competed for control over the Jews and their fate, and in which geography and the course of the war played important roles in determining exactly which authority they faced.[14]

Of course it was not only the type of authority they had to face that left its mark on Jewish leadership; the individual German personalities whom they encountered also came into play. For example, Hans Frank, the head of the Generalgouvernement, was a veteran Nazi who was engaged in a constant struggle for primacy in his bailiwick. He was adept at bending with the times in order to maintain his position. It was Frank who, in a speech at Berlin University in November 1941, suggested that Jews who performed useful labour for the Reich would continue to do so. However, less than a month later on 16 December, he called for the 'successful destruction' of all the Jews.[15] These two speeches were given at just about the time the Final Solution had been decided upon, and show how Frank himself was digesting the new policy, explaining it to his colleagues and bending with the winds.

Adolf Eichmann was a figure that Jewish leaders encountered at various times and places throughout the Holocaust period. As we now know from the most recent scholarship about him, Eichmann was neither a simple cog in the machinery nor the most important single force behind the murder of European Jewry, as contradictory portraits by writers in the first few decades after the Holocaust portrayed him.[16] Eichmann was a man who went about his job knowing full well what he was doing, and always aware of his place as an essential bureaucrat in the mechanism of Jewish persecution. But on a professional level, he also developed over time. In Vienna in 1938, Eichmann was out to prove himself. He displayed much creative initiative in finding ways to coerce Austrian Jews to leave. In Hungary, nearly six years later, he was a seasoned, poised veteran of the murder apparatus who wanted, perhaps more than anything else, to finish the job of destroying the last bastion of Jews in Nazi-dominated Europe.

Different from Eichmann was Odilo Globocnik, the SS and police leader in Lublin in 1942. Globocnik was directly responsible for the implementation of Aktion Reinhardt, the crusade to murder Polish Jewry. He was hell-bent on fulfilling his assigned task and lining his pockets. He did both very thoroughly and mercilessly, although the latter was a serious infraction of SS rules. Most probably because of his success in murdering Jews, instead of being severely reprimanded when his scandalous behaviour could no longer be ignored, Globocnik was promoted up and out to a less critical post in Trieste.[17]

A personality that combines some features of both Globocnik and Frank was Wilhelm Kube, the *Reichskommissar* for Belorussia. Like Frank, Kube was a veteran Nazi who held both party and governmental positions before the outbreak of the war. Like Globocnik, apparently he was not against lining his own pockets. Kube lost his most senior pre-war post, the governorship of the Brandenburg–Berlin district, as a result of party infighting owing to the suspicion that he had embezzled funds. Rehabilitated and given the post of *Reichskommissar*, Kube went so far as to complain about the murder of Jews and the draconian treatment of civilians in Belorussia in autumn 1941. His complaint had nothing to do with moral scruples. Kube objected because things were being done without his being consulted. Like Frank, his struggle with the SS for authority over matters concerning the Jews was spirited and eventually ended in compromise.[18]

Jewish leaders had both direct and indirect contact with men such as these, who had much power over the fate of individual Jews and entire Jewish communities. Undoubtedly, their idiosyncrasies and influence on their subordinates made an impression on Jewish leaders. The demeanour and deeds of men such as these could be a factor in how Jewish leaders interpreted specific directives and actions, or how they evaluated the situation of their communities at a given time.

Not only were the Nazis who held positions of authority a variegated lot, the leadership structures imposed on the Jews also differed from place to place. Generally, because the use of the term has become so common, we think of all Jewish leaderships to have been *Judenraete* (Jewish councils) of the type established in Poland based on Reinhard Heydrich's infamous *Schnellbrief* of 21 September 1939. In that order Heydrich called for the establishment of councils of Jewish elders, to include up to 24 'authoritative personalities and rabbis', depending on the size of the community.[19] These Polish Jewish councils were local, except for the one set up in Zaglembia, which was regional. In other places, however, the Jewish leadership was broader, countrywide in scope, with branch offices. This is the kind of structure that was imposed upon the 500,000 Jews of Germany when the Reichsvertretung der Deutschen Juden ('Reich Representation of German Jews') was set up in 1933. It became the model for the Ustredna Zsidov ('Jewish Centre') in Slovakia, the UFIG in France, the Association of Belgian Jews and the Zsido Tanacs ('Jewish council') in Hungary.

The number of Jews for whom the Jewish leaders were responsible also varied. The Reichsvertretung was accountable to half a million Jews in 1933 and the Zsido Tanacs in Hungary oversaw roughly 800,000 Jews in 1944, whereas the Association of Belgian Jews was only responsible for about 66,000 Jews in 1940. The Jewish councils in the individual ghettos also assumed responsibility for a wide array of populations. In Warsaw, at its height, the Jewish council was held accountable for some 445,000. In Lodz over 204,000 Jews lived in the ghetto at some point. In Rovno in the Ukraine there were only about 30,000 Jews and in Drogobych, near Lwow, there were only 10,000 Jews. Some ghettos were even smaller; for example, in Tuczyn, also in the Ukraine there were only about 3,000 Jewish inhabitants. Undoubtedly the scope of their responsibilities influenced Jewish leaders.

In addition to the officially constituted Jewish leaderships, there were alternative unofficial leadership groups that evolved in some localities. Occasionally, they became the *de facto* leaders of a given community. In other places they worked in co-ordination with the official Jewish leadership, and in some localities they formed a sort of opposition to the official leadership. Sometimes the same person was a member of both an official body and an unofficial body, as were Oskar Neumann and Gisi Fleischmann in Slovakia.

In the Warsaw ghetto, various Jewish organizations generally worked in parallel and sometimes in tandem with the official Jewish council. These organizations included formations that emanated from political parties and organizations such as the Bund, or the various factions of the Zionist youth movements, as well as the American Jewish Joint Distribution Committee, which worked through ZTOS (Polish initials for 'Jewish Mutual Aid Society') to address welfare needs in the ghetto. ZTOS in turn co-ordinated its activities with the *Judenrat*. In the wake of the great deportations from Warsaw in summer 1942, various factions formed the main Jewish underground fighting organization, the ZOB (Polish initials for 'Jewish Fighting Organization'). After its first clashes with the Germans in January 1943, the ZOB became the *de facto* leadership body in the Warsaw ghetto.[20]

In Slovakia, at the time the deportations were about to begin in early spring 1942, several members of the Jewish Centre, along with figures outside the official leadership, formed an alternative leadership group. This body came to be known as the Working Group. It was the Working Group that made great efforts to prevent, and then later try to stop, the ongoing deportations from Slovakia. As part of this process the Working Group entered into ultimately unsuccessful negotiations with the SS to stop the transports to Poland from throughout Europe. Eventually, the Working Group essentially took over the Jewish Centre when Oskar Neumann, an active member of the Working Group, assumed the mantel of leadership of that official body.[21]

In Hungary, the alternative leadership evolved from a committee that originally tried to help Jewish refugees who reached Hungary and later tried actively to bring Jews to a safe haven in Hungary. The Relief and Rescue Committee, under Israel (Rezso, Rudolph) Kasztner and Otto Komoly, began to work in 1942, and late in 1943 became formally aligned with the Jewish Agency. Soon after the German occupation of Hungary in March 1944, it became the *de facto* leadership of Hungarian Jewry. Among its other activities were negotiations with the SS.[22] All the while, the Zsido Tanacs continued to exist and the two bodies maintained contact, co-ordinating their activities to a certain extent.[23]

Although it is not possible within the framework of an article to present an all-encompassing overview of Jewish leadership during the Holocaust, it is worthwhile to provide a few thumbnail sketches of Jewish leaders, their circumstances and their activities. Such a foray should provide further insights into the complexity of the issues and the personalities involved. It may also help to elucidate the dilemmas Jewish leaders faced and the decisions they took.

Shortly after Hitler came to power, the Reichsvereinigung was established to be the representative body of all German Jews. Among its leaders, until his deportation to Theresienstadt in 1943, was the Reform rabbi, philosopher and educator Leo Baeck. Baeck served as president of the Reichsvereinigung. Although not a Zionist, Baeck was not an outspoken opponent of Zionism. He was considered a man of great learning and integrity. Twice arrested by the Gestapo, he nevertheless refused all offers to arrange his emigration from Germany. In the Theresienstadt ghetto, he also was recognized as an outstanding leader.[24]

Baeck and his fellow leaders faced many dilemmas in the first years of the Nazi era before the November 1938 orgy of anti-Jewish violence that came to be known as *Kristallnacht*. For the most part, the measures taken against the Jews in Germany were public knowledge. The regime promulgated the decrees that separated and isolated the Jews from other Germans in the light of day. Everyone could see and was meant to see the park benches designated for Jews only, or the exclusion of Jewish performers from the stages of Germany. The creeping takeover of Jewish businesses and property could be openly observed, especially when previously Jewish-owned firms advertised themselves under new Aryan names. Baeck and his peers did not face a problem of gaining access to information as much as they faced the problem of interpreting the meaning of the flood of anti-Jewish restrictions.

A key point in this pre-pogrom period came in September 1935 with the passage of the Nuremberg Laws. These laws sought to define Jews by racial criteria. They also relegated Jews to the status of protected subjects of Germany, taking away their citizenship in the process. They proscribed sexual contact between Jews and Aryans, they prohibited the employment of German women under the age of 45 as domestics in Jewish homes and they forbade Jews to fly the German flag.

In response to the laws, which redefined the status of German Jews after many months of deterioration, Baeck and his organization, recently renamed the Reichsvertretung, set forth their main goals. They declared that the laws were a heavy blow against German Jewry, but perhaps offered a vehicle for arriving at a 'tolerable relationship' between Jews and the authorities. They called for a strengthening of the Jewish educational system and its redirection towards vocational subjects that would prepare Jews to be able to make a living in the new socio-economic reality of Nazi Germany. Since Jews were being systematically ousted from German cultural activities, they proclaimed an alternate framework must be created for Jewish artists and entertainers. The Nazi economic decrees were leading to the growing impoverishment of German Jews and therefore welfare work, they said, must be enhanced. Last, they held it was the job of Jewish leadership to foster emigration, especially to Palestine. This statement provided a sort of blueprint for Baeck and his colleagues for the next three years. But in November 1938, after the violent outbreak against the Jews, it became largely useless as a guide. Following *Kristallnacht*, the overriding response to the worsening plight of German Jews became emigration. Baeck and his colleagues recognized that the circumstances had changed drastically, and they focused on fostering escape from Germany to any possible destination.

The period, from the establishment of the ghettos in Poland until the advent of the systematic mass murder that struck the Jews in the ghettos, provides another moment in the history of the Holocaust that is worth exploring regarding the issue of Jewish leadership. The Warsaw ghetto was established in the autumn of 1940 and in July 1942 was struck by a massive wave of deportations, primarily to the Treblinka extermination camp. The head of the Warsaw *Judenrat* was the engineer Adam Czerniakow. Czerniakow was not among the most salient pre-war leaders of Warsaw Jewry – he was a figure of the secondary rank. However, many of the more prominent Jewish leaders fled at the onset of the German invasion; and the result was that Czerniakow was among the few experienced Jewish leaders left on the scene. The Nazis appointed him head of the *Judenrat* and Czerniakow, with his engineer's logic, approached the task with pragmatism and forthrightness. In Warsaw as in other Polish ghettos, the *Judenrat* was meant to implement Nazi orders. In addition, they had to assume the duties of a local city government, most aspects of which the Jewish community had never had to handle by itself. Thus, under Czerniakow the *Judenrat* dealt with issues of housing, sanitation, welfare, food distribution, health care, policing, emergency services, education and courts of law. Some of these areas of responsibility were shared with already existing Jewish communal organizations, and at times there was an element of competition between the official Jewish leadership and these organizations. But having the overall responsibility for all of these activities was a new and, given the circumstances of the brutal German occupation, a generally daunting task for Czerniakow and the *Judenrat*.[25]

In the first year of the Warsaw ghetto's existence, the Nazis basically wanted the ghetto to be self-sustaining. However, they were willing to invest little in it in the way of materials and money. Czerniakow and his colleagues concluded that being productive, even though it meant working for the enemy, was in the ghetto's best interest and might lead to increased investment in the ghetto economy and thereby an improvement in conditions. For the most part the German ghetto commissioner, Hans Auerswald, also encouraged this view of ghetto productivity. As we have seen, Hans Frank, the head of the entire Generalgouvernement, embraced this outlook until the policy of the Final Solution was adopted in autumn 1941.

One of the earliest challenges the *Judenrat* faced revolved around the issue of Jewish labour. In the weeks following the Nazi occupation, Jewish men were picked up randomly for forced-labour details in Warsaw and later in forced-labour camps. Czerniakow and his people decided to try to organize this better, in order to distribute the burden more rationally for the sake of the individuals and the entire community. To do this meant volunteering to perform a service for the enemy, in the hope that this would ameliorate conditions. Assuming this responsibility also opened up the way for protectionism; those with more pull could sometimes be released from this onerous obligation. For the most part the intervention benefited the community, even if it tainted the hands of the Jewish leadership and often earned more resentment than praise from the ghetto inhabitants.[26]

If the *Judenrat* could sometimes improve a situation, at other times it was helpless in the face of insurmountable obstacles. Despite attempts to foster more hygienic conditions, improved health care and more equitable food distribution, the death rate in the ghetto skyrocketed. In the summer of 1941 over 5,000 Jews a month died from the combined effects of starvation and disease. All told, about one out of every five residents died before the wave of deportations hit the Warsaw ghetto in July 1942.

On the eve of the deportations many rumours about the impending disaster took wing in the ghetto. Czerniakow tried to clarify whether the rumours were true and Auerswald assured him they were not. Finally, however, the authorities asked Czerniakow to provide lists of Jews for the deportations. Rather than comply, he committed suicide. Manek Lichtenbaum, now virtually unknown to all but scholars of the ghetto, became the new head of the *Judenrat*.

Was Czerniakow's suicide an act of moral strength or was it cowardly? Did Czerniakow draw the proverbial line in the sand which he would not cross, or did he abandon his community in its time of greatest need, leaving a vacuum in leadership that would only be filled by the armed underground many months later? These questions are not easily answered, and they remain a source of debate among survivors, students and scholars of the Holocaust.

Let us turn to another ghetto story, which leaves us with similarly difficult questions to answer. In Vilna, the dominant Jewish leader after the German invasion of June 1941 was Jacob Gens.[27] During the first wave of murder that struck Vilna from July through to December 1941, Gens was the head of the Jewish police. In autumn 1941, the Nazis set up two ghettos – one for non-workers and a second for workers. At first they liquidated the non-workers' ghetto and then they selected out the less fit from the workers' ghetto. By the time this spate of murder had ended in December 1941, Gens was the *de facto* leader of the remaining Jews of Vilna. Finally, in July 1942 Gens was officially appointed head of the *Judenrat*.

Unlike Czerniakow in Warsaw, who ended his own life on the eve of the start of mass systematic murder, Gens, like all the Jews in Vilna, faced murder from the beginning of the Nazi presence. His challenge, similar to all Vilna Jews, was to evaluate the meaning of the course the murderous actions followed: indiscriminate mass shootings followed by the establishment of the two ghettos with their distinction between workers and non-workers, the complete liquidation of the non-workers' ghetto, the partial liquidation of workers' ghetto and, finally, the halting of the killing operation.

At the end of this long phase of murder in December 1941, an underground newspaper of the time declared that the 'pogrom' had ended. Seeing the murder as a pogrom, something that Jews in Vilna and other areas of the former Russian Pale of Settlement knew from their past, implied that the murder had come and gone and, like a pogrom, would not necessarily return. Others, such as the Zionist Youth who met with Abba Kovner in a convent on the outskirts of Vilna, believed that something else was happening. They believed that the murder would resume because all the Jews were slated for destruction. Kovner and his colleagues really lacked a sound basis for formulating their conclusion. They didn't know about the fate of Jews from faraway places, and they couldn't possibly know about Nazi plans for the destruction of the Jews from Nazi sources. They made a sort of leap of imagination in concluding that the Jews of Europe were facing a new, and all-encompassing, kind of violence.

Based on events in Vilna, Gens believed the Nazis valued Jewish labour and that thus, by being productive, the ghetto could forestall further murderous actions. When he became the official head of the *Judenrat* on 12 July 1942 Gens declared: 'The basis of the existence of the ghetto is work, discipline and order. Every resident of the ghetto who is capable is a pillar on which our existence rests.'[28] In other words, Gens believed in working for the Germans. He hoped that the remaining Jews of Vilna would be considered sufficiently important to be allowed to live long enough to see their liberation.

Czerniakow, in the reality of pre-murder Warsaw, was only willing to go so far in his co-operation with the German authorities to ameliorate conditions, and he stopped short of providing lists for deportations. However, living in Vilna, which had already experienced mass murder, Gens was even willing to be a party to murder if it would lessen the blow and help others live. Given the choice of participating in the round-up of Jews from the neighbouring ghetto of Oszmiana, and thereby reducing the quota from 1,500 to 400, Gens chose to send his police to take part in the round-up. In his report on events in Oszmiana Gens said:

> The Jewish police saved those who must live. Those who had little time left to live were taken away, and may the aged among the Jews forgive us. They were a sacrifice for our Jews and for our future. I don't want to talk about what our Jews from Vilna have gone through in Oszmiana. Today I only regret that there were no Jews [i.e. Jewish police] when the *Aktion* was carried out in Kiemieliszki and in Bystrzyca. Last week all the Jews were shot there without distinction ... I don't know whether everybody will understand this and defend it, and whether they will defend it after we have left the ghetto, but the attitude of our police is this – rescue what you can, do not consider your own good name or what you must live through.[29]

Gens's attitude to the Jewish underground in Vilna and his relationship with it were complex. On the one hand, he agreed that at the time of the final liquidation of the Vilna ghetto the underground should rise in rebellion. On the other hand, he also worried that the underground's existence endangered his policy of rescue through work. The well-known incident involving Yitzhak Wittenberg in July 1943 illustrates this well.

Wittenberg was a communist and the leader of the armed resistance in the ghetto. When a communist resistance member outside the ghetto was arrested, he named Wittenberg as a member of the communist underground. The German authorities demanded that Gens hand over Wittenberg. Wittenberg went into hiding and the ghetto residents, fearing reprisals, encouraged him to turn himself in. Wittenberg eventually gave himself up to Gens, who provided him with a cyanide tablet. Rather than fall into the hands of the Germans, Wittenberg swallowed the poison and died. The incident severely strained the relationships between Gens and the underground, and the underground and the rest of the ghetto.

Later that summer, in September, the underground came to believe (we now know erroneously) that the final liquidation of the ghetto was at hand. Owing in part to the Wittenberg incident, the ghetto inhabitants did not support the attempted uprising. Gens also believed the time for fighting had not yet arrived. Because of the uprising, the Germans arrested and executed Gens. Most of the fighters, led by Abba Kovner, escaped to the forests and the ghetto was liquidated.

Had the uprising not broken out in September 1943, might Gens have succeeded in steering most, or at least some, of the ghetto inhabitants to a safe harbour through his policy of rescue through work? Of course hypothetical situations are merely that. But, as Christopher Browning has demonstrated in his book *Nazi Policy: Jewish Workers, German Killers,* even those among the Nazis who advocated exploiting Jewish labour, believed that ultimately the labourers, too, would be subjected to the Final Solution.[30] Of course Gens could not really have known this; just as Kovner could not have known that his assessment of the arrival of the final liquidation of the ghetto was wrong.

In Slovakia the alternate leadership body, the Working Group, became the real leaders of the Jewish community, displacing the officially comprised Jewish Centre, under the very weak leader Arpad Sebestyn. The Working Group was as dynamic as it was heterogeneous. The two foremost members of the Working Group could hardly have been more dissimilar. Rabbi Michael Ber (Dov) Weismandl was a strictly Orthodox Jew, the son-in-law of the head of the world-renowned Nitra Yeshiva, and Rabbi Shmuel David Halevi Ungar. Dressed in traditional eastern European Jewish garb replete with side-locks, hat and knee-length coat, Weismandl was, nonetheless, not an average ultra-Orthodox rabbi. Before the war he had spent time in Britain studying rare Jewish manuscripts.[31] His counterpart was a relative by marriage, Gisela (Gisi) Fleischmann. Gisi Fleischmann was the head of WIZO, the Women's Zionist Organization in Slovakia. Before the advent of the deportations, she actively aided Jewish refugees who had reached Slovakia. A modern woman, who had removed her two daughters out of harm's way by sending them to Palestine, she still observed basic Jewish traditions. Offered several chances of escape from Slovakia during the war years, Gisi Fleischmann refused to leave her post.[32] Others closely involved in the Working Group included Oskar Neumann, a veteran Slovak Zionist leader who, in December 1943, became the head of the Jewish Centre, and Rabbi Armin Frieder, an Orthodox Rabbi who gravitated towards Zionism and a more modern version of Jewish practice.

On the eve of the start of the transportations from Slovakia, the people who would later form the Working Group learned from a Slovak official that deportations were impending. Thinking that the Slovak government itself was behind the planned measures, they approached various members of the regime in an attempt to convince them to cancel their plans. According to at least one scholar, they might even have tried to bribe Slovak officials.[33] At roughly the same time they pursued another track in the hope of forestalling the planned anti-Jewish action. They approached the Papal Nuncio in Slovakia, Giuseppe Burzio, asking him to forward a plea to Pope Pius XII to intercede with the head of the Slovak government, Father Tiso.[34] Neither of these attempts bore immediate fruit and on 27 March 1942 the deportation trains began to roll toward Poland.

The first transport to leave Slovakia consisted of slightly less than 1,000 young women aged 16.[35] Leaders of the Zionist Youth movements asked themselves what was the meaning of these transports that included their sisters and friends. Given their understanding of events in the First World War, when women had been sent to the front to act as prostitutes for the soldiers, they concluded that the transport from Slovakia were bound for the Eastern Front and the women were destined to be abused for the pleasure of the soldiers. For the Zionist Youth leaders, this was intolerable. They decided to disrupt further transports. Turning to the nascent communist underground, they begged for explosives to blow up the railway tracks leading to the front. The communist leaders, however, demurred, claiming that were the explosives to be traced back to them, their incipient plans for an armed uprising against the Slovak fascist regime would be foiled. Thinking again, the young Jewish leaders decided the next best course of action would be escape.[36] They began to organize escape routes out of Slovakia to neighbouring Hungary where, at the time, the situation was much better. After all, Slovakia had been part of the old Austro-Hungarian empire before its break-up after the First World War. Many Slovak Jews spoke Hungarian and many had family ties on the other side of the border. Ultimately, in both organized and improvised acts of flight, up to 8,000 Slovak Jews reached Hungary before March 1944. These border crossings were frequently funded by the Working Group and invariably had their blessing. As long as Hungary remained free of a German presence on their soil, these Jews, if hidden suitably from the authorities, were safe. Of course, on 19 March 1944, when the Germans occupied Hungary, their situation, like that of all Jews in Hungary, deteriorated radically.[37]

Returning to the spring of 1942, while the transport trains continued to carry their unfortunate passengers from Slovakia toward their bitter destinies, the members of the Working Group tried another path in the hope of saving Jews from deadly exile. Since the Slovak government had announced that the Jews were being sent out of Slovakia to work, the Working Group tried to convince Slovak leaders that Jewish labour could be put to better use within the country's borders than outside them. From this intercession sprang the idea of transforming labour centres that already existed in Slovakia into a haven for Jews. In the camps Novaky, Sered and Vhyne some 6,000 Jews were eventually safeguarded from the deportations while they worked on projects that profited the Slovak regime.[38]

In the camps themselves, Jewish underground cells came into being in preparation for a time when the work camps might be liquidated. Via the Working Group, these cells were put in contact with the anti-fascist underground that was preparing for what would become the Slovak National Uprising. The Working Group also provided money to the cells for the purchase of arms and ammunition. In late August 1944, when the uprising broke out, Jews from the camp undergrounds joined in the fighting. Over 200 Jewish fighters fell in battle before the Germans cold-bloodedly quashed the rebels.

Turning back once again to the period of the deportations in 1942, there was yet another line of rescue pursued by the Working Group. Rabbi Weismandl and his colleagues decided to approach Dieter Wisliceny, Adolf Eichmann's representative in Slovakia. Their unsuccessful attempt to convince the Slovak authorities to cancel the planned deportations apparently led them to conclude that the Germans might be playing a more central role in the anti-Jewish campaign than they had thought previously. Weismandl sounded out Wisliceny about stopping the deportations for money. Wisliceny took the offer seriously. He discussed it with his superiors in Berlin, and they gave him the go-ahead to embark upon negotiations with the Working Group. Within a short time it was agreed that for a sum of US$50,000 the Germans would stop the deportations from Slovakia. For most of the summer the Working Group strove to obtain the required sum, which was not easy given the robbery to which the Slovak Jewish community had been subjected by the Tiso government. The final payment was made in October 1942 on Yom Kippur, the Day of Atonement, the holiest day in the Jewish calendar. Lo and behold, the deportations then stopped.

In the meantime, having sent couriers to discover the fate of the Jews already deported to Poland, the Working Group heard tales of terrible suffering and mass death. They also were told that Jews from all over Europe were being transported to Poland. Given this information, they decided to make another offer to the Nazis in autumn 1942. Wisliceny took this offer seriously as well, and it soon developed into what has become known as the Europa Plan. Essentially for the sum of US$2 million, of which 10 per cent was to be paid up-front, the SS said it would stop the deportation of Jews to Poland from all points outside the country. Over the course of the next year the Working Group struggled to amass the necessary US$200,000. They managed to obtain a large portion of it, but not all the required sum. In the meantime

Wisliceny was posted to Greece, where he took part in the destruction of the local Jewish community, and the contact between him and the Working Group petered out. The idea, however, did not die; it simply lay dormant and would surface again in spring 1944 in Hungary.

The story of Slovak Jewry and the Working Group would not be complete without discussing the effect of the Slovak National Uprising on both. Neither the Working Group nor any other Jewish body initiated the National Uprising, although the Working Group was involved in its organization to a certain degree and Jews fought in it. On a theoretical level, among all of the rescue schemes the Working Group attempted, it could be said that participation in the National Uprising was the definitive rescue attempt. It was definitive because once begun, there was no turning back. As soon as Jews participated in the uprising, they closed off all their other options for rescue. It was definitive in another way as well: were the uprising to succeed, and were the fascist regime to collapse, all the remaining Jews in Slovakia would be saved. But this is not what happened. The Slovak National Uprising was pitilessly suppressed. Some 13,500 Jews were deported to Theresienstadt or Auschwitz in the wake of the fighting. Rabbi Weismandl was among the deportees, and on the way to Auschwitz he managed to jump from the train, leaving his family behind to their gruesome fate. Gisi Fleischmann was also put on a train bound for Auschwitz, with the specific instructions that her return was not wanted. Needless to say, she never returned from the extermination camp. Some 4,500 Jews in Slovakia managed to survive in hiding until the Red Army arrived.

To tie together the last threads of the story, one must ask: why did the SS stop the initial wave of deportations from Slovakia? Was it the money paid to them? Was it because of Vatican intervention or some other reason? Yehuda Bauer, among others, has written about this. According to his logic, which is very persuasive, the money could hardly have been the chief factor. For Heinrich Himmler and the SS, with the treasures of Europe lying at their feet, what was US$50,000? There is some indication that the Vatican may have played a role in pressuring the government of Father Jozef Tiso into stopping the deportations. Most likely, however, is a reason that has only recently come to light. A Slovak researcher, Eduard Niznansky, has uncovered a document that suggests that before the onset of the deportations the Slovaks and the Germans agreed to the number of 64,000 deportees. This is just about the number of Jews who had been deported when the deportations ended in October 1942, minus the number of Jews in labour camps in Slovakia itself.[39] In other words, although there may well have been various kinds of pressure and persuasive arguments brought to bear on the Slovak and German authorities to end the deportations, the main reason the deportations ended in autumn 1942 was because the quota had been filled.

The story of the Working Group is that of a dynamic leadership group. On their own or with others, they tried just about everything that was possible to save Jewish lives. For the most part, they failed. They failed because the destructive power arrayed against them was so great that they really could do nothing to stop it from crushing Slovak Jewry. Despite all the efforts of the Working Group, and despite their perceptions of those efforts at the time and afterwards, it is most likely that the course the deportations followed had been determined before the first train crossed the border into Poland. No effort, no matter how valiant or how creative by Jewish leaders, could alter that devil's pact and its consequences for Slovak Jewry. In the end the story of the Working Group stands as a paradigm for Jewish powerlessness in the face of the Holocaust.

The destruction of the Jews of Hungary is a heart-wrenching, dramatic, at times contentious, and almost always thought-provoking chapter in the history of the Holocaust. The crux of the story occurred in 1944, some three years after the advent of the mass and systematic murder of the Jews had begun and 14 months before the war in Europe ended. It is this time frame perhaps more than anything else that defines the events.

The official Jewish leadership in Hungary, the Zsido Tanacs, played a notable role during the period, but the primary leadership function belonged to the Budapest Relief and Rescue Committee, under Kasztner and Komoly. To tell their story fully would take not just an article, it would require a long and rather intricate book. Kasztner was not among the recognized Jewish leaders before the war, and Komoly barely belonged to the fringes of the Jewish élite. They became the *de facto* leaders largely owing to the dormant, but not yet dead, negotiations between the Working Group and the SS.

When the German forces occupied Hungary, Dieter Wisliceny found his way there as well. Armed with a letter from Rabbi Weismandl claiming that he was a serious partner for negotiations, the SS officer eventually made contact with the Kasztner group. For their part, cognizant of the negotiations that had occurred in Slovakia, the Kasztner group was seeking out just such a contact. Much has been written about the Hungarian chapter in these negotiations, their by-products and the controversy surrounding them.[40]

For our purposes, the most salient feature of the negotiations is that they were an attempt to rescue Jews. In fact, the thrust of the activity of the Relief and Rescue Committee, and the Zionist Youth underground with which they maintained contact and a considerable degree of co-operation, was to rescue Jews. Kasztner, Komoly and many other adult and youth leaders had a pretty firm understanding of the danger posed to Hungarian Jewry by a German occupation, even before it began. Among other sources, they received information from the Working Group and Jewish refugees who had reached Hungary. They also knew about the Warsaw Ghetto Uprising and about less successful uprisings in other localities, such as Bedzin- Sosnowiec. Although there was a certain amount of preparation for Jewish armed resistance in Hungary, it was minimal compared to rescue activities. Jewish leaders focused on rescue because they apparently understood that armed resistance was suicidal whereas mass rescue in Hungary was possible.[41]

Even at the height of the first wave of deportations from mid-May to early July 1944, rescue in Hungary seemed feasible for several reasons. The international community intervened from the moment the Germans set foot in Hungary to dissuade the Hungarians from taking part in anti-Jewish persecution, and their intervention was common knowledge. Although it took several months, and in the meantime hundreds of thousands of Jews were deported, a few Western countries eventually designated special representatives to aid Jews on Hungarian soil. The names of Raoul Wallenberg, Charles Lutz and George Perlasca have become well known, although other diplomats were also involved in rescue work. The contact with the SS suggested that this avenue of rescue might also bear fruit. The Hungarian ruler, Admiral Miklos Horthy, declared an end to the first wave of deportations in early July 1944, and offered to let a limited number of Jews leave Hungary. The offer never reached fruition, but it did have important side effects. In the meantime, Allied forces had landed in France and Soviet forces were making great headway in the east, both clearly signalling that the Nazi empire would not hold out for much longer.

The result was that the Relief and Rescue Committee, the Zionist Youth underground and the diplomats managed to safeguard scores of thousands of Jews in the capital of Budapest, where the last Jews remained after the end of the first wave of deportations. They used a variety of methods chiefly based on various kinds of protective documents. Mostly as a consequence of Horthy's rescue offer, the Hungarian authorities recognized the validity of the documents. No less important, when Admiral Horthy ended the deportations and made his offer, he charged the International Red Cross with the responsibility for maintaining the welfare of the Jews of Budapest. Many of the protected Jews, housed in special buildings, thus lived under the auspices of either a foreign embassy or the International Red Cross. These special houses, generally in one part of the city, came to be known as the International Ghetto. Among the Jews enjoying international protection were some 6,000 children in houses established under the wing of the International Red Cross and run by Zionist Youth working for Otto Komoly.[42] During the summer of 1944 most of this network, based on diplomatic protection, was established and consolidated.

In October 1944, when Admiral Horthy tried again to extricate Hungary from the alliance with Nazi Germany, the result was his humiliating dismissal. This also resulted in the advent of new deportations organized by the Hungarian Arrow Cross, the fascist party under Ferenc Szalasi that was placed in power by the Germans. It was during the last months of 1944 and the first two months of 1945 that the rescue network went into high gear. Scores of thousands of Jews were shot on the banks of the Danube river, mostly by members of the Arrow Cross. So many bloody corpses filled the river that it is said that it ran red. Scores of thousands more were deported, mostly by foot to Austria. But scores of thousands were also helped – they were extricated from columns heading toward Austria, guarded from deportations and given food, clothing and shelter. Unlike the situation in Warsaw, where rescue from the deportations entailed keeping Jews alive for nearly three more years, the rescue in the last phase in Hungary meant keeping bodies and souls together for only a matter of weeks. The ingenuity and *chutspa* of Kasztner, Komoly and their colleagues, the international backing they enjoyed and the writing on the wall that declared the war was soon to be lost by Germany and her allies, all combined to make mass rescue in Hungary a reality – of course a far from perfect reality, since about two-thirds of the Jews from greater Hungary were murdered.[43]

The few examples presented here do not comprise an overall survey of Jewish leadership during the Holocaust. They do help clarify, however, many factors that influenced decisions made by Jewish leaders. They show that each situation had its own constellation of events, cast of characters, chronology and momentum. Any given Jewish leadership group in the Holocaust period faced events somewhat differently to other similar groups. The understanding of the situation and the range of options considered varied with each scenario.

One factor, nevertheless, seems to be present in almost every situation. On their own, Jewish leaders lacked the political power necessary fundamentally to change the fate that awaited their communities. This is true before the advent of murder and even more so once the Nazis had adopted the Final Solution. Jewish leaders could not stop the machinery of death in its tracks. At most, with the help of an outside force, they could slow it down or deflect it partially, as they did in Hungary toward the end of the war. Despite this fundamental axiom of powerlessness, Jewish leaders pursued many avenues of rescue and resistance, from rescue through work, to fostering mass escape, to outright armed confrontation. That they generally failed says less about the quality of their leadership than it says about the zealous destructive force that fuelled the Nazis' murderous crusade against the Jews.

NOTES

1. R. Hilberg, 'The *Judenrat*, Conscious or Unconscious Tool', in I. Gutman (ed.), *Patterns of Jewish Leadership in Nazi Europe, 1933–1945* (Jerusalem: Yad Vashem, 1979), pp. 31–44 and *The Destruction of the European Jews, Revised and Definitive Edition* (New York: Holmes and Meier, 1985).
2. H. Arendt, *Eichmann in Jerusalem, A Report on the Banality of Evil* (New York: The Viking Press, 1963).
3. Y. Weitz, *Ha-Ish She-Nirtsach Paamaim, Hayav, Mishpato, u-Moto shel Yisrael Kasztner* [The Man Who Was Murdered Twice, The Life, Trial and Death of Israel Kastner], (Jerusalem: Keter, 1995).
4. J. Melchman, 'The Controversy Surrounding the Jewish Council of Amsterdam from its Inception until the Present Day', in I. Gutman (ed.), *Patterns of Jewish Leadership in Nazi Europe, 1933–1945* (Jerusalem: Yad Vashem, 1979), pp. 235–57.
5. I. Trunk, *Judenrat: The Jewish Councils in Eastern Europe Under Nazi Occupation* (New York: Macmillan, 1972).
6. A. Weiss, 'Jewish Leadership in Occupied Poland, Postures and Attitudes', *Yad Vashem Studies*, XII (1977), pp. 335–65.
7. Y. Weitz, 'Changing Conceptions of the Holocaust: The Kasztner Case', *Studies in Contemporary Jewry* (1994), pp. 211–30.
8 D. Pohl, 'The Murder of the Jews in the General Government', in U. Herbert (ed.), *National Socialist Extermination Policies: Contemporary German Perspectives and Controversies* (Oxford: Berghahn Books, 2000), pp. 83-103.
9. For basic documents concerning the destruction of Slovak Jewry see L. Rothkirchen, *Churban Yahadut Slovakia, Tiur Beteudot* (Jerusalem: Yad Vashem, 1961) [in Hebrew].
10. For more on the Hungarian Labour Service System see R. Braham, *The Hungarian Labor Service System, 1939–1945* (Boulder, CO: East European Quarterly, 1977) and *The Wartime System of Labor Service in Hungary: Varieties of Experiences* (New York: The City University of New York, 1995).
11. For the most comprehensive account of the Holocaust in Hungary see R. Braham, *The Politics of Genocide: The Holocaust in Hungary*, revised and enlarged edn (New York: Columbia University Press, 1994) (originally published in 1981).
12. For more on Himmler see R. Breitman, *The Architect of Genocide: Himmler and the Final Solution* (London: The Bodley Head, 1991). For more on the earlier stages of the police–SS relationship see S. Aronson, *The Beginnings of the Gestapo System: the Bavarian Model* (Jerusalem: Israel Universities Press, 1961).
13. M. Steinberg, 'The *Judenpolitik* in Belgium within the West European Context: Comparative Observations', in D. Michman (ed.), *Belgium and the Holocaust: Jews, Belgians, Germans* (Jerusalem: Yad Vashem, 1998), pp. 199–221.
14. Several excellent books have been written about the Holocaust in France. For a thorough discussion about French anti-Jewish policies see M. Marrus and R. Paxton, *Vichy France and the Jews* (New York: Basic Books, 1981). For a detailed treatment of the Jewish leadership see Y. R. Cohen, *The Burden of Conscience: French Jewish Leadership During the Holocaust* (Bloomington: Indiana University Press, 1987), and for a comprehensive study of the experience of Jews in France during the Holocaust see R. Poznanski, *Jews in France During World War II* (Hanover, NH: Brandeis University Press, 2001).
15. Y. Arad, Y. Gutman and A. Margaliot (eds), *Documents on the Holocaust* (Jersualem: Yad Vashem, 1981), pp. 246–9.
16. For an up-to-date discussion of Eichmann and his staff see Y. Lozowick, *Hitler's Bureaucrats: The Nazi Security Police and the Banality of Evil* (London: Continuum, 2002). For more on Eichmann the man see D. Cesarani, *Eichmann: His Life and Crimes* (London: Heinemann, 2004).
17. T. Friedman (ed.), 'Introduction', in *Himmler's Teufels General SS–Und Polizeifuehrer Globocnik in Lublin: Dokumenten Sammlung* (Haifa: Institute of Documentation, 1977), no page citations.
18. C. Gerlach, *Kalkulierte Morde: Die Deutsche Wirtschafts- und Vernichtungspolitik in Weissrussland 1941 bis 1944* (Hamburg: Hamburger Edition, 1999), p. 580.
19. Arad *et al.*, *Documents*, pp. 173–8.
20. I. Gutman, *The Jews of Warsaw, 1939–1943, Ghetto, Underground, Revolt* Bloomington, IN: Indiana University Press, 1982), pp. 77–94, 102–6 and 285–306.

21. For a detailed presentation about Slovak Jewish leadership see G. Fatran, *Haim Maavak Al Hisadrut, Hanhaga Yehudit Beslovakia, 1938–1944* [A Struggle for Survival? Jewish Leadership in Slovakia 1938–1944] (Tel Aviv: Moreshet, 1992) (in Hebrew).
22. For a detailed discussion of the negotiations see Y. Bauer, *Jews for Sale, Nazi–Jewish Negotiations: 1933–1945* (New Haven, CT: Yale University Press, 1994).
23. J. Molnar, 'The Foundation and Activities of the Hungarian Jewish Council, March 20–July 7, 1944', *Yad Vashem Studies*, XXX (2002), pp. 93–124.
24. Several studies have appeared about Leo Baeck. Among the most well known are: L. Baker, *Days of Sorrow and Pain: Leo Baeck and the Berlin Jews* (New York: Macmillan, 1978) and A. H. Friedlander, *Leo Baeck, Teacher of Theresienstadt* (New York: Holt, Reinhart and Winston, 1968).
25. I. Gutman, 'Adam Czernkiakow, the Man and his Diary', in I. Gutman (ed.), *The Catastrophe of European Jewry* (Jerusalem: Yad Vashem, 1976), pp. 451–89.
26. Gutman, *The Jews of Warsaw*, pp. 22–4.
27. For more on the Vilna ghetto see Y. Arad, *Ghetto in Flames: the Struggle and Destruction of the Jews in Vilna during the Holocaust* (Jerusalem: Yad Vashem, 1980) (later published in New York: Holocaust Library, 1982).
28. Arad *et al.*, *Documents*, p. 438.
29. Ibid., pp. 442–3.
30. C.R. Browning, *Nazi Policy: Jewish Workers, German Killers* (Cambridge: Cambridge University Press, 2000), pp. 58–88.
31. A. Fuchs, *The Unheeded Cry: The Gripping Story of Rabbi Weismandl* (Brooklyn, NY: Messorah Publications, 1984), pp. 17–26.
32. J. Campion, *In the Lion's Mouth: Gisi Fleischmann and the Jewish Fight for Survival* (New York: University Press of America, 1987), pp. 3–40.
33. Yeshayahu Jelinek, 'The Vatican, the Catholic Church, the Catholics and the Persecution of the Jews in World War II, the Case of Slovakia', in B. Vago and G. L. Mosse (eds), *Jews and Non-Jews in Eastern Europe* (New York: J. Wiley, 1974), pp. 257–70.
34. A. Fuchs, *The Unheeded Cry*, p. 142.
35. R. Y. Buechler, 'The Deportation of Jews to the Lublin District of Poland, 1942', *Holocaust and Genocide Studies*, 6, 3 (1991), pp. 151–66.
36. Yaacov Rosenberg Testimony (OA/8), 'Slovak National Uprising', Oral History Archive (Jerusalem: The Institute of Contemporary Jewry, Hebrew University).
37. A. Cohen, *The Hehalutz Resistance in Hungary, 1942–1944* (Boulder, CO: Social Science Monographs, 1986), pp. 19–25.
38. G. Fatran, *Haim Maavak*, pp. 92–105.
39. Professor Niznansky presented this idea to a forum of scholars at Yad Vashem on 5 June 2002. The document on which he bases his analysis may be found in the Slovak National Archives, 'Ministry of the Interior', Ministry of the Interior Bill, 1 April 1942, carton 267, 406-560-13.
40. In several of his books, Yehuda Bauer has explored these negotiations; see Y. Bauer, *The Holocaust in Historical Perspective* (Seattle, WA: University of Washington Press, 1978); *The Jewish Emergence from Powerlessness* (Toronto: University of Toronto Press, 1979); *American Jewry and the Holocaust: The American Jewish Joint Distribution Committee, 1939–1945* (Detroit: Wayne State University Press, 1981) and *Jews for Sale*.
41. R. Rozett, 'Jewish and Hungarian Armed Resistance in Hungary', *Yad Vashem Studies*, XIX (1988), pp. 269–88 and A. Cohen, 'The Dilemma of Rescue or Revolt', in R. L. Braham and S. Miller (eds.), *The Nazis' Last Victims: The Holocaust in Hungary* (Detroit, MI: Wayne State University Press, 1998), pp. 117–36.
42. R. Rozett, 'Child Rescue in Budapest, 1944–5,' *Holocaust and Genocide Studies*, 2, 1, (1987), pp. 49–59.
43. R. Rozett, 'International Intervention: The Role of Diplomats in Attempts to Rescue Jews in Hungary', Braham and Miller, *The Nazis' Last Victims*, pp. 137–15.

5
Learning from Personal Accounts of the Holocaust

Personal accounts have come to comprise a significant niche in the documentation and published literature of the Holocaust. It is hard to say how many individual testimonies have been taken from survivors, but over the years many tens of thousands of eyewitness accounts have been documented. At Yad Vashem there are over 30,000 such testimonies, and the Shoah Foundation alone, at the end of the 1990s, recorded some 50,000 eyewitness accounts. Thousands of testimonies were collected by the Soviet authorities at the end of the Second World War and in the post-war years by many governmental authorities involved in judicial proceedings against war criminals. Published memoirs about the Holocaust first appeared during the last years of the war and many shorter personal stories began appearing in the memorial books that were written to commemorate destroyed communities.[1] It may be estimated that nearly six thousand book-length memoirs by Jews have been published that touch in some way on the events of the Holocaust years.[2] In addition to memoirs, several hundred diaries written by Jews during the Holocaust have come to light, some of which have been published and many which have not.[3]

Given this large body of material, it should come as no surprise that scholars have addressed the significance of these accounts. In the last few years, several books were published that discuss the ultimate meaning of first-hand accounts of the Holocaust, their use and misuse, and what one can expect to learn from them. In this most recent discussion, it is noteworthy that although the Holocaust is an historical event, most of the writers concerned with first-hand accounts do not come from the field of history, but from other academic disciplines.[4]

WHAT CAN WE LEARN FROM FIRST-HAND ACCOUNTS? – THE 'NON-HISTORICAL' APPROACH

David Patterson, a professor of comparative literature at the University of Memphis and Director of that university's honors programme, has attempted in his book *Sun Turned to Darkness: Memory and Recovery in the Holocaust Memoir* to uncover the deeper meaning of what he calls the 'Holocaust memoir'. Patterson's discussion of the Holocaust memoir is predicated on a very narrow definition of which Jews actually suffered the Holocaust. In his spiritual, metaphysical discussion about the 'Holocaust memoir', he includes the writings of Jews who were in camps, in hiding and in ghettos, but he does not include the stories of Jews who fled to the partisans, those who were not deported even though they lived in Nazi-dominated areas, or those who fled from Nazi-dominated areas. Patterson is not really concerned with the historical debate that such a narrow definition might raise. For he focuses on the nature and deeper meaning of Holocaust memory, not on the historical details that may be gleaned from individual memories.[5] His approach can be seen clearly in the bibliography that he furnishes at the end of the book; it does not contain any works by historians.

Patterson bases his interpretive method to a large degree on his reading of Emile Fackenheim's steps for the *Tikkun* (mending) of the world:

1. the recovery of Jewish tradition
2. the recovery from an illness and
3. the open-ended nature of the first two processes of recovery.[6]

The Holocaust memoir, in Patterson's view, recovers memory, which is the substance of tradition, and thereby it recovers tradition.[7] In his interpretation, the 'illness' from which the Holocaust memoir can help us recover is that of indifference.[8] The main symptom of this illness is silence, and even by remembering the silence by writing about it, that symptom is overcome and convalescence is promoted.[9] Patterson believes that the existence of the Holocaust memoir is an integral part of the observance of Fackenheim's 614th commandment: 'Jews are forbidden to hand Hitler posthumous victories … '.[10] In Patterson's words: 'The essence of memory in the Holocaust memoir, therefore, entails not just a memory of time but a recovery of the eternal in time through the observance of the 614th commandment.'[11]

According to Patterson's view, the Holocaust memoir has great power. Memoirs can revive and transmute the traditional role played by Jews as a light unto the nations.[12] In this age, where G-d has been pushed aside, apparently in no small measure because of the Holocaust, Patterson believes that memoirs can heal the soul and bring back the centrality of G-d's presence.[13] In Patterson's opinion, it is only by dealing with the frightful past of the Holocaust, through the Holocaust memoir, that there can be a future: 'This is the last and most important point to be made about the essence of memory in the Holocaust memoir,' he writes, '[it] is that here memory moves from perception of the past toward a recovery of the future, which is a recovery of time, through a relation to the other.'[14]

Patterson looks to Jewish tradition to bolster his view of the Holocaust memoir. For example, in discussing the loss of parents during the Holocaust, he looks to Jewish thought regarding their roles. According to his reading of Jewish sources, the loss of a mother is the loss of creation, since it is the mother with her motherly love who lies at the root of creation, i.e. birth. Moreover, the world in which the Nazis murdered Jewish mothers was a world that was diametrically opposed to the love and compassion represented by the mother in Jewish sources.[15] In his interpretation, the loss of the father is the loss of the essence of memory. In Jewish tradition, according to Patterson, the father is the custodian and transmitter of memory. He writes:

> The father is the guardian of one of the avenues of G-d's revelation. There is no murder of the father, then, that does not entail a murder of G-d the Father. And there is no memory of the loss of the father that does not include the memory of G-d.[16]

Patterson is quite sure that his analysis of the deeper meaning of the Holocaust memoir is correct, and he criticizes those who would disagree with him. In his opinion, Lawrence Langer, Professor Emeritus of Literature at Simmons College, is too concerned with what took place and not concerned enough with *why* it took place. He contends that James Young, also a professor of literature who has written widely about memory and the Holocaust, is wrong to say that the self has been removed from the Holocaust memoir; rather, Patterson maintains, in memory one finds the 'recovery of the living soul from the dead datum of experience'.[17] To Patterson's mind there is only one conscientious way to read the Holocaust memoir: 'Either Torah or Auschwitz – that is the existential necessity confronting the Jew and underlying the recovery of tradition. And neither the Holocaust memoir nor a responsible reading of it can avoid this either/or.'[18]

Although Patterson's book is thought-provoking at times, it is a deeply flawed work. The root of his problem is his eschewing of historical method for the sake of finding deeper meaning in the Holocaust memoir, while at the same time using examples from historical events.

Because Patterson seems to lack the craft of a trained historian, he makes many mistakes that a person with more finely tuned sensibilities regarding the nature of historical thinking and historical sources might have avoided.

One of the first problems in Patterson's analysis is that he discusses *the* Holocaust memoir versus Holocaust memoirs. Although many memoirs may have common points, no two stories are identical, just as no two individuals are identical. It is clear that memoirs were written not only by individuals, each with their own Holocaust experience, but also at many different times, in different places and in different languages. This great variation makes it extremely hard, if not impossible, to discuss one archetypal Holocaust memoir.

A fundamental problem in Patterson's writing is his uncritical use of sources. Several times in his book, he quotes supposed 'authorities' about Nazi policies and intentions even though they had no real way of knowing such things. For example, Patterson writes that according to the survivor Nathan Shappel: 'The Germans obviously understood only too well the family structure of the European Jew', and he implies they therefore sought to undermine it.[19] Shappel is undoubtedly an expert about his own experiences during the Holocaust years, but since he almost certainly never took part in the discussions held by Nazi leaders about their plans for the Jews, and since he is not a historian who writes about that period based on documentation, he cannot be considered an authority on Nazi intentions. To the best of my knowledge, researchers have yet to uncover documentation that shows the Nazis ever discussed how best to destroy Jewish families. So Patterson is on thin ice when he claims 'the Nazi project aimed at the devastation of the home took a variety of forms' without providing some sort of documentary evidence.[20]

The same problem is present when Patterson quotes Emile Fackenheim, who writes: 'The Nazi state had no higher aim than to murder human souls while bodies were still alive. The *Muselmann* was its most characteristic, most original product.'[21] Although Fackenheim is considered to be one of the foremost Jewish philosophers of the twentieth century, he is not a historian nor does he use purely historical methods. His statement about Nazi intentions should not be taken uncritically as a historical fact, because Fackenheim assumes intentions from acts and their results. Neither he nor Patterson offers evidence from Nazi documentation about a premeditated plan to turn Jews into *Muselmanner*. Indeed, as far as we know from the published scholarship, the Nazis did not explicitly order the dehumanization of the Jews, nor did they overtly design a process of dehumanization that was to be employed as such. Rather, their racial and political ideologies were the principle progenitors of the brutality in the ghettos and camps that led to dehumanization of Jews and others. This is the kind of issue about which some non-historians seem to be unaware when they engage in interpretation.

Two other statements made by Patterson go beyond a simple lack of a historian's sensibilities. According to Patterson, when the Nazis devised the system of using numbers instead of names in the camps, they did so with an awareness of Rabbi Nachman of Braslav's dictum: 'You must watch over your name and your soul.'[22] It is ludicrous to think that, when Theodore Eicke first established the model for future concentration camps in Dachau, he or any of his staff was aware of Rabbi Nachman or his dictum.[23]

In discussing the Nazi total disregard for Jewish life, Patterson writes: 'Like a stone, the body of the Jew in the antiworld was raw material for soap, fertilizer, clothing and lamp shades.'[24] This statement, without any accompanying explanation, is simply irresponsible coming from a scholar in the 1990s. Of course Patterson is not the only one to claim uncritically that Jewish fat was used to make soap. Survivors have been known to write of the existence of such soap. For example, in his book *Saving Children: Diary of a Buchenwald Survivor and Rescuer*, Jack Werber writes about Buchenwald in 1940:

> Once a week, usually on Sunday, we were able to take hot show-
> ers with soap. The soap was engraved 'RJF.' The *Stubdienst*
> explained to us that the letters stood for Reine Juden Fat, mean-
> ing that fat from dead Jews was used to produce the soap. Even
> in the showers, the Nazis had to remind us of our ultimate fate.[25]

Professor Henry Huttenbach has explained clearly the source of this misinformation. The Germans commonly used soap during the war stamped 'RIF', which meant '*Reichs-Industrie-Fett*', 'Reichs Industrial Fat'.[26] Patterson, even if he had not seen Huttenbach's article, should have been aware that the existence of soap made from Jewish fat has long been considered controversial. Most serious scholars consider it a myth, and any allusion to it demands some sort of explanation.

Patterson's book is a prime example of a well-known problem present in writing about the Holocaust.[27] When applying a discipline other than history to the study of the Holocaust, one must first have a firm footing in historical methods and sources, and one must have a solid understanding of the historical events that comprised the Holocaust. Without this firm footing, the resultant analysis, no matter how thought-provoking, simply does not hold up.

In his book *On Listening to Holocaust Survivors: Recounting and Life History*, the psychologist and playwright Henry Greenspan does not focus on the historical details present in first-hand accounts of the

Holocaust for the sake of uncovering facts or yielding abstract lessons; rather his interest is in the process itself of recounting by survivors.[28] Greenspan's method is to listen to the same few survivors over and over again as they recount their experiences. His goal is to understand how survivors tell their stories, to uncover the problems inherent in their telling and to learn to listen better.

Having listened intently to his group of survivors, Greenspan concluded that each individual speaks in a voice that is multidimensional and complex. With great sensitivity he writes:

> Survivors' voices are thus compound voices. In some uncertain balance, each contains both earlier identifications and their reductive transformations; both a primary theme and its opposite; echoes of both the murders and the dead ... survivors' voices often have a uniquely orchestral quality, reflecting the complexity. They may become vibrant ... Yet the fuller they become, the more they risk breaking against the memories that no single voice can articulate. At these moments, the silence comes not so much 'between the words' as erupts within them, sometimes taking them over again.[29]

Like Patterson, Greenspan acknowledges that silence is part of the recounting, as it is a part of the orchestral music that he uses as a metaphor for the complex voices of survivors. But unlike Patterson, he does not try to impute to silence a grandiose meaning. He writes:

> In entering into survivors' voices and stories ... we also find 'I's' inside of 'I's,' memories inside memories, with 'I's' and memories interchanging, interweaving, but attaining no final integration. We also find conscience becoming silence and peace. But the silence and peace ... are not those of redemption.[30]

Greenspan reminds us that there are simply some things that words, even a flood of words, cannot convey.

In his analysis of the survivors and their stories as stories, Greenspan arrives at several other valuable insights. In order to recount their experiences, survivors try to fashion stories out of events that do not necessarily fit into a story format and they often struggle unsuccessfully to find the words to express themselves. One of the survivors to whom Greenspan listened illustrates this point clearly with his stuttering attempt to give voice to his experiences:

> People don't want to listen to the, the –, how do I describe the –? Corpses that were lying around there, like, like, like garbage. Or

> the stench … the agony –, the, the, the –, the sorrow. I don't know if there is a word. For the pain. To describe –[31]

Greenspan also reminds us of a central point about the special perspective of survivor recounting. Since they are survivors, and they survived, all of their narratives are ultimately narratives of survival. These accounts are linked to the concept of legacy, the passing on of their experiences. Although he does not say it outright, he implies that the murdered have no voice nor can they pass anything on, since there is no way to hear them tell their stories. Moreover, Greenspan explains that the narratives written by historians based on the testimony of survivors are inherently narratives of survival. Greenspan also sees survivor accounts as having a role in redemption, but a less bombastic role than that assigned to them by Patterson. In his view, historical narratives hold the 'promise of redemption from an eternity of wandering or loss'.[32] This also seems to be tied to his theory that the concentric circle of stories recounted by a survivor constitute a monument to what once was and no longer is.[33] Perhaps for this reason, Greenspan believes the most important thing about listening to survivors is simply to listen to them: 'No other purpose is required. Just as none would be required to listen to any other people who endured what they endured in the world we share; with whom we share everything except those agonies and memories.'[34]

Greenspan himself does not suffer from the misuse of historical data, since he does not relate to the stories or the voices of the survivors he has interviewed as factual information that needs to be put into its historical context, or needs to be interpreted for its greater meaning. He may be right in saying that there are some things that survivors simply cannot recount in a way that we can understand, and because of that we cannot grasp the essence of their experiences. He may also be right in his implied criticism about those who would draw lessons from personal accounts of the Holocaust and use them to teach tolerance.[35] But do the problems inherent in survivor accounts preclude us from learning anything about the history of the Holocaust from them? There are definitely things we can learn from personal accounts of the Holocaust despite their limitations. But we must do so with a strong awareness of those limitations and proceed carefully despite them.

If any author has cogently argued for the importance of understanding the limitations of survivor accounts, it is Lawrence Langer. Langer is one of the most important writers about the nature of survivor testimony. In his most recent book, *Preempting the Holocaust*, Langer discusses at length what he believes we can or cannot learn from first-hand accounts of the Holocaust.[36] Lest readers be swept up by pretentious ideas of what can be learned from such accounts, Langer starkly brings them back to earth:

> All efforts to find a rule of hierarchy in that darkness, whether
> based on gender or will, spirit or hope, reflect only our own need
> to plant a life-sustaining seed in the barren soil that conceals the
> remnants of two-thirds of European Jewry. The sooner we aban-
> don this design, the quicker we will learn to face such chaos with
> unshielded eyes.[37]

For Langer, even those who search only for facts and seek to place
them in their immediate historical context must take care. He writes:

> Literalist discourse about the Holocaust – and I must stress that I
> am speaking only about the Holocaust – leads nowhere but back
> into the pit of destruction. At least it has the grace to acknowledge
> that we learn nothing from the misery it finds there.[38]

But what does Langer mean by 'we learn nothing'? He himself
shows us that we can learn important things by looking at first-hand
accounts. Discussing the diary of David Sierakowiak,[39] a youth in the
Lodz ghetto, Langer makes a point that certainly adds to our understanding of the kind of experiences Jews suffered in the ghettos.
Several times in his diary, Sierakowiak complains and expresses his
anger about how his father has taken more than his share of the food.
Most readers, one may assume, would side with the boy against his
father and tend to blame the father for being selfish. Langer, however,
reminds us that it is not the father who is at fault, but the 'starving man'
the German regime created.[40] Langer has obviously learned something
valuable from the diary and his work with first-hand accounts about
perspective, responsibility and critical reading that he can pass on.

Perhaps Langer's feeling about the difficulty of learning comes in
part from misplaced frustration. He writes:

> Taking or watching Holocaust testimony is a humbling experi-
> ence. You begin with the hope of creating order out of chaos,
> finding patterns in the survival narrative that can be organized
> into what some call a 'syndrome.' You imagine you can design a
> new template of evil to gain insight into the motives that lead to
> mass murder.[41]

Langer has, however, fallen into the same trap as Patterson, trying to
learn something from the wrong source. First-hand accounts of the
Holocaust given by Jews cannot teach us about the nature of Nazi evil,
the motives for their brutal acts and plans for carrying them out. From
their perspective as witnesses, Jews who went through the Holocaust
cannot be experts about such matters. Their accounts can only teach us

about the affect of the horror on the individual victims and the experiences of the victims facing the horror.

ISSUES REGARDING PUBLISHED MEMOIRS

As is true for other sources upon which the writing of history is based, there are inherent limitations and problems present in published memoirs about which both scholars and lay readers need to be aware. The simple fact that published memoirs must go through the process of publication raises a set of issues about which readers need to be mindful.

Published manuscripts are usually edited for content and language. Moreover, the account may be abridged to meet the needs of the publisher, and that abridgement might result in the exclusion of information the survivor thought important to impart to the reader. The result may also be in a change in proportions or emphasis in the published work. Even language editing, to make the text more readable, may inadvertently cause a change in meaning.

In setting down their memoirs on paper, survivors often engage in self-editing. In his own memoir, Elie Wiesel expresses this very eloquently.[42] Some survivor memoirs were actually collated by their children, based on a manuscript or several partial manuscripts left behind by survivors before their death. Others have been ghost-written by their children or professional writers.[43] All of these processes make published memoirs very different from oral testimony, which is more spontaneous, and from unpublished diaries, which were written at the time of the events described in them. Published diaries, of course, may also be subjected to editing. The various versions of Anne Frank's published diary illustrate this clearly.[44]

The issue of perspective, as Greenspan observes, is crucial to our reading and use of published first-hand accounts. At a conference held at Yeshiva University in 1993, Professor Nechama Tec made a point regarding children's diaries from the Holocaust, which is germane to all similar material. She reminded her listeners that children's diaries from the Holocaust do not represent the experiences of all children during the period, but represent the small segment who write diaries and whose diaries surfaced after the war.[45]

Another aspect of the issue of perspective has already been broached: the witness is an expert about that which he experienced himself. Therefore, during the Holocaust, Jews were almost never in a position to have first-hand information about Nazi intentions regarding anti-Jewish policies. The problem of expertise, however, is not only a problem regarding Nazi intentions. Sometimes survivor accounts move from the first person singular to the first person plural without elucidation of the change in voice. When a survivor says 'we' it is not always clear in just whose name he or she is talking. Morris Wyszogrod, for example, writes the following:

> When the British and the French entered the war a few days later, *we* [emphasis added] thought it would be over very quickly. The happiness of the population was beyond description. But as the days passed, *we* came to realize that there would be no quick end to the war.[46]

Here Wyszogrod is speaking in the name of the population. But which population: the Jews of Warsaw, all of Warsaw, or perhaps all of Polish Jewry? Readers cannot judge the veracity of his statement without knowing in whose name he is speaking; it is doubtful that he had firsthand information about people's thoughts beyond his most intimate circles.

Herman Wygoda, speaking in the plural third person, draws our attention to a similar problem of voice and perspective. He writes: '... those who had experienced World War I knew the difference between the Fuehrer and the Kaiser, and their fear and anxiety were correspondingly great.'[47] It is not realistic that he could make an unqualified and sweeping statement like this based on first-hand knowledge. Were he to qualify his statement with phrases such as 'my impression at the time was ...' or 'among the people I knew ...', or were he to introduce some sort of corroboration, his statement would pose much less of a problem for readers and researchers alike. But as it stands, the reader has no alternative but to look upon Wygoda's declaration with a certain degree of scepticism and at best to relate to it as an extrapolation.

Post-war first-hand accounts are open to another problem related to that of perspective: the mixing-in of information learned after the war with that which was learned through personal experience during the war. Of course such mixing, when the writer or witness clearly points it out to the reader or listener, does not necessarily present a problem. But when it occurs without the benefit of a clear road sign, or when the post-war assessment itself is deeply flawed, the problem is more substantial.

Jack Werber in his memoirs makes several such awkward statements. Writing about a job he received, probably late in 1939 or early in 1940 from the context, he says: 'Since they needed furriers they ordered me to come the next day. They were already thinking about invading Russia and they wanted warm clothing for their soldiers.'[48] It is exceedingly hard to believe that, more than a year before the start of Operation Barbarossa, the German invasion of the Soviet Union, Werber knew about the Germans' plans.

Somewhat earlier in his story, Werber makes it reasonably clear that he was offering a post-war assessment concerning his position at the outbreak of the war. After having explained that the outbreak of the war found him away from his home town Radom on business in Vilna, Werber says: 'If I had stayed in Vilna, I probably would have made it safely through the war, since it was possible to travel from Vilna to Shanghai, where many Jews found a safe haven throughout the war period.'[49] His assessment is clearly based on after-the-fact – but even at that only partial – information about the flight to Shanghai from Vilna. Several books and articles have appeared on the subject of flight to Shanghai. From them it is clear that only a small percentage of the Jews of Vilna even tried to go to Shanghai, and that most of the Jews who were in Vilna at the time of the Nazi invasion in the summer of 1941 were eventually murdered. In other words, the chances that Werber might have survived the Holocaust by having fled to Shanghai from Vilna were extremely slim.[50]

Because published memoirs are not necessarily the only source of information about the story of an individual, it is sometimes possible to discern discrepancies in the different accounts. In a fascinating article about the diary and memoirs written by Rabbi Y. M. Aharonson concerning his experiences in the Konin labour camp, Esther Farbstein shows that most of the information in the two texts corresponds, but that there are some discrepancies. She astutely points out that these derive in part from the difference in the nature of the two media. The diary, written under the pressure of events and the fear of discovery, goes into less detail than the memoir, which was written under much less tense circumstances shortly after the war. In this case, the diary often reflects more about 'public experiences' and the memoir more about 'private' experiences.[51]

Mark Roseman, of the University of Southampton, has written an absorbing biography of a young Jewish woman who hid in Germany during the war, Marianne Ellenbogen, *née* Strauss. The question of different accounts of events in her life is a central theme in his book.[52] Before she died, Roseman interviewed Strauss, read a short memoir she had written and saw a few letters she had kept. After her passing, he discovered that she had many letters from the Nazi period and a diary she had written while in hiding from 1943 until the end of the war. In addition, Roseman sought out many of the people mentioned by Strauss in the various sources and interviewed them. He also found documents relevant to her story in historical archives.

Among the discrepancies that Roseman discusses in his book are different versions of Strauss's experiences at school before the outbreak of the war. Various accounts show her as happy, well liked and enjoying school, versus being withdrawn, isolated and suffering from prejudice. Roseman concludes that the 'many discrepancies did, in fact faithfully reflect different contemporary perceptions of events'.[53] In other words, divers people saw her differently at slightly different times, and she herself may have emphasized one self-image over another of her fluctuating situation. This notion seems to be a kind of variation on that of the multiple voices that Henry Greenspan found among the survivors he interviewed.

Two other episodes that Roseman explored revolve around Strauss's separation from those she loved: her parting from her fiancé Ernst Krombach when he was deported to Izbica, and her flight from her family home when the Gestapo came to deport her and her family. Both episodes have more than one rendering. Roseman theorizes that by offering different versions, Strauss was trying to deal with the pain of these awful separations. He writes:

> It seemed to me that the inaccuracies in Strauss's memory were evidence of her pain and loss and a sign that she had sought to control the past within her, just as she sought to limit communication about it to the outside world. The stories had been gently changed into metaphors. As 'parables' of her and her family's fate, they were very slightly more bearable.[54]

In a sense this also echoes Henry Greenspan's idea that survivors often have a very difficult time articulating their experiences and must somehow fit them into a story format.

WHAT CAN A HISTORIAN OF THE HOLOCAUST GLEAN FROM PERSONAL ACCOUNTS?

Nechama Tec may be right in saying that even though some events are so strong as to be indelibly etched in an individual's memory, in later survivor accounts especially, the chronology of events and dates may be somewhat confused.[55] Indeed, anyone who has worked with post-war first-hand accounts has quickly learned that it can be frustrating trying to use them for determining very small precise details, such as the name, rank and unit of a perpetrator. Although some post-war first-hand accounts are loaded with details about various episodes from the Holocaust years, it can be exasperating to try to use them alone to construct a historical narrative of events or fill in a gap in a narrative. The corroboration of information, either by comparing multiple first-hand accounts or by comparing first-hand accounts with other types of documentation, is crucial when using first-hand accounts as sources for 'hard' historical information.

If 'hard' facts are not always the strongest point in published memoirs and post-war testimony, such material is often a good source for other kinds of information that traditional documentation does not always yield. In first-hand accounts, Jews who went through the Holocaust often provide researchers and readers with small glimpses into that which they experienced. These glimpses are often similar to snapshots or vignettes in the kind of data they can impart. Like snapshots, they communicate information from a fixed perspective – that of the witness to events.

In published memoirs, most writers say something about their pre-war lives. Occasionally these descriptions can be very idealized. When Jack Werber writes, 'Even though life was very difficult and people had to struggle hard to make a living, they never lost their sense of humor, their ability to laugh at life',[56] it is clear that the rough edges have been shaved away to form a romanticized picture of the pre-war Jews of Radom. His description is eerily reminiscent of the Jewish practice of only speaking well of the dead.

Other writers, however, tell a more realistic story about their lives before the war. Moshe Prywes, for one, ruthlessly describes the trials and tribulations of Jewish youth who wanted to study medicine in Poland during the 1930s. He writes of the great effort spent in trying to gain acceptance to the university, which severely limited the number of Jewish medical students accepted each year. He describes the daily brush with antisemitism in the form of Jewish benches in the classroom. And he also writes about the occasional physical attacks by nationalistic Christian students on their Jewish peers and the small minority of students and teachers who came to their aid.[57]

Life in the ghettos and camps, experiences in hiding and in underground formations and the treatment meted out by individual Nazis or local residents all find expression in the first-hand accounts from the Holocaust years. The survivor Morris Wyszogrod opens his memoir with a scene that evokes a powerful image of tradition and continuity within momentous change. It also describes a profound 'spiritual' response to the dreadfulness of the ghetto. The scene is the first night of Passover 1942, one year before the outbreak of the Warsaw Ghetto Uprising and several weeks before the advent of mass deportations from the ghetto to Treblinka. Everything in the house has been made kosher for the holiday. The meal comprises 'water boiled with coarse black salt and some rotten cabbage leaves'.[58] The father says *Kiddush* on water, since there is no wine or matzoth,[59] and he reads the traditional Passover ceremony from the *Haggadah*. Wyszogrod writes:

> He wanted so much to believe that the miracle of our people's deliverance from Egypt would occur for us too … To the last

moment, he believed with all his might that some miracle would occur and we would be spared from death. He tried to convey this to us. 'Children,' he says, 'don't fall into despair' … and my father began to recite the *Shfoch Chamoscho*, the passage in the *Haggadah* entreating God – 'Pour out Your wrath on the nations who do not acknowledge You.' My father's *Shfoch Chamoscho* was the most powerful curse I ever heard in my life. It was his rage, his hatred, [and] his belief that the enemy could be mortally wounded with his words. He hurled it at the enemy with all his remaining strength, the last breaths of life left to a man dying in agony. At that moment, his curse was also mine. I too was killing the enemy …[60]

Wyszogrod offers another image of his father's prayer, this time more subtle, but still compelling. His father has retreated into himself to cope with the awful situation he is facing:

I have a particularly sharp recollection of my father. He would get up early in the morning, wrap himself in *tallis* [prayer shawl] and *tfillin* [phylacteries] and begin his prayers. He prayed for a very long time. Before the war, he prayed quickly because he had things to do. Now he had nowhere to go. The synagogues were not functioning any more and it seemed that the *tallis* also gave him warmth because we had no coal to heat the oven and our apartment was terribly cold. It was painful to watch my father in a motionless position, deep in thought. All I heard were deep sighs and groans. I felt the world was coming to an end.[61]

In many of the ghettos, the dominant feature of life was hunger and search for food. In the diary kept by a teenager in the Lodz ghetto, David Sierakowiak, the reader can find many descriptions of slow starvation and its effects on Sierakowiak and his family. In particular, as has been mentioned by Lawrence Langer earlier, the starvation induced by Nazi decrees caused great strife within the Sierakowiak family. David himself found some solace in reading and writing.

Of course, suffering was not only the lot of those who lived in the ghettos of eastern Europe. The great torment Jews in hiding encountered is described in many first-hand accounts. Some of these accounts are reminiscent of the well-known story of Anne Frank, since they are stories of Jews being hidden by Christians in secretive and confined spaces. Sometimes a single sentence conjures up a powerful image of the misery that such hiding entailed. In her memoir, Fanya Gottesfeld Heller describes life hiding in the barn of Sidor, a Polish friend of her Ukrainian boyfriend Jan in Skala, Ukraine. The inability to wash was a constant agony, and she writes: 'There were so many lice that my hair was moving.'[62]

Marianne Strauss had a very different experience of hiding from that of Anne Frank or from that of Fanya Gottesfeld Heller. Posing as an Aryan, with the help of members of an underground German organization called the *Bund*, she actually lived quite openly. Strauss, with her dark hair bleached blonde and armed with one document that identified her as an Aryan, travelled on the trains of Germany, going from one safe house to the next. Occasionally, eating in restaurants obviously meant for Aryans only, she would find a spot at an SS man's table and flirt with him.[63] She is certainly not the only Jew who sought to survive by entering the lion's den and sidling up to the lion. Hermann Wygoda's story is about a Polish Jew who posed as a *Volkesdeutsch*. He thereby managed to eventually reach Italy and safety by working for Organization Todt. Saloman Perel's story – that of a Jew in the Hitler Youth Movement – became famous when his book, *Europa Europa*, was made into a movie.[64]

Posing as Aryans was not always dramatic, and sometimes it had to do with trying to live a quiet life from day to day. The Starkopf family – Adam, his wife Pela and their daughter Jasia – spent the last two years of the war posing as Aryans in several villages not far from the Treblinka extermination camp. They suffered much stress because of the fear they might be found to be Jews. In the late autumn of 1943, after two other Jewish families posing as Poles and living near them in the village of Sadowne had been discovered, they heard rumours that some of their neighbours thought they might also be Jews. The Starkopfs decided to pretend nothing was amiss. They continued playing their roles as Polish Christians and just waited for the rumours to die down – which is what eventually happened. Only in the spring of 1944, after the rumours had died down, did they dare to move on to a village near Siedlce.[65]

Certainly one of the most central questions in Holocaust research is: what was known about the Holocaust; who knew about it when and where? For understanding the responses of Jews under Nazi domination to their unfolding situation, this issue is vital. It is also one of the hardest questions to answer.

Professor David Engel undertook a study to determine what was known in the Warsaw ghetto through an examination of 11 diaries written there. At the same conference at Yeshiva University where Nechama Tec appeared, Engel clearly explains the challenge that evaluating their situation posed to residents in the ghetto. He writes:

> They had to evaluate not merely the veracity of such data [about Nazi anti-Jewish measures] but their significance. They had to

determine what the purpose of such actions was, and what was the thinking that underlay them. They had to ask themselves whether the actions had been taken impulsively on individual initiative, or as part of a program directed from Berlin. If the latter, they had to guess what the program might be, in order to determine the likelihood of the actions being repeated and of their affecting any particular Jew directly. And the operative word was always 'guess,' for they could never confirm their inferences with hard evidence until it was too late. [66]

Engel's conclusions might be surprising to some. He came to believe that the diaries he examined could not help determine what the ghetto as a whole understood. They could only shed light on the understanding of individuals. He writes:

In the final analysis it may be that a particular diarist's perception of the threat facing Warsaw Jewry was primarily a reflection of his own individual psychological makeup and was thus ordained from the beginning of the war, no matter what the diarist may of subsequently observed. [67]

It may be possible to reach an understanding of what was known and understood in the Warsaw ghetto, he suggests, but not through the use of diaries. [68]

Diaries from the Holocaust years, however, do provide us with glimpses into how individuals evaluated their situation. Various entries in David Sierakowiak's diary, for example, show how his frame of mind fluctuate over the many months he was enclosed in the Lodz ghetto. On 23 October 1941, several months before the first deportations to Chelmno began from Lodz, he is optimistic about his future. He writes: I'll start my work in the saddlery workshop tomorrow ... My student career has been suspended, at least for a while. Will I ever again be a student? I don't know. I dare to doubt it. But perhaps? The main thing now is to make an income and survive poverty. Just to hold out, just to keep going. The war will take a long time, and our task now is to fight with all our strength to stay alive. The immediate goal: overcome the winter. I'm certain that a wonderful, shining life is waiting for us. [69]

By early April 1942, however, Sierakowiak has seen many Jews deported from Lodz and is facing a growing gnawing hunger. At that point he hopes only somehow to survive: 'Thursday, April 2 [1942], Lodz ... May there be no more deportations and may something substantial arrive to eat. Potatoes are the main thing. To eat, think, study, write and work. Just to get to the end!'[70]

By the end of April, the situation has deteriorated further and Sierakowiak is less sure than ever that he will survive:

> Wednesday, April 29 [1942], Lodz. It is really bad at home. There is no fuel, and we are eating our May ration of potatoes in April. No one knows what will happen in May. Nothing good, that's for sure. Again I don't have any will, or rather any strength, for studying. I want to do something, but everything is exceptionally difficult for me, so I just stick to reading most of the time. Time is passing, my youth is passing, my school years, my power and enthusiasm are all passing. Only the Devil knows what I will manage to save from this pogrom. I'm slowly beginning to lose my hope of coming back to life or even of holding onto the one I'm living now.[71]

Several months later in August 1942, Sierakowiak feels that he is trapped, but once again he finds some reserve of hope that he may survive. He writes: 'Monday, August 3 [1942], Lodz … Meanwhile, trembling with fear for what remains of our strength, we anxiously calculate our abilities and chances of getting out of this trap. Perhaps we'll make it after all!'[72] Ultimately, however, he experienced more pain until finally dying. First in September 1942 his mother was deported, and then in March 1943, after many months of anguish, his father died. David Sierakowiak, too, would not live out the year.

How did David Sierakowiak understand what was happening to Lodz Jewry in general? In April 1942, he characterizes what is happening to the Jews of Lodz as a 'pogrom'.[73] Of course this term was used by other Jews in order to describe what they were experiencing during the Holocaust. For example, in Vilna the Jewish press used the word to describe the initial six months of killing that struck the community, and then stopped. Pogroms, of course, were part of recent Jewish history for eastern European Jews, especially those carried out during and immediately after the First World War. Pogroms may be characterized as an intense and capricious eruption of violence. A pogrom may return to a given community at a later date, may strike another community or may not come back at all. This of course is fundamentally different from the Nazi implementation of the Final Solution, which often hit a given community piecemeal, but was intended to come back as often as was necessary to destroy all the Jews.

In May 1942, Sierakowiak writes about the fate of Jews from the Reich and surrounding Jewish communities who had been brought to Lodz, as well as the Jews from Lodz itself. Sierakowiak really seems to have no clear idea about what was in store for the Jews at this point. He writes:

> There are rumors about an enormous ghetto for all the Jews from the Reich, but only for those who can work. Nobody knows what the Germans do with the children of those unable to work. The Pabianice Jews also know nothing about their elderly, their sick and their children. Children were torn away from their mothers in the most brutal way. We are not considered humans at all: cattle for work or slaughter. No one knows what happened to the Jews deported from Lodz. No one can be certain of anything now.[74]

Throughout the summer, it is clear that the Sierakowiaks still did not have a clear understanding of the meaning of deportations. They are not even sure if they were necessarily bad. As a result, Sierakowiak's father debates whether he should volunteer for a transport or not. He knows the situation in Lodz is terrible, but is uncertain if going on a transport will make things better or worse for himself. Ultimately he decides not to go voluntarily.[75]

Later, in winter 1943, Sierakowiak mentions the extermination of the Jews in his diary. In February, he notes a newspaper report that says that Hitler had plans to exterminate the Jews.[76] In March he writes: 'Every day is worse in the ghetto ... There are no new food rations. Extermination is approaching.'[77] It is hard to say if this means that he understood that the Nazis really were trying to murder all the Jews. The last entry in his diary, however, suggests that he felt that he himself, along with all the Jews in Lodz, had little chance of surviving. He writes:

> Thursday, April 15 [1943], Lodz ... In the evening I had to prepare food and cook supper, which exhausted me totally. In politics there's absolutely nothing new. Again, out of impatience I feel myself beginning to fall into melancholy. There is really no way out for us.[78]

By 8 August 1943, having found no way out, David Sierakowiak died from the ravages of starvation and disease.

In the case of David Sierakowiak, Engel's insight seems to apply: the 'operative word' was to 'guess' the meaning and implication of events. But for Marianne Strauss, the sources of information were much clearer at some junctures in her life under Nazi rule and she had to engage in much less guesswork. One of the clearest pieces of information she had was about the impending murder of her parents. In her diary in June 1944, she writes that she heard a BBC broadcast that said

Jews who had been deported from Germany to Theresienstadt after 18 December 1943 were slated to be sent to Auschwitz-Birkenau to be gassed. Strauss knew that her parents had been deported to Theresienstadt on 18 December 1943, and thus were to be murdered in Auschwitz. Mark Roseman corroborated this entry in her diary with material from the BBC archives that showed there had been such a broadcast very near the time of the diary entry.[79]

Linked very closely to the issue of information and the analysis of that information, is the subject of personal decision-making by Jews during the Holocaust. Personal decisions, one would assume, were based on how Jews assessed their situation at a given time. André Stein, however, in a symposium on Simon Wiesenthal's book, *The Sunflower*,[80] suggests that decisions taken by Jews under Nazi rule were not normative decisions. He says:

> In the absurd culture of the death camp where every moment was saturated with its own premature ending, all decisions were by necessity the consequence of planned randomization of meanings. Nothing could be taken for granted on the basis of previous stock of knowledge. Any act, decision, compliance with an order could as easily be life-affirming as life-threatening. Nothing made sense. The victims were evicted from their own destiny.[81]

The gist of Stein's statement might be correct, and Lawrence Langer, for one, seems to accept it.[82] But in its details, Stein overstated his case and some of what he said requires qualification. It would be hard to prove that the Nazis actually planned randomization of meanings, even in the death camps.[83] Like Fackenheim's statement that the Nazi system purposely created *Musselmanner*, documentary evidence from the perspective of the perpetrators that could support the idea of a plan to muddle all meaning has yet to surface. It would be equally difficult to demonstrate that absolutely 'nothing made sense' to any Jew in any camp. It is clear, however, in looking at personal decision-making as described in first-hand accounts of the Holocaust, not only those written about the death camps, that almost 'nothing could be taken for granted on the basis of previous stock of knowledge'.[84]

Explaining his decision to pose as a *Volksdeutscher*, Herman Wygoda writes:

> There were no rules to go by. No handbook had ever been written or ever will be written that could be of use to a man who is hunted like a wild animal just because he was not born an Aryan. There were no rules of safety to follow to save one's life; all our choices had to be quick, ad hoc decisions made as each case

presented itself. One important factor remained in my favor: I was born in Germany and spoke German without an accent. In Kossow, which was 80 percent Jewish and where practically everyone knew me, I had no valid reason to use this asset. Yes, I began to think of my fluent German as an asset, and then I thought of a way to make use of it.[85]

Here, Wygoda made his post-war assessment clearly, that in his situation 'there were no rules to go by'. Yet, during the war, he came to understand that in his new situation, his knowledge of German was an asset. It was this knowledge that allowed him to begin his ruse and carry it out – steps that ultimately contributed significantly to his survival.

Wygoda's decision to pose as a *Volksdeutscher* also included the decision to flee his home town. In many memoirs of survivors, the decision to flee or stay put is presented. Morris Wyszogrod, nineteen years old at the time, describes the discussion in his family about fleeing Warsaw at the start of the war. Ultimately, for a number of reasons that he points out, they decided to stay put. The Wyszogrod family discussion reflects many ideas that were noted by later historians, who have discussed the basis on which Polish Jews assessed their situation at the time of the German invasion. Wyszogrod writes:

> People advised us to leave too, but we never did. We had no money. We had no place to go, no one in any villages to run to. In addition, although my father was influenced by socialist ideas, he did not altogether trust the Soviet Union. The memory of Russian pogroms was too strong … Finally, although people tried to convince me to run away with them, I would not leave my parents, and they did not believe things would get so bad that they should run away. They trusted their memories of the way Germans had behaved during World War I. Back then the Germans were considered a better occupier than the tsar, who was no hero to the Jews … So, all things considered, my father believed that, in the worst case, we would get ration cards and have to do forced labor.[86]

Jack Werber's family also decided to stay put and not to escape from Radom to the section of Poland that the Soviet Union had occupied. In his case, as the family loaded their wagon and realized how many personal possessions they would have to leave behind, they decided to stay.[87] Two months after the start of the war, the Sierakowiaks also discussed leaving their home in Lodz. Money was their main problem. They decided to try to sell their possessions to obtain the necessary sum to fund their flight, and they even considered having the father go first, in the hope that from a better venue he would be able to arrange the flight of the rest of the family. But they were unable to sell anything and ended up staying put.[88]

Adam Starkopf's story of flight is much more complex and includes a series of decisions over several months. With the outbreak of the war Starkopf, like many other Polish citizens, answered the government's call to gather at Brzesc to join the Polish armed forces. Leaving Warsaw, and travelling mostly on foot, Starkopf and several others encountered trouble on the road to Brzesc. Owing to the fighting, some of the men were killed on the way. After five days of walking, Starkopf and several others reached the town, only to discover that it was aflame. From there, they crossed into territory that soon was to be occupied by the Soviet Union. Learning of the fall of Warsaw in mid-October, Starkopf decided to return to his wife and the rest of his family. Back in Warsaw, he discovered that his mother had died and his brother-in-law, who also had left to join the Polish army, was missing; most probably he was in the Soviet sector. Once again Starkopf set out for the far side of the Bug River – for Soviet territory. Once there, he discovered that his brother-in-law had died and he then decided to bring the rest of his family to the Soviet area. His wife's parents and his father, however, refused to come. In his book, he explains their decision: 'Most of the Jews of our parents' age did not take kindly to the idea of becoming penniless, unwanted refugees under the Russians, whom they viewed with suspicion.'[89] (Here too, one must be a bit sceptical about the plural voice, but can accept this explanation for Starkopf's immediate family.) When his wife arrived in December 1939, and learned that her brother had died, she decided that they must return to her parents in Warsaw.

After the establishment of the Warsaw ghetto and the birth of a daughter, Jasia, Starkopf again began to think the family should escape from Warsaw. In the meantime, deportations had begun and Starkopf set the date for their escape, 31 July 1942. His chief thought was to do what was best for his daughter. But it was far from certain to him, his wife or their parents that flight was the best alternative. On the night before the planned escape, they had second thoughts:

> Did I have the right to risk the life of my child? Even if we escaped without being caught, what assurance did I have that I would be able to keep Jasia alive? How could I be certain that she would not get sick, or starve? Would our escape really give her a chance to survive the war and grow to maturity, or would it only bring her prolonged agony ending in a horrible death?[90]

Nevertheless, despite their hesitations, the Starkopfs decided to escape. With the help of false papers and a complicated ruse, they managed to slip out of the ghetto through the Gesia Street cemetery. Starkopf, his wife and child reached the Soviet sector. This time his father and his in-laws were willing to come, but they did not succeed in their escape attempt. Once in the Soviet sector, Starkopf and his small family posed as Polish Christians and lived in a series of villages. They let it be known that, because of Adam Starkopf's past association with the Polish underground (which he invented), they must be discreet. There is no indication in the story on the eve of their escape the Starkopfs had the slightest inkling that Warsaw Jews were being deported to their deaths in Treblinka. Apparently, they did not need to know this in order to decide to run away from the ghetto with an infant; what they had already experienced in the ghetto was more than enough to fuel their decision.

In Marianne Strauss's narrative, the decision to flee is confronted twice. The first time, her parents had to decide whether or not to send their two children, Marianne and her younger brother Richard, to Britain alone as part of the *Kindertransports*. Early in 1939, shortly after the father Siegfried was released from Dachau, where he had been imprisoned with other Jewish men on *Kristallnacht* in November 1938, the parents discussed the idea. They decided it was not yet bad enough to abandon hope that the entire family might still get out of Germany together and thus they decided not to send their children to Britain.

Mark Roseman comments regarding the decision: 'What seems evident is that despite Dachau, Siegfried still had not fully realized what the regime was capable of.'[91] As careful as Roseman is to try to see things from the point of view of those about whom he is writing, here he loses this perspective. Siegfried Strauss had indeed been a prisoner in Dachau. The issue is if that experience should have led him to the conclusion that sending his children to Britain was a better option than trying to arrange the emigration of the entire family together. In Dachau, he was subjected to a brutal regime, which at the time was designed to break the spirit of the opponents to the regime. He was in the camp as a Jewish male, with other Jewish males. Although he would have learned that the Nazi regime could be incredibly cruel to men, there was no reason that he should have come to the conclusion that it would be as cruel to women and children. He may well have learned that he, and thus his family, had no future in Germany, and that they should leave sooner and not later. However, it seems he had no reason to surmise, based on his personal experiences, that his children were in the kind of immediate danger that demanded breaking up the family for an undefined period.

The second time that Marianne Strauss faced a decision about fleeing was on the fateful day in August 1943 when the Gestapo came to her house to take the family for deportation. Although, as has been mentioned previously, there is more than one version of the sequence of events, it is clear that Strauss had to flee without much time to decide. In her written account, she describes her flight with the following words:

> Unable to say good-bye to my parents, my brother and my relatives, I followed the impulse of the moment and ran out of the house just as I was, with a few hundred mark notes which my father had stuffed into my pockets moments before. I ran for my life, expecting to hear a pistol shot behind me at any minute. But to go in that way seemed to me a much better fate than the unimaginable one awaiting me in Auschwitz or Lodz, in Treblinka or Izbica. But there was no shot, no one running after me, no order, no shouting.[92]

In addition to some inconsistencies in the various accounts – whether the Gestapo was in the family's cellar when she fled from her kitchen, or whether they were in the living room and she fled from the kitchen after having asked for permission to take a loaf of bread – the most extraordinary part of her written account is her mentioning of Auschwitz, Lodz, Treblinka and Izbica and her apparent knowledge of them. Her account certainly raises this question: could a young Jewish woman sitting in Essen in August 1943 have known about these places? It is easy to picture Mark Roseman raising his eyebrows the first time he read her account of the escape. But as extraordinary as it may appear, Strauss probably did have a pretty clear image of at least some of these places as she ran from her home that August day.

In May 1942, Strauss received a letter by way of the regular mail from her fiancé, Ernst Krombach, who shortly before had been deported with his family to Izbica, near Lublin.[93] For the next few months, with the help of a mechanic Christian Arras, who frequently travelled from Essen to Izbica for his work, Strauss managed to send Krombach packages and letters and receive letters in exchange. In August 1942, responding to many of her questions about Izbica, Krombach sent Strauss what can be described best as an 18-page report about conditions there. As the following excerpt suggests, he described much of the sad reality to her:

> 'Hygiene' is a joke. Everything filthy, lice (particularly clothes lice that spread typhus), fleas, bugs. There are few latrines. Sewage flows through unpaved streets (stench, illness). One illness is very common here: a high temperature with no other symptoms. It goes as quickly as it comes, but leaves you weaker. Diarrhea is equally common …[94]

Later, through Arras, Strauss learned that Krombach's parents had been deported from Izbica and that he had been blinded, either in an accident or as a punishment of some sort.[95]

Given that German Jews had been deported to Lodz for some time before August 1943, it is quite conceivable that Strauss knew something of that as well – at least on the level of rumour. The sources for the inclusion of Treblinka and Auschwitz in her list of horrors to be avoided, however, are much less clear. The Jews from Izbica were mostly murdered in Belzec and Sobibor, as Roseman points out. Had Strauss mentioned either of these places as being in her mind when she fled the Gestapo, it is reasonable that she might have heard something about them from Arras. But since Jews from Izbica were not deported directly to either Treblinka or Auschwitz, it is not apparent that she learned about these places from him. Nevertheless, there was some information about Auschwitz available in Germany in the summer of 1943 to the 'man in the street'. Lili Hahn, a journalist, mentions Auschwitz and Birkenau in her diary in May 1943.[96] It may be that like Hahn, Strauss also had heard of Auschwitz, or it may be that she mixed in later information in this account of her flight. When she first might have heard about Treblinka is much less clear. But even if Auschwitz and Treblinka are later additions to her account, Strauss already knew enough about the horrors of Izbica to risk her life by running from the Gestapo. As luck would have it, Strauss's escape did not benefit her family. They were about to be deported, and that is what happened. They continued to live in Theresienstadt for a while and then were murdered in Auschwitz, not because of Strauss's escape, but because they were caught in the gears of the Nazi murder machine.

Unlike Strauss at her time of escape, David Matzner confronted the possible ramifications of his escape attempt more directly. In the late 1930s he had fled from Germany to Belgium and, before the Nazi attack on western Europe, to France. The French authorities interned Matzner in Le Benet. He was released apparently some time late in 1940 and was given permission to live with his brother, who was in France legally. After several months (Matzner does not give a date), very early one morning, French policemen came to arrest him. Matzner fled and hid, but when he became aware that if he did not come voluntarily, his brother and his brother's family might be arrested, he gave himself up. Caught between a rock and a hard place, Matzner made a very conscious choice. His choice led to his imprisonment in Drancy, and his subsequent deportation to Auschwitz.[97] One may assume that, except for having learned from his previous period of incarceration that internment was to say the least unpleasant, Matzner had no way of knowing what would be the specific repercussions of his arrest.

Did individuals learn new rules from their experiences under the

Nazis that helped them make decisions to improve their situation? In the memoirs there are examples of Jews who sometimes deciphered new rules that aided their decision-making. There are also examples of Jews who tried to apply the new rules they thought they had learned only to have a factor change that caused the rule not to hold. The few vignettes presented here are not sufficient for building a general theory; however, they do give us insight into the difficulties camp prisoners faced when they had to make a decisions in a reality that was so different from that which they had known before the war.

Working in a quarry in Buchenwald, Jack Werber describes the kind of 'tricks of the trade' one could pick up to help ease the daily grind of slave work. He writes:

> Crucial to survival was learning how to select and hoist onto your shoulder the right stone in a split second. It took me about a week to master how to carry the stones. If you took a stone that was too small, they beat you up for being a loafer. And if you chose one that was too large, you ran the risk of collapsing under its weight. After a while, I learned how to select stones that looked big but were lighter because they were a little hollow on the inside.[98]

But just because Werber found one way to make his work easier without the guards noticing, did not mean that he would succeed with another work-saving idea. Werber and three friends realized that, by using a rope to hold the rocks, they could work more efficiently and with less strain. But when a guard saw their innovation, he shot one of them and punished Werber and two friends by having them 'hung in a fiendish manner'.[99]

Werber, however, continued to look for ways to make his life easier. When he learned that some prisoners would be taught bricklaying, he decided to risk volunteering. Weber reasoned that since it would take time to learn the craft, he might be spared the worst outdoor work during winter. He could not have known when he signed up for the course that it would prove his salvation from the deportation to Auschwitz that struck many Jewish prisoners in October 1942.[100]

In his memoir, Werber expresses his feelings about his ability to manoeuvre to help himself. He writes:

> One of the reasons I survived is probably because I was very observant. I watched everything around me. I tried to follow orders and not stick out too much. Also, I could adjust very easily. I learned quickly what needed to be done in each new situation. Since I had no hope that I would ever be free, I said to myself 'I'm a slave; I was born a slave.' It's hard to explain it. I don't know. But

above all else, it was luck, or coincidence. I did very few things on purpose to survive.[101]

In Werber's assessment one needed to be sharp in order to learn and apply new rules, but one also needed luck. It may be that what he calls 'luck' or 'coincidence' also includes the notion that one needed to apply rules in circumstances where they were valid – circumstances that were often fleeting.

David Matzner recounted two incidents where he was faced with the decision of whether or not to tell the truth. In the first instance an SS man in the camp told him to lie to the camp commandant about seeing two Jewish senior prisoners light his cigarette, lest the SS man be found guilty of fraternization with prisoners. Matzner lied. The camp commandant knew he was lying and beat him severely. In the second incident, an SD investigator asked Matzner if he had told other prisoners that Munich had been bombed, and how did he hear about the bombing in the first place? Matzner decided to tell the truth and nothing happened to him.[102] In the first incident one may assume that if he had told the truth, the SS man would later have beaten him instead of the commandant, although it is impossible to say for sure. In the second incident, the fact that he was not punished may have more to do with the whim of the SD man than anything else, since Matzner had broken camp rules and breaking rules often led to severe punishment.

If Matzner seemed to have concluded, based on his first experience, that telling the truth was better than lying, in another earlier incident he saw that the outcome of two similar situations could be devastatingly different. In Auschwitz one day a German gave Matzner bread. Sometime shortly afterward while he was working, he saw the same German and asked him again for some bread. Several hours later the German returned with bread for Matzner. But this time the guard saw Matzner talking to the German. For this he was beaten severely, and from that time onward the deputy camp commander would beat Matzner whenever he saw him. The constant violence wore Matzner down so much that he considered himself to have become a *Muselmann* for a while.[103]

Of course, throughout the Holocaust years, in many different situations, Jews had contact with the Gentiles around them – from camp guards to neighbours. Their encounters obviously ran the gamut of possible experiences and, as we have already seen, comprise an important element in first-hand accounts. Some of the acts of kindness have already been alluded to: the aid received by Marianne Strauss from her friends in the *Bund*, the bread given to David Matzner by the German in Auschwitz and the prolonged help provided to the family of Fanya Gottesfeld Heller by her Ukrainian lover Jan and Jan's Polish friend

Sidor. Yet in many memoirs it is the descriptions of cruelty that stand out.

Adam Starkopf describes a scene of particular heartlessness that happened when he and his family were hiding in the village of Sadowne, on the railroad line to Treblinka. One night, early in January 1943, some Jews jumped off the train bound for Treblinka. Starkopf's landlord and his family came to his door and called to him by his assumed name:

> 'Mr. Budovski! Mrs. Budovski!' they chorused. 'Didn't you hear the commotion outside? Some Jews just escaped from a train and the Germans started to shoot at them! They must have hit quite a few. Just think – all those Jews lying on the ground, ready for the taking! It's a windfall! We can go out, pick them up and turn them over to the Gestapo. We'll take their clothes, clean out their pockets and on top of that we'll get a reward from the Germans for bringing them in. Come on! Everybody else in the village is going, too, so we'd better hurry! Otherwise there'll be no Jews left for us to catch.' [104]

Feeling like strangling his landlord and the family, Starkopf summoned his self-control and made an excuse so as not to join them. Although it is unlikely that Starkopf remembered the exact words that he heard that night, the substance of his rendition seems genuine and presents a picture of vile behaviour. The next day at work, he witnessed further unbridled viciousness against the wretched Jews who had jumped from the train, and one incident of restraint.

Fanya Gottesfeld Heller writes in her memoir several times about the sexual abuse of women by Germans. This is a touchy subject, especially since sexual contact between Germans and Jews was so completely against Nazi ideology as to cast doubt on many such descriptions. The first time she mentions this topic, she says that the Skala Jewish Council was forced to provide beautiful women for the Germans. It is difficult to accept her statement as hard-and-fast evidence since she was neither on the Jewish Council nor close to it, and she was not one of the women approached, because she was still a young high-school girl.[105] The next time she broaches the subject, it is about an incident that happened to her. She describes a scene in which a *Volksdeutscher* caressed her and then, when she protested that she was only sixteen years old, let her go with a tirade of verbal abuse.[106] In addition to her personal confrontation, Gottesfeld Heller writes about the rape of her aunt. Her aunt told her that a Wehrmacht non-commissioned officer named Gottschalk, from Vienna, had raped her.[107] Finally, she tells the story of her friend Zhenia, who began working as a maid for an SS man and then became his mistress. Gottesfeld Heller visited her friend and writes of her: 'an SS man, defying the non-fraternization rule, set her up in her own little room and provided her with food and clothes.'[108] The SS man eventually shot her dead to prove to his colleagues, who had badgered him about his Jewish lover, that she meant nothing to him.[109] Despite a necessary sensitivity one should retain about such accounts, the last three seem to contain enough detail and internal integrity to be taken seriously.

Sometimes the stories presented in first-thand accounts go beyond mere questionability, but are out and out impossible. Such is the case for Jack Werber's belief that he had showered with soap made from Jewish fat. Werber made another claim that seems to have no real basis: in 1940 the coffee served to prisoners in Buchenwald was poisoned.[110] It is quite possible that this is what prisoners believed, and it may well have been one of their explanations for why they felt so awful, became sick and often died. But most likely they fell sick because of the horrible and cruel conditions in the camp.

David Matzner made a much more demonstratively inaccurate claim in his memoir. As the registrar in the Wolfsburg camp, Matzner claimed that he spoke with the Satmar Rebbe several times to help arrange a Kol Nidre service on the eve of Yom Kippur in 1944.[111] There was really such a service in the camp, and a prayer book for the high-holidays was produced there, which Yad Vashem published in a facsimile edition.[112] But the Satmar Rebbe, Joel Teitelbaum, never was in Wolfsburg. He was one of the over 1,680 Jews who left Budapest for Switzerland, by way of the Bergen Belsen camp in the summer of 1944, on the so-called Kasztner train.

Unquestionably there are wilful distortions in some first-hand accounts. The memoir of the former Chief Rabbi of Romania, Alexandre Safran, seems to be a case in point. According to a scholar of Romanian Jewry, Jan Ancel, who spoke at a symposium of the Yad Vashem International Institute for Holocaust Research soon after thousands of new documents about the Holocaust in Romania became available in the 1990s, Safran greatly inflated his role in the rescue of the Jews of the Romanian heartland, the Regat, in his memoir. However, few, if any, have gone as far as Binjamin Wilkomirski, who apparently fabricated his entire memoir.[113] Rather, more commonly, according to Nechama Tec: 'Divergent information often reflects subjective perceptions, subjective experiences, rather than willful distortions.'[114]

Undoubtedly, many inaccuracies can be explained. In Matzner's case, there are several potential explanations for his error, in addition to the possibility that he may have knowingly falsified information. He may have simply made a mistake at the time he was in the camp, and assumed that the leader of the Satmar Hassidim he met there was the Rebbe. Or perhaps, in retrospect, as he reconstructed events to compose his memoir, he may have thought that the man he had met in the camp was Rabbi Teitelbaum.

Especially where the misinformation serves no apparent purpose, a reader can assume that an innocent mistake was made. Nevertheless, it is important that readers be aware of such gaffes and that they remember that they are an inherent problem in first-hand accounts. The explanations offered by Greenspan, Roseman and Tec all shed light on the roots of these kinds of discrepancies. Diaries, testimonies and memoirs about the Holocaust should not be put on a pedestal or treated as though they were sacred. They need to be approached with an understanding of their inherent strengths and weaknesses. Like any other historical source material, they need to be read critically. But it also behoves those who read first-hand accounts of the Holocaust to remember that they are not just another recounting of another historical event. They do embody a deeper meaning. Their mere existence is important for, among other reasons, as Ruth Wisse has written, 'individualizing the Holocaust undoes the leveling work of the Nazi regime'.[115] When we read first-hand accounts about the experiences of Jews in the Holocaust, we are involved not only in a learning process, but also in commemoration.

NOTES

An abbreviated version of this essay was published in *Studies in Contemporary Jewry*, Vol. 18, 2002, pp. 219–31.

1. One of the earliest publications was B. Habas, *Shnaim Asar Plitim* [Twelve Refugees] (Tel Aviv: Am Oved, 1943) [in Hebrew]. In English one of the first accounts was J. Bernard, *The Camp of Slow Death* (London: Gollancz, 1945) (the French-language version was published in 1944). The Yad Vashem library has nearly 1,200 memorial books in its collection.
2. The database on memoirs compiled by the Yad Vashem library listed nearly six thousand items in December 2002.
3. As of July 2001, the computerized index of the Yad Vashem archives listed 480 diaries and the Yad Vashem library listed 446 published diaries. It also should be noted that not all of these diaries were necessarily kept by Jews, and that there is an overlap between some of the published and unpublished diaries.
4. H. Greenspan, *On Listening to Holocaust Survivors: Recounting and Life History* (Westport, CT: Praeger, 1998); L. Langer, *Preempting the Holocaust* (New Haven, CT: Yale University Press, 1998); D. Patterson, *Sun Turned to Darkness: Memory and Recovery in the Holocaust Memoir* (Syracuse, NY: Syracuse University Press, 1998); R. M. Shapiro (ed.), *Holocaust Chronicles: Individualizing the Holocaust through Diaries and Other Contemporaneous Personal Accounts* (Hoboken, NJ: Ktav, 1996). Greenspan is a psychologist, and Langer and Patterson are scholars of literature. The papers published by Shapiro include those of Betty Jean Lifton (psychology), David Roskies and Ruth Wisse (literature), Magdalena M. Opalski and Nechama Tec (sociology), Jan Tomasz Gross (political science), Rafael Scharf (law), Yitzhak Arad, David Engel, Daniel Grinberg, Samuel David Kassow, Dina Porat and Robert Moses Shapiro (history), and a number of authors of literary works.
5. Patterson, *Sun Turned to Darkness*, p. 9.

6. Ibid., p. 22.
7. Ibid., p. 94.
8. Ibid., p. 27.
9. Patterson, *Sun Turned to Darkness*, p. 123.
10. E. L. Fackenheim, *God's Presence in History: Jewish Affirmations and Philosophical Reflections*, (Northvale, NJ: Jason Aronson, 1997), p. 84.
11. Patterson, *Sun Turned to Darkness*, pp. 21–2.
12. Ibid., p. 16.
13. Ibid., p. 18.
14. Ibid., p. 19.
15. Ibid., p. 42.
16. Ibid., p. 75.
17. Ibid., p. 8–10.
18. Ibid., pp. 24.
19. Ibid., p. 37. See Nathan Shappel, *Witness to the Truth* (New York: David Mackay, 1974).
20. Patterson, *Sun Turned to Darkness*, p. 53.
21. Ibid., *Sun Turned to Darkness*, p. 6. See also E. L. Fackenheim, *To Mend the World: Foundations of Post-Holocaust Jewish Thought* (Bloomington, IN: University of Indiana Press, 1994).
22. Patterson, *Sun Turned to Darkness*, p. 166.
23. I. Gutman (ed.), *Encyclopedia of the Holocaust* (New York: Macmillan, 1990), pp. 339–43.
24. Patterson, *Sun Turned to Darkness*, p. 168.
25. J. Werber, *Saving Children: Diary of a Buchenwald Survivor and Rescuer* (New Brunswick, NJ: Transaction Books, 1996), p. 41.
26. H. Hutenbach, 'The Myth of Nazi Human Soap', *The Genocide Forum*, 1, 6 (1994).
27. Perhaps the most famous work that suffers from similar problems is H. Arendt, *Eichmann in Jerusalem: A Report on the Banality of Evil* New York: Viking Press, 1963).
28. Greenspan, *On Listening to Holocaust Survivors*, p. xv.
29. Ibid., p. 17.
30. Ibid., p. 90.
31. Ibid.,p. 154.
32. Ibid., pp. 146–7.
33. Ibid., pp. 163–5.
34. Ibid., p. 171.
35. Ibid., p. xv.
36. Langer's other books include *The Holocaust and the Literary Imagination* (New Haven, CT: Yale University Press, 1975); *Holocaust Testimony: The Ruins of Memory* (New Haven, CT: Yale University Press, 1991); *Admitting the Holocaust: Collected Essays* (New York: Oxford University Press, 1995).
37. Langer, *Preempting the Holocaust*, p. 58.
38. Ibid., p. 22.
39. A. Adelson (ed.), *The Diary of Dawid Sierakowiak: Five Notebooks from the Lodz Ghetto* (New York: Oxford University Press, 1996).
40. Langer, *Preempting the Holocaust*, p. 135.
41. Ibid., pp. 78–9.
42. E. Wiesel, *All Rivers Run to the Sea: Memoirs* (New York: Knopf, 1995), p. 17.
43. For example, see D. J. Azrieli, *One Step Ahead, David J. Azrieli (Azrylewicz), Memoirs: 1939–1950* (Jerusalem: Yad Vashem, 2001); Werber, *Saving Children*; H. Wygoda, *In the Shadow of the Swastika* (Urbana, IL: University of Illinois Press, 1998); M. Wyszogrod, *A Brush With Death: An Artist in the Death Camps* (Albany, NY: State University of New York Press, 1999).
44. Among the various English-language editions of Anne Frank's diary are A. Frank, *The Diary of a Young Girl* (Garden City, NY: Doubleday, 1952); *The Diary of a Young Girl: The Critical Edition* (New York: Doubleday, 1989); *The Diary of a Young Girl: The Definitive Edition* (Garden City, NY: Doubleday, 1995).
45. Shapiro, *Holocaust Chronicles*, p. 271.
46. Wyszogrod, *A Brush With Death*, p. 29.
47. Wygoda, *In the Shadow*, p. 11.
48. Werber, *Saving Children* p. 28.

49. Ibid.
50. Y. Arad, *Ghetto in Flames: The Struggle and Destruction of the Jews in Vilna in the Holocaust* (New York: Holocaust Library, 1982); D. H. Kranzler, *Japanese, Nazis and Jews: The Jewish Refugee Community of Shanghai, 1938–1945* (New York: Yeshiva University Press, 1976); E. Zuroff, 'Attempts to Obtain Shanghai Permits in 194: A Case of Rescue Priority during the Holocaust', *Yad Vashem Studies*, XIII (1978), pp 321–51; 'Rescue via the Far East, The Attempt to Save Polish Rabbis and Yeshiva Students, 1939–1941', *Simon Wiesenthal Annual*, 1 (1984), pp. 153–83; and *The Response of Orthodox Jewry in the United States to the Holocaust: The Activities of the Vaad ha-Hatzala Rescue Committee, 1939–1945* (New York: Yeshiva University Press, 2000). It should be noted that the last work mentioned by Zuroff would not have been available to Werber at the time he wrote his memoir.
51. E. Farbstein, 'Diaries and Memoirs as a Historical Source – The Diary and Memoir of a Rabbi at the "Konin House of Bondage"', *Yad Vashem Studies*, XXVI (1998), pp. 87–128.
52. Roseman, *A Past in Hiding: Memory and Survival in Nazi Germany* (New York: Metropolitan Books, 2001).
53. Ibid., p. 66.
54. Ibid., p. 411.
55. Shapiro, *Holocaust Chronicles*, p. 273.
56. Werber, *Saving Children*, p. 14.
57. M. Prywes, *Prisoner of Hope* (Hanover, NH: Brandeis University Press, 1996), pp. 30–71.
58. Wyszogrod, *A Brush With Death*, p. x.
59. Normally the blessing, called *Kiddush*, is made over wine or grape juice. It can also be made over bread or matzoth, which take precedent over the wine and are thus covered while the blessing over the wine is recited.
60. Wyszogrod, *A Brush With Death*, p. xi.
61. Ibid., pp. 53–4.
62. F. Gottesfeld Heller, *Strange and Unexpected Love: A Teenage Girl's Holocaust Memoirs* (Hoboken: Ktav, 1993), p. 192.
63. Roseman, *A Past in Hiding*, p. 289.
64. S. Perel, *Europa, Europa* (New York: John Wiley, 1997, first published in France, 1990). The movie version, directed by Agnieszka Holland, was released in 1991.
65. A. Starkopf, *Will to Live: One Family's Story of Surviving the Holocaust* (Albany, NY: State University of New York Press, 1995), pp. 196–7.
66. Shapiro, *Holocaust Chronicles*, p. 73.
67. Ibid., pp. 79–80.
68. Ibid., p. 81.
69. Adelson, *The Diary of Dawid Sierakowiak*, p. 143.
70. Ibid., p. 151.
71. Ibid., pp. 160–1.
72. Ibid., p. 203.
73. Ibid., p. 160.
74. Ibid., pp. 69–70.
75. Ibid., pp. 174–91.
76. Ibid., p. 251.
77. Ibid., p. 259.
78. Ibid., p. 268.
79. Roseman, *A Past in Hiding*, pp. 303–8 and 370–2.
80. S. Wiesenthal, *The Sunflower: On the Possibilities and Limits of Forgiveness*, revised and expanded edition (New York: Schocken Books, 1997).
81. Quoted in Langer, *Preempting the Holocaust*, p. 178.
82. Langer, *Preempting the Holocaust*, p. 178.
83. It is hard to know just to which camps Stein is referring. Does he mean the six extermination camps (Auschwitz, Belzec, Chelmno, Majdanek, Sobibor and Treblinka) or does he have other camps in mind. Sometimes all the Nazi camps are referred to generically as 'death camps'.
84. Langer, *Preempting the Holocaust*, p. 178.
85. Wygoda, *In the Shadow*, p. 19.
86. Wyszogrod, *A Brush With Death*, p. 31.
87. Werber, *Saving Children*, p. 25.

88. Adelson (ed.), *The Diary of Dawid Sierakowiak*, pp. 65–6.
89. Starkopf, *Will to Live*, p. 53.
90. Ibid., p. 111.
91. Roseman, *A Past in Hiding*, pp. 91–2.
92. Roseman, *A Past in Hiding*, pp. 2–3.
93. Ibid., p. 176.
94. Ibid., pp. 195.
95. Mbid., *A Past in Hiding*, pp. 211–17.
96. David Bankier, 'The Germans and the Holocaust', *Yad Vashem Studies*, 20 (1990), p. 72.
97. D. Matzner, *The Muselmann: The Diary of a Jewish Slave Laborer* (Hoboken, NJ: KAVT, 1994), pp. 7–29.
98. Werber, *Saving Children*, p. 44.
99. Ibid., p. 49.
100. Ibid., pp. 54–6.
101. Ibid., p. 65.
102. Matzner, *The Muselmann*, pp. 124 and 138–9.
103. Ibid., pp. 50–6.
104. Starkopf, *Will to Live*, p. 160.
105. Gottesfeld Heller, *A Strange and Unexpected Love*, p. 73.
106. Ibid., p. 74.
107 . Ibid., p. 81.
108. Ibid., p. 120.
109. Ibid., p. 204.
110. Werber, *Saving Children*, p. 34.
111. Matzner, *The Muselmann*, p. 104.
112. B. Gutterman (ed.), *Machsor Wolfsburg, 1944, Machane L'Avoda Kfia, Germania, 1944* [Wolfsburg Machsor, 1944, A Forced Labour Camp, Germany, 1944] (Jerusalem: Yad Vashem, 2000) [in Hebrew].
113. S. Maechler, *The Wilkomirski Affair: A Study in Biographical Truth* (New York: Schocken Books, 2001).
114. Shapiro, *Holocaust Chronicles*, p. 274.
115. Ibid., p. xviii.

6
Using and Abusing History:
The Holocaust, the Press
and the Middle East

In the spring of 2002, a wave of articles appeared in the press that linked together the Israeli–Palestinian conflict and the Holocaust. In particular many appeared adjacent to *Yom Hashoah* (Holocaust Remembrance Day). At the time, there was a rash of suicidal attacks by Palestinians on Israelis and a vigorous response by Israel that was called Operation Defensive Shield. The writings were from different vantage points, sometimes standing in diametrical opposition to each other. Many of the articles were polemical, whereas only a handful of them were analytical. Some represented well-thought-out ideas, whereas others could be generously called glib propaganda. Among the articles were those that reflected a deep identification with the Holocaust and the suffering that attended it. Others cynically used the Holocaust, its events and terminology as tools of hateful invective. The common denominator, the juxtaposition of events in Israel with the Holocaust, suggests how deeply the Holocaust has entered the consciousness of people throughout the world and become a point of reference – albeit in vastly different ways. This essay is not a comprehensive survey of all of those writings but an attempt, through an investigation of a selection of Hebrew and English-language articles to try to understand how the Holocaust is presented in the press in the context of the Israeli–Palestinian conflict.

ATTACKING ISRAEL WITH HOLOCAUST IMAGERY

Many of those who attack Israel in the press summon to their purpose a large arsenal of terms taken directly from the Holocaust, or from events and motifs related to it. Among the authors are Muslims, Christians and Jews from all over the world, including Jews who live in Israel and write for Israeli newspapers. In almost all cases, the comparisons made are baseless or are so distorted as to lack all merit. Essentially the Holocaust is employed for its rhetorical punch.

In his seminal report prepared for the American Jewish committee, entitled *Muslim Antisemitism: A Clear and Present Danger*, Professor Robert Wistrich presents and discusses Muslim antisemitism of the late twentieth and early twenty-first centuries.[1] Of course this is not the first study of Arab and Muslim antisemitism; Wistrich's earlier books and articles and the writings of Bernard Lewis, among others, offered serious analysis of the phenomenon in the 1980s and 1990s.[2] These authors have shown how canards like 'Blood Libel' and the *Protocols of the Elders of Zion*, which were cornerstones in the Nazi armoury of hate, have become staples of anti-Israel and antisemitic propaganda throughout the Arab and Muslim worlds.[3]

The use of the Holocaust and associated terms in the press by Arab and Muslim opponents of Israel frequently revolves around the axis of Holocaust denial and the acceptance of the Holocaust to some degree. As Wistrich shows clearly in his report, the outright denial of the Holocaust by Arab and Muslim writers stems principally from the simplification that Israel was created because of the Holocaust and on the backs of the Palestinians. If the Holocaust can be shown to be false, according to this argument, then Israel's existence can be shown to have no legitimacy whatsoever. Holocaust denial became a mainstay among Arab intellectuals in the 1980s, according to Wistrich. To a large extent, he writes, this was a response in the Arab world to the decisive Israeli victory in the 1967 Six Day War.

More complex than outright denial is the use of the Holocaust for propaganda purposes, while not accepting it as a valid historical event. A sophisticated example of rejecting the veracity of the Holocaust, but nevertheless using it as a tool to bash Israel, appeared on 29 April 2002 in the Egyptian daily *Al-Akhbar* under the byline of Fatma Abdallah Mahmoud. The article, entitled 'Accursed Forever and Ever', declares that there was never a Holocaust, but had there actually been one, it would have been nice if Hitler had finished the job of murdering the Jews. An English-language excerpt is quoted on the Internet site *CNSNews.com* in an article entitled 'Hating and Killing Jews' by Alan Caruba, author of a study on militant Islam.[4] Mahmoud writes:

> They are accursed in heaven and on earth. They are accursed from the day the human race was created and from the day their mothers bore them. They are accursed also because they murdered the Prophets. They murdered the Prophet John the Baptist and served up his head on a golden platter to the singer and dancer Salome. Allah also cursed them with a thousand curses when they argued with and resisted his words of truth, deceived the Prophet Moses, and worshiped the golden calf that they created with their own hands ... With regard to the fraud of the

Holocaust … Many French studies have proven that this is no more than a fabrication, a lie, and a fraud … But I, personally and in light of this imaginary tale, complain to Hitler, even saying to him from the bottom of my heart, 'If only you had done it, brother, if only it had really happened, so that the world could sigh in relief [without] their evil and sin … Since their birth, the Jews [have amassed] hatred and hostility towards Islam and the Muslims. They have always laid traps for the Muslims, woven conspiracies and crimes against them, and been biased in favor of their enemies and occupiers …' They always try to warp and distort everything fair and beautiful!! Basically, they are a model of moral ugliness, debasement, and degradation. If only Allah would curse them more and more, to the end of all generations. Amen.

As this excerpt illustrates, one need not accept that there was a Holocaust to use it and its images as a weapon against Israel and Jews. Here the writer relates to the Holocaust as a myth or legend, citing the 'many French studies' that disprove the existence of the Holocaust. She is most probably referring to the works penned by the notorious Holocaust deniers, Robert Faurisson, Paul Rassinier and Roger Garaudy.[5] Mahmoud then harnesses the myth to her purposes. For her, Hitler is a soulmate, and she combines traditional Muslim anti-Jewish themes with a veneration of Nazism.

Of course not all Arab or Muslim writers assume a position of Holocaust denial, or relate to the veracity of the Holocaust at all. Abdelwahab El-Affendi, a senior research fellow at the Centre for the Study of Democracy, University of Westminster, apparently accepts that there was a Holocaust, although in his rendition the focus is on the deportations and not the murder. Writing in the Lebanese newspaper *Daily Star*, he places the Holocaust at the centre of the current Israeli–Palestinian conflict and considers it the unjustified reason not only for the creation of Israel, but for continued Western support for Israel. He writes:

It is the West that bears the primary responsibility. First, the West persecuted its Jewish citizens and drove them from their homes, dumping them unceremoniously in Palestine … [The Western world's support of Israel] is motivated by a commitment to the security of the State of Israel, which represents a haven and compensation for the survivors of the Holocaust.[6]

One may certainly argue that the western world bears a responsibility for the Holocaust, that the West played a role in the establishment of

Israel and that these two processes are related. It is specious, however, to characterize these related phenomena as an algorithm that proceeded from 'persecution' of Jews, to their 'dumping', to a guilt-ridden 'commitment' of unequivocal support for Israel.

In an article entitled 'How Palestinians were Dispossessed', under the byline of M. Shahid Alam in the Pakistani publication *Dawn*, the author never really admits to the veracity of the Holocaust. He simply sidesteps the issue while using a distorted version of the creation of the State of Israel to slam contemporary Israel. He writes:

> Ironically, the Nazi terror had provided two vital inputs into the creation of Israel. By fuelling Jewish emigration from Europe, it gave Israel the population it needed to create an exclusive Jewish state. A similar and simultaneous flow westward strengthened the power of the Jewish community in the United States – the new hegemon [sic] whose resources and power would become Israel's most important assets in its colonizing project. The Zionists would make capital out of the Holocaust in their campaign to shield Israel from critics.[7]

Like El-Affendi, Alam coldheartedly shifts the focal point of the Holocaust from the murder of six million innocent people to its byproduct, the immigration of the saving remnant to Israel and the United States.

The equation of Israeli Prime Minister Ariel Sharon with Adolf Hitler and the equation of the Palestinian suffering to events of the Holocaust are ideas commonly employed in much Arab writing about the Israeli–Palestinian conflict. In particular, when Israeli troops entered Jenin during Operation Defensive Shield and rumours (which later proved to be false) surfaced that Palestinians had been massacred, such accusations gained great currency.[8] Writers outside the Middle East also co-opted these claims.

Jeff Johnson of *CNSNews.com* quotes a statement in this vein by Hasan Abdel Rahman, the Palestinian Representative to the United States, on the situation in the wake of Operation Defensive Shield. Rahman does not deny the Holocaust. Rather he inverts it, accusing the Jews of making a transition from victim to perpetrator: 'Those same people who were the victims of the holocaust – an appalling crime that was committed against the Jews of Europe – are doing to the Palestinians similar actions … and I don't hesitate to say that.'[9] Needless to say, such inversions trivialize the Holocaust and the suffering of the Jews without contributing at all to clarifying the true situation of the Palestinians.

A statement similar to Rahman's appears in an article entitled

'Another Holocaust in the Making', which appears on a Pakistani Internet news site *Paknews.com*.[10] The author accepts that there was a Holocaust, and in the same breath he squarely accuses Israel of perpetrating similar Nazi-like crimes against the Palestinians. Tellingly, the author, like many others who equate Palestinian suffering to the Holocaust in their writings, uses a small 'h' for the word 'Holocaust' in the body of the article. This use intentionally dilutes the moral impact of the Holocaust by negating its singularity and placing sundry unrelated events under its rubric. He writes:

> The World War II holocaust of Jewish people by Nazis is a reminder of systematic and state sponsored atrocities and genocide based upon intense hate and rage ... While United Nations and world leaders urge on 'restraint' and 'withdrawal' to Israel, the holocaust continues this very minute. This is a devastating reminder of brutal massacres in Sabra and Shatila refugee camps, not surprisingly under the familiar Israeli leadership of Sharon. Shockingly, this holocaust is being conducted by the same nation whose ancestors lived and fortunately survived through a holocaust ...

Unquestionably the massacres at Sabra and Shatila were a great tragedy in which many innocent people lost their lives and in which Israel played a role, albeit a secondary one. Nevertheless, the author assigns immediate blame to Israel for killings that were carried out during the 1982 Lebanese war by Christian militiamen, who were allied to Israel but not directly under their control. Terming the catastrophe of Sabra and Shatila a Holocaust is, at the very least, hyperbole. The underlying factors, the actual crime and the context of the crime are profoundly dissimilar to the Holocaust.

In the *Arab News*, the Saudi Arabian English-language daily, Tariq A. Al-Maeena likens Israeli actions in Jenin to those of the Nazis, and the fate of the Palestinians to Jews, who suffered through Nazi camps in the Holocaust. He writes: 'This is indeed a current day holocaust, one that evokes painful memories of Auschwitz and Dachau!' This proclamation is similar to the statement made by the Portuguese author and Nobel Prize Laureate, José Saramago, comparing the situation in Ramallah in spring 2002 to Auschwitz. As many writers pointed out in light of Saramago's poorly chosen analogy, one would be hard pressed to find a real commonality between the situation in Jenin during Operation Defensive Shield and the extermination camp in Auschwitz-Birkenau, or commonality between Jenin and the regime in Nazi concentration camps such as Dachau, for that matter.[11] Like many other writers who attack Israel, Al-Maeena also accuses Sharon of being like Hitler. In his words, Israel feared that allowing a UN commission into Jenin would 'simply disrupt the bloodthirsty goals of a butcher no less evil than Adolf Hitler, and let the Americans witness this blood thirst first hand'.[12]

The news agency *WAFA* is the official organ of the Palestinian Authority. On numerous occasions it, too, has likened Israel to the Nazis in press releases. Regarding the battle over the Church of the Nativity in Bethlehem, in which Palestinian gunmen holed up in the building fought Israeli troops for several weeks, *WAFA* declared the following: '[The] so called "Defensive Shield" is still continuing its savage and brutal terrorist aggression against the entire Palestinian Occupied Lands where our people and their property and Holy places are subjected to the Israeli Nazi practices ... '.[13] Later, in June, when Israel again entered the Palestinian Authority territory in response to attacks on Israeli citizens, *WAFA* likened closures and curfews to the brutal regime of the Nazi camps.[14]

In the wake of President George W. Bush's speech, calling for fundamental reforms in the Palestinian Authority before the process of creating a Palestinian state could begin, at least one Arab pundit proclaimed the call for the establishment of a democratic Palestinian Authority under new leadership 'a new Holocaust'. Dr. Afnan Hussein Fatani, writing in the *Arab News*, opined:

> As if the Palestinian Holocaust of 1948 and 1967 weren't enough, Bush's speech formally announced the official start of the Third Palestinian Holocaust replete with 24-hour curfews, a 350-kilometer barrier of fences, trenches and walls, house-to-house searches, deprivation of food and water, the rounding up of Palestinian men aged between 15 and 50, rape, vandalism, ethnic cleansing, transfer of population, torture, demolition of homes, mass executions of alleged would-be suicide bombers and the mass expulsion of their entire families from the West Bank.[15]

For Fatani every tragedy the Palestinians have suffered is a Holocaust, regardless of whether they can be called by that term logically. For him even a plea for democratic reform can be seen as a call for mass systematic murder of an entire people.

A motif that is clear in Fatani's article is the jumbling together of the Palestinian experience and the Holocaust, claiming they are one and the same. When examined out of context, some elements of the Palestinian experience bear a certain similarity to that of the Jews under the Nazis. But other aspects, even divorced of their immediate circumstances, have not the slightest relation to the Holocaust. For example, the suggestion that the Nazis destroyed Jewish homes is simply factually incorrect; generally Jewish homes were given to non-Jews. Therefore, Fatani's comparison between Nazi practices and Israel's destruction of the homes of terrorists is based on a false premise. More telling, however, is the comparison of the alleged mass execution of would-be suicide bombers to the mass murder suffered by the Jews in the Holocaust. It is true that Israeli security forces assassinated Palestinians who were primed for murder or had carried out murderous actions. In other words, these people were killed because they had committed or planned to commit acts of great violence and evil. The Jews murdered by the Nazis, however, were not killed because of anything they had done, but simply because they were Jews. This is a basic truth that is routinely overlooked by many who seek to link the Israeli-Palestinian conflict to the Holocaust.

Anne Frank is an outstanding symbol of the wholly unwarranted suffering of innocent Jewish youth in the Holocaust. Her diary has been translated into numerous languages and has been performed on stage and screen for millions of people. Yusef Agha, writing in *Arab News*, uses the image of Anne Frank as a paradigm for the suffering of Arab youth under Israel. In his article, Agha likens the plight of teenage women who are being held in Israeli gaols for having planned attacks on Israelis, to Anne Frank. He intertwines quotes from Anne Frank's diary with descriptions of the Palestinians' plight, and he writes about the indignities of prison life.[16] Of course, his presentation and analysis, like that of Fatani, is flawed at its core. It, too, glosses over the distinction between victimization based on mere perceptions and ideology, and punishment for crimes committed, planned or reasonably suspected.

Attacks against Israel employing Holocaust imagery are not published only in the Arab and Muslim press. An official government statement from China directly accuses Israel of perpetrating a Holocaust against the Palestinians.[17] In the year 2000, the Chinese premier, Jiang Zemin, and his entourage received a guided tour through Yad Vashem. Despite efforts to the contrary, it would seem that either they came away with a most superficial picture of the Holocaust or whatever they learned had no impact at all on the official press of their country.[18]

An article in the British daily the *Independent*, on Yom Hashoah, juxtaposes the Holocaust and the plight of the Palestinians in a much more sophisticated but no less biased way than the other items reviewed here. Basically, Robert Fisk uses the Holocaust and its commemoration as a vehicle for berating Israel. Fisk interviews a Holocaust survivor living in Givat Shaul, a Jerusalem neighbourhood that now stands in place of the Arab village Deir Yassin. During the 1948 War of Independence, Israeli troops apparently forced the village's residents to flee for their lives. Fisk asks if the two can or should be compared. He writes:

> So a visit to Mr Kleinman's [the survivor] home raises a serious moral question. Can one listen to his personal testimony of the

greatest crime in modern history and then ask about the tragedy which overwhelmed the Palestinians at this very spot – when the eviction of the Arabs of Palestine, terrible though it was, an act of ethnic cleansing in our terms, comes nowhere near, statistically or morally, the murder of six million Jews?

Fisk tries to get the survivor to make the comparison for him, but Mr Kleinman refrains from drawing parallels. The author ultimately makes the comparison himself, by virtue of his questions and by quoting the organizers of a Holocaust memorial ceremony in St John's Wood in London:

> Many Jews may not want to look at this [the comparison with Deir Yassin], fearing that the magnitude of their tragedy may be diminished. For Palestinians there is always the fear that, as often before, the Holocaust may be used to justify their own suffering.[19]

Fisk suggests that Jews are insulted by any attempts to compare the Holocaust to other events, particularly if they are of different magnitude. He appears to be woefully unaware of the large body of reflective literature, often written by Jewish scholars, that compares and contrasts the Holocaust to other events in an attempt to understand it better. Fisk does not seem to recognize that the magnitude of the Holocaust is only one element in understanding its totality, and not necessarily one of the most important. Nor does he explain the vastly different contexts of the events he compares. The result is that he makes an analogy that is far slicker than it is thoughtful.

For Nobel Peace Prize Laureate Desmond Tutu, the Holocaust and the suffering of his people during the era of apartheid in South Africa are bludgeons with which to bash Israel. In an opinion piece in the *Guardian*, Tutu compares Jewish treatment of Palestinians to apartheid and the Holocaust. He writes:

> My heart aches. I say why are our memories so short? Have our Jewish sisters and brothers forgotten their humiliation? Have they forgotten the collective punishment, the home demolitions, in their own history so soon? Have they turned their backs on their profound and noble religious traditions? Have they forgotten that God cares deeply about the downtrodden? … Hitler, Mussolini, Stalin, Pinochet, Milosevic, and Idi Amin were all powerful, but in the end they bit the dust.[20]

Not only does Tutu declare sanctimoniously that Jews have forgotten their suffering and religious heritage, and are callously perpetrating a

Holocaust on the Palestinians, he also suggests that Sharon belongs in the pantheon of great villains, along with Hitler. Like many of the anti-Israel propagandists over the last decades, he does not differentiate between Israel, Jews and Zionists. By so doing, he holds all Jews everywhere responsible for Israeli policies and actions.

Moreover, Tutu, like other critics of Israel, muddles the facts of the Holocaust and the Palestinian experience. Without regard for historical precision, detail or background, he overlays the experience of Jews in the Holocaust and the experience of his own people in South Africa onto the Palestinian experience. Like other writers who criticize Israel, he apparently does not realize that the persecution of Jews in the Holocaust, like the persecution of native South Africans, had nothing to do with their actions or ideas. He glosses over the point that in both cases the persecution was grounded in a hateful racial ideology whereas, in the case of the Palestinians, their suffering is a consequence not of a racial ideology but of a conflict over land and sovereignty and a result, at least in part, of the decisions of their political leadership. Nor does he distinguish between callous discrimination laced with a great deal of violence, which was the experience in South Africa, and systematic mass murder, which was the lot of the Jews in the Holocaust. By lumping the Holocaust, apartheid and the Palestinian experience together, and making ill-conceived correlations, Tutu does more to obscure than to clarify shared issues. Ultimately, Tutu comes across as extremely prejudiced against Israel and only tangentially concerned with thoughtful analysis based on demonstrable facts.

A columnist in the African newspaper the *Sunday Nation*, while defaming Israel, also adopts a peculiarly African approach to the relationship between the Israeli–Palestinian conflict and the Holocaust. In a convoluted discussion about the antisemitic acts that struck Europe in the spring of 2002, the author shuffles together Christian crimes against the Jews, European colonialism and neo-Nazism. His foremost explanation for the upsurge in European antisemitism, however, is 'Zionism's continuing crimes in Palestine'. In timeless antisemitic fashion, invoking the classical stereotype of Jewish avarice, he blames the Jews for the hatred directed against them. He writes:

> Delirious greed is what drives all this historic folly. It is what allows the Zionist Jew to agree to be used by his erstwhile slaughterer to slaughter another nation today. He cannot see that, sooner or later, it will boomerang. If anti-Judaism is surging again in Europe, other nations are becoming increasingly enraged by the Zionist abattoir in Palestine and could soon be goaded into victimizing their Jewish compatriots.[21]

Some of the most forceful attacks on Israel use caricature or photo montage to make their point. The Israeli newspaper *Maariv* reproduced an illustration from a Spanish weekly that juxtaposes two photographs. One shows the famous photograph from the Stroop Report (which is displayed in the Yad Vashem museum), of a young boy who was smoked out of hiding during the Warsaw Ghetto Uprising. The boy is holding his hands in the air in front of a German soldier, who is training his gun on him and several other Jews. The second photograph, placed at its side, is of a Palestinian child with his arms raised in the air.[22] Obviously the message is that the Israelis are doing to the Palestinians what the Nazis did to them, and the Intifada is a new version of the Warsaw Ghetto Uprising. Like many other images used in this way, the differences are simply varnished over. The boy in the Warsaw Getto lived in horrible circumstances where, over the course of two and a half years the population was reduced drastically. Some 20 per cent of the nearly half a million Jews in the ghetto died of disease and starvation, and almost all the rest – about 350,000 – were deported to the Nazi extermination camp in Treblinka. It is only after this massive slaughter that an armed uprising took place, in which the remnant of the ghetto was eventually burned to the ground by German forces. This course of events cannot be reasonably compared to the Intifada, Operation Defensive Shield or the suffering of the Palestinians. The latter, replete with much anguish, has its own sequence of events, rationale and background.

Some Jewish opponents of Israel and its policies, or of the Zionist enterprise, also use imagery derived from the Holocaust to maul Israel. A common motif in this kind of writing is to present first the writer's credentials as a Jew, a Holocaust survivor or a child of Holocaust survivors, as a supposed certificate of objectivity and clarity. This is to imply that the experience of surviving the Holocaust or being born to a Holocaust survivor automatically imbues one with a special power that guarantees a deeper understanding of events or a purer impartiality of judgement. Several articles in this tone have been published in the *Arab News*, generally after having been re-edited from their original source.

The full version of Lucien Heichler's article 'A Jewish View of a Jewish State' first appeared in the journal *American Diplomacy*.[23] Reprinted in the *Arab News*, with all criticism of the Palestinians deleted, both the original and the reworked articles squarely accuse Israel of acting like Nazis.[24] Heichler writes:

> Can there be a more cruel historical irony than Jews inflicting on Palestine's native population forms of harassment, suffering and horrors reminiscent of what their forefathers were condemned to experience at the hands of the Nazis half a century ago? A plague on both their houses …

Both in the body of the article and the short biography of the author, his status – as a Jew who lived under the Nazis – is cited to justify Heichler's censure of Israel. He writes:

> As a Jewish refugee from the Nazis who narrowly escaped the Holocaust, I feel free to express negative views of the Zionist experiment, Israel's policies, and one-sided US support of Israel without fear of being instantly branded a Jew-hater. Jewishness, I insist, does not require I may belong to a minority, but I count myself among the Jews who oppose the Zionist movement. Perhaps it was in part because of Nazi insistence on defining me as a member of a different, 'non-Aryan' race that already as a boy I came to regard Judaism as first and foremost a religious faith and community. As a young teenager in Nazi-occupied Austria, I was offended by what struck me as parallels between Nazi and Zionist definitions of the Jews as an ethnic group.

Heichler openly uses the Holocaust and his personal experiences to berate Jewish organizations that defend Israel, lumping together legitimate mainstream organizations such as AIPAC (the American Israel Public Affairs Committee) with the marginal and extremely controversial Jewish Defense League. He writes:

> Having suffered Nazi hatred and persecution at first hand, I am like the child 'once burned, twice careful,' and I worry that, fed by blind support of Israeli policies and actions by many American Jews, and by powerful lobbies like AIPAC and even the terrorist gang known as the Jewish Defense League, Anti-Semitism may increase rapidly in America.

The article 'After Jenin' by Israeli poet Yitzhak Laor appeared in the Saudi daily *Arab News*, after having first been published in the *London Review of Books*.[25] In the opening paragraph, the author announces that his point of view and sensitivity to the plight of the Palestinians derives from being the child of a Holocaust survivor. He writes, 'I know: my father was a German Jew.' According to Laor, Israel cannot bear to lose the status of Holocaust victim, and thereby justifies its acts against the Palestinians. In his opinion this tells

> us more about ourselves as victims, and how we must be forgiven for every atrocity we commit. As my friend Tanya Reinhart has written, 'it seems that what we have internalized' of the memory of the Holocaust 'is that any evil whose extent is smaller is acceptable'.

Laor tars all Israelis (apparently himself included) with the brush of cruelty and moral relativism.

Although Laor does not declare outright that Israel is using the same methods as the Nazis to destroy the Palestinians, he attacks them for doing so nonetheless. He says there are other ways than those of the Nazis to precipitate genocide: 'Gas chambers are not the only way to destroy a nation.' He asserts: 'It is enough to destroy its social tissue, to starve dozens of villages, to develop high rates of infant mortality'. Like others before him, despite his supposedly inherited innate understanding of the Holocaust and human suffering, Laor does not seem concerned in the least with why Jews suffered in the Holocaust and how this compares to the cause of Palestinian suffering. Since he does not address this issue, he does not see any difference between the two. Of course this is an example of pure post-modernism, which analyses end results without relating to their historical context.

Writing in the Kenya-based newspaper *Daily Nation*, Betty Caplan first establishes her credentials before criticizing Israel for its policies in the West Bank. Having grown up in Australia as a child of survivors who supported Israel, she then declares her empathy with Palestinian suicide bombers. Caplan also believes there was not one Holocaust, but many, and that the Palestinians have experienced a Holocaust similar to that of the Jews. She writes: 'There can be no competition when it comes to persecution; approximately 13 million slaves were dragged from their countries and treated so inhumanly that the results are still felt in many parts of the world today.'[26] Caplan apparently does not appreciate that classifying tragedies under different headings is a tool for trying to understand each better and not a form of 'competition'.

Israel Shamir is a journalist based in Jaffa, Israel, who maintains his own website. His articles severely criticizing Israeli policies have been picked up by a variety of radical left-wing and extreme right-wing journals and websites. Among the venues in which his writings have appeared is the Saudi *Arab News*. Being an Israeli does not prevent Shamir from misrepresenting the Holocaust and its background in his onslaught. In an article entitled 'The Beginning of the End of the Jewish Post-war Ascendancy?' he writes:

> Until now, the Jews were divided in their tasks and purposes. In Palestine, they created a toxic, ferociously nationalist and religiously fanatic entity based on Adolf Hitler's Nuremberg Laws. Elsewhere, in France as well as in Britain, they promoted the pseudo-liberal paradigm of dismantling European national and cultural content in favor of the Judeo-American spirit. In Palestine, they shot at the church; in France, they undermined it by subterfuge.[27]

In addition to the pure nonsense he writes about France and Britain, Shamir ties together the Israeli–Palestinian conflict, the Holocaust, anti-Americanism and anti-globalization. Like Desmond Tutu and others, he does not make a distinction between Israel, Zionists and Jews – for him, they are all the same. It is worth pointing out that by his formulae, Shamir himself is part of the supposed evil he seeks to unveil.

HOLOCAUST IMAGERY AND SYMPATHY FOR ISRAEL

The exercise of Holocaust imagery in defence of Israel or to reproach the Palestinians ranges from straightforward and simplistic to a complex usage of terms and events. Even the most eloquent defences of Israel, however, suffer from a certain misuse of the Holocaust; chiefly owing to lack of precision in historical details and flawed comparisons.

Among those who sympathize with Israel and who harness the Holocaust and its terminology to their task, the most crude simply call Arafat 'Hitler' and the Palestinians 'Nazis'. Former Israeli Prime Minister Benyamin Netanyahu frequently employs such characterizations of Arafat and the Palestinians in his speeches, and his words are often reported in the press as news items.[28] It may well be that the 'man in the street' in Israel tends to agree with Netanyahu's portrayals. On Yom Hashoah, Anton La Guardia of the *Daily Telegraph* interviewed a number of Jews in Jerusalem, and only one expressed disagreement with the equation of Arafat with Hitler.[29]

Suzanna Fields, a columnist for the *Washington Times*, primarily addresses the issue of the similarity between the evil of the Taliban and the Nazis in an article entitled 'The Ghosts of Auschwitz', but she also touches on the Palestinians.[30] Several of her comparisons are to say the least, shallow. For example, she writes:

> Hitler finally killed himself in his bunker beneath Berlin as the Third Reich was pounded into a pile of rubble. Bin Laden furrows deep into his cave in the Afghan wilderness as his acolytes are picked off one by one.

Although this may be true, it sheds no significant light on the true nature of either.

Comparing Arafat to Hitler, and Arafat's followers to the Nazis, Fields rightly implies that both the Nazi murder and the Palestinian murder of Jews is grounded in ideology. She writes:

> Mr. Arafat and his fanatics believe, as Hitler and the Nazis before them, that they are right and eager to kill infinite numbers of

civilian innocents to make their point. While decent men and women everywhere are outraged because the targeted victims of the suicide bombers are civilians, the terrorists see them, as the Nazis did, as merely Jews.

Although ideas played a central role in Nazi crimes and are important for Palestinian actions as well, Fields neither articulates the specific ideas involved, nor does she compare and contrast them.

Fields sees Hamas and all Palestinians as being the heirs of the Nazis. The only salient difference between them, she writes, is that Hamas does not have the means to carry out their Nazi-like plans: 'Hamas, fortunately, does not have the technology the Nazis had, nor the ability to drive Jews to an Auschwitz or a Bergen-Belsen. But the anti-Semitism that drives Palestinian hatred is no less real, no less virulent.' One may assume that Fields refers to the camps Auschwitz and Bergen-Belsen in order to compare the murderous nature of the Nazis and Palestinians. She does not seem to grasp, however, that Auschwitz and Bergen-Belsen were very different places. Auschwitz was a large labour camp system, which included an extermination centre for Jews at Birkenau. Auschwitz or, more precisely, Birkenau, embodies industrialized murder as the 'factory of death,' to borrow a phrase from Ota Kraus and Erich Kulka.[31] Bergen-Belsen was a special camp set up for Jews the Nazis hoped to exchange for Germans stuck in Allied territory. At the end of the war, Bergen-Belsen became a dumping ground for tens of thousands of inmates from other camps brought there on the Death Marches. In the awful conditions of neglect in Bergen-Belsen at the end of the war, thousands of Jews perished. Ultimately, both camps were places of mass death; but the mechanics of death were different. So what does Fields really mean? If they could, would Hamas or the Palestinians like to kill Jews in an industrialized fashion, or by neglect, or by both?

As Fields asserts, Palestinian antisemitism is certainly venomous and certainly has been proven murderous. However, she does not seem to fathom that Palestinian antisemitism, in its essence, is different from Nazi antisemitism. It is not based on a racial theory. Neither does it necessarily seek to destroy all Jews everywhere, as the Nazis did. Rather, it predominately focuses on the Jews living in Israel and on ridding Israel of a Jewish presence. Lumping the two together in the way she does, Fields does little to add to our understanding of either.

The editor of the *National Review Online*, Jonah Goldberg, makes a more discerning comparison of the Nazis and the Arab world. He never says that all Arabs are Nazis. But he demonstrates that Israelis, who are often termed Nazis, less frequently use Nazi-related themes in their political writing than do the Arabs. In his own words:

Now, I spent just a few minutes looking for examples of Nazi-like rhetoric and actions and found so many examples – of Arab mobs chanting 'death to Jews'; Arab governments endorsing the blood libel against Jews (Syria is making a movie about the 'Protocols of the Elders of Zion', based on their foreign minister's book on the subject); *Mein Kampf* being a perennial bestseller in the Arab world; Jews being likened to vermin, poison, bacteria, disease, and so on, in grade-school textbooks and children's TV shows – that I could use up the entire NRO server just listing examples … The Palestinians are the Arab world's Sudeten Germans. The 'liberation' of their coreligionists and ethnic brothers is used as a utopian carrot guiding brainwashed donkey after brainwashed donkey to murder and suicide. I am not saying that Arabs or Muslims generally are Nazis or Nazi-like. That would be absurd. But I am saying that the Arab world is the only place left on this planet which bears a reasonable resemblance to Germany in the 1930s, with the open and accepted dissemination of Nazi-like ideas and ambitions.[32]

It is not only the actions and writings of the Palestinians that are equated to those of the Nazis. Some authors liken the current suffering of the Jews in Israel to the torment of the Jews during the Holocaust. In mid-June 2002, over the course of a few days, there was a spate of attacks on Israelis by Palestinians: in the community of Itamar in Sumaria and two suicidal attacks in Jerusalem. In response to these rampages, a rather long article appeared on the website *DEBKAfile* that discusses these events. The article says:

The slaughter of innocents inflicted on Israel this week by Palestinian murderers is unparalleled since the days of Nazi Germany. No longer are Israelis murdered singly; whole families are being wiped out while asleep, riding buses, celebrating. The terror stalking every corner of the country lends the term Holocaust a fearful, intimate meaning for the offspring of those who survived the Nazis and in 1949 founded a Jewish state and a national defense force, vowing that never again would Jewish children die defenseless.[33]

In the writer's opinion, the relationship of events in Israel to the Holocaust is complex. On the one hand, the murder of Jews by the Palestinians is like the Holocaust, and on the other hand, the trauma of the Holocaust itself heightens anxiety among Israelis.

Many writers, assuming a pro-Israel stance, compare the world's response to the Holocaust to contemporary reactions in light of suicide bombings and European antisemitic acts during the second Intifada. Such parallels are often problematic, especially when they are formulated as generalities. As such, they tend to present a less than precise picture of the Holocaust – a picture that does not stand up to scrutiny regarding the history they invoke.

On the most superficial level, some writers simply believe that 'the world' that allowed the Holocaust to occur has not changed one iota. In their opinion nothing was done to stop the murder of Jews in the Second World War and nothing is done today to protect Jews. For example, in a news item that appeared in the Israeli daily *Haaretz*, the Israeli prime minister, Ariel Sharon, states that examining European responses to attacks on Israel and Jews in Europe, one can better understand the essence of European passivity in the Holocaust.[34]

Jeremy Rapke, a Queen's Counsel writing in the Australian publication *The Age*, also makes a claim in this vein. He asserts, when 'the world' does say something, it is in defence of the murderers:

> The voices that were silent when Jews were being slaughtered in their dozens can now be heard complaining when the murderers are hunted down and the infrastructure that permitted and, indeed, encouraged their proliferation is dismantled. What shameless hypocrisy! ... The cry 'Never again!' that resonated in the death camps and ghettos of Europe after their liberation at the end of the Second World War can again be heard in the streets, schools and homes of the state of Israel. And if that upsets the leaders and churches and political agencies of the world, I, for one, don't care.[35]

Similarly, an editorial in the *Jerusalem Post* chides Europe for forgetting its role in the Holocaust, while Europeans hasten to the support of Arafat and criticize Israel.[36] These arguments, of course, are based on the commonly held formulae that during the Holocaust 'the world stood idly by', or did 'too little, too late'.

It is undeniably true that the readiness of the world to save Jews from the Nazi machinery of persecution and murder was not nearly commensurate to the Nazi desire to persecute and murder them.[37] Nevertheless, one must remember when assessing the attitude of the Allies and local European populations during the Holocaust that the picture is multifaceted, and that it changes over geography and time. The fact that more than 20,000 individuals have been awarded the status of Righteous Among the Nations by Yad Vashem shows that attitudes towards the Jews during the Holocaust era were far from black and white. The aid rendered Jewish children by French peasants, attempts made by Italian soldiers in Yugoslavia and Italian authorities in southern France to safeguard Jews from the Nazi clutches, the pressure of Bulgarian leaders to save Bulgarian Jews and the rescue of scores of thousands of Hungarian Jews are only some of the activities that need to be considered before making sweeping, blanket statements about attitudes towards Jews in the past and present.

Writing in *Hatsofe* in the context of the stand-off in the Church of the Nativity in Bethlehem, Gonen Ginat focuses his wrath on the Catholic Church, then and now. He stops two letters short of making an unreserved accusation, ever so slightly buffing it with the word 'if'. He writes: 'If the Church feels comfortable that it has turned into a fortress for slaughterers of Jews, it would appear that nothing has changed since the days of collaboration with Hitler.'[38]

Accusing the Church in its entirety of collaboration with Hitler is no less problematic then accusing the whole world of passivity in the face of the murder of the Jews during the Holocaust.[39] The Catholic Church and individual Catholics bear much responsibility for the murder of the Jews in the Holocaust, but many Catholics were involved in rescue. Again, nuances in our understanding are very important. There was a formal agreement between the Church and the Nazis – the Concordat signed in July 1933. This treaty, however, was signed many years before the Nazis adopted the policy of the Final Solution, and it cannot be seen as a sign of imminent Catholic complicity in the 'slaughter of Jews'. It is also true that there were explicitly Catholic regimes that participated to a very large extent in the murder of the Jews. Chief among them were the Slovaks and the Croatians. Moreover, societies steeped in Catholicism, such as Lithuania and France, not to speak of Austria and large parts of Germany, were very involved in the murder. Nevertheless, one must bear in mind that many members of the Catholic clergy made valiant efforts to rescue Jews. The Papal Nuncios in Hungary and Turkey have both been recognized as Righteous Among the Nations. A significant body of priests and nuns throughout Europe risked their lives to hide Jews, especially children, in monasteries and convents. Individual Catholics, because of their religious convictions, succoured Jews. Some, such as the Portuguese consul in Bordeaux, France, Arista de Sousa Mendes, destroyed their careers because they proffered Jews aid. These acts of rescue render simplistic formulations about the Church useless for genuine evaluation of the role of Catholics in the Holocaust and such formulations used as a yardstick for events in our own time have little or no real value.

The Israeli daily *Maariv* blames Europe not only for its silence, but for forgetting its collaboration with the Nazis in the murder of the Jews:

> It is especially infuriating that among the states of Europe, which were the valley of death for our people and where almost all collaborated in the murder of Jews, that they are the first and

chief factor to voice unwarranted, hypocritical and bothersome criticism of Israel instead of being the first to understand that especially we, of all people, have a right to self defense.[40]

Needless to say, the same problem of generalization applies here as it does regarding the Catholic Church.

The noted Italian journalist Oriana Fallaci, who in the past trenchantly criticized Israel, comes to Israel's defence in an extremely powerful article that was published in the Italian newspaper *Corriere della Sera*.[41] Fallaci recites a long litany of European hypocrisy towards the Jews in the context of the Israeli–Palestinian conflict, often touching on the Holocaust and Mussolini as points of reference. From an intensely personal angle she writes:

> And disgusted by the anti-Semitism of many Italians, of many Europeans, I am ashamed of this shame that dishonors my Country and Europe. At best, it is not a community of States, but a pit of Pontius Pilates. And even if all the inhabitants of this planet were to think otherwise, I would continue to think so.

As compelling as her writing is, Fallaci, too, suffers from a certain mishandling of the facts of the Holocaust. The following paragraph, despite its forceful language, illustrates the problem of historical inaccuracies in her article. Like Fields of the *Washington Times*, Fallaci is apparently confused or uninformed about the nature of specific Nazi camps. She writes:

> I find it shameful that in Italy there should be a procession of individuals dressed as suicide bombers who spew vile abuse at Israel, hold up photographs of Israeli leaders on whose foreheads they have drawn the swastika, incite people to hate the Jews. And who, in order to see Jews once again in the extermination camps, in the gas chambers, in the ovens of Dachau and Mauthausen and Buchenwald and Bergen-Belsen etcetera, would sell their own mother to a harem.

Although it is true that some of the camps she cites had crematoria for burning the bodies of the dead, none of them is considered an extermination camp – the kind of camp set up by the Nazis for the industrialized murder of Jews.[42] It may well be that Fallaci herself and her editor simply did not know enough to notice there was a problem with the list of camps she uses. This in turn suggests that, ironically, those who wield the Holocaust as a tool in their writing, even with great rhetorical and ethical impact, do not necessarily know much about it.

On a very different level of discussion, Walter Reich argues that the Holocaust and the history of Jewish persecution prove that a Jewish state is necessary and must be defended. In his article entitled 'Israel an Indispensable Haven', Reich, the former director of the United States Holocaust Memorial Museum, states that he believes the dearth of aid given to Jews during the Holocaust by the enlightened world, especially the United States, bears directly on the plight of Israel and the Jews in 2002. He writes:

> But it's what happened to the Jews in their archipelago of exile – throughout those two millenniums but especially during the last century – that gives the inhabitants of the modern state of Israel, in addition to the right to live there, the urgency and necessity to do so. Very simply, they were murdered again and yet again … Given the moral stakes, it's clear that Jews will never have secure homes anywhere unless they also have a national home in Israel – a haven to which they can escape from wherever they are if the beast of anti-Semitism is ever again given the power to put its passions in murderous gear.[43]

Reich's plea is impassioned and shared by others.[44] Past Jewish suffering may have been a necessary factor for the creation of Israel and it may still be a factor in its defence, but it is not sufficient by itself to justify the existence of the state. The rekindling of many aspects of Jewish life and tradition, along with the simple fact of the existence of an independent Israel, are no less important pillars on which Israel stands. If one does not take these other factors into account, the dreary picture of Israel facing the second Intifada takes on an even bleaker tone and the meaning of events in Israel, and its survival, become distended.

THROUGH THE PRISM OF THE HOLOCAUST

Many of the articles that juxtapose the Israeli–Palestinian conflict and the Holocaust do so in an attempt to understand events, the conflict itself and its repercussions through the prism of the Holocaust. Other articles seek to assess and critique these interpretations. Some of the analyses are rather flippant, others are more reflective, and a few bear the mark of serious scholarly thought.

On the shallowest level, some commentators make comparisons between the second Intifada and the Holocaust era, pointing out only external differences between the two. Yehudit Desberg, writing in *Hatsofe*, believes that Arafat hates Jews no less than Hitler did. She concedes, however, that there is a difference between the Nazis and the

Palestinians – the Nazis did not use suicide bombers. Desberg herself is aware that her own family history (her father and others hid from the Nazis in Czechoslovakia) colours her view of the situation. In part, she admits, it is this personal history that brings her to make visceral generalizations about the Holocaust and the Israeli–Palestinian conflict.[45]

Mark Steyn, writing in the *Sun Times*, also compares these events, while at the same time he acknowledges differences between the situation in the Holocaust era and the early twenty-first century. For him, a salient difference between the two periods is that at the start of the twenty-first century there are simply many fewer Jews in Europe then there were on the eve of the Holocaust. Another important difference in Steyn's eyes concerns the portrayal of Jews in the European press. He writes: 'The big difference is that, whereas in the '30s the Jews were David, now they're Goliath – the massive military sledgehammer crushing an oppressed and captive people'.[46]

Michael Elliot, in *Time*, considers these same two related ideas to be fundamental for understanding Europe's response to attacks on Israel and twenty-first century anti-Semitism in its midst. Moreover, he believes that the mere physical presence of Jews in America has made America far more supportive of Israel than is Europe. He writes:

> Put at its crudest, most Europeans know very few Jews; they killed too many of them. In America there is a thriving community for whom the survival of Israel is a passionate commitment; in Europe there isn't. No number of school lessons or church sermons about the Holocaust can overcome that humdrum truth … So why do Europeans and Americans see the Middle East in such different ways? Above all, because the shadow and shame of the Holocaust reaches out of the past and lays a cold hand on our present understanding. All the prayers in the world won't make that grim truth go away.[47]

Victor Davis Hanson, in the *National Review Online*, offers a reflective critique of the linking together of the Holocaust and the Israeli–Palestinian conflict by those who attack Israel.[48] In his opinion, comparison between current events and history is often legitimate. But such comparisons must be made within certain boundaries of accepted discussion:

> All essayists at times invoke history to reflect upon the present. And there is often legitimate disagreement among historians as to the validity of particular historical allusions. Nevertheless, there are still generally agreed parameters of historical accuracy that must be respected – and suggesting that suicide bombers are akin

to our [American] Founding Fathers, or that Jenin is a Stalingrad, are well outside the plausible and so only bring ridicule to the purveyors of such nonsense.

Hanson emphasizes that it is not just the historical facts that the Palestinians distort in their comparisons. They also misrepresent the context in which the facts should be set, and thereby reach conclusions that are far off the mark. He writes:

> The Palestinians' historical analogies with the Holocaust and Nazis are completely false in order of magnitude, wicked in their shameless efforts to invoke the Nazis to denigrate Holocaust survivals, and spurious in their equation of industrial murder on a continental scale with the minimal collateral damage of war. The only possible affinity with Nazi atrocity in the Middle East could be a similarity in the technique of liquidation, albeit not of magnitude, of Saddam Hussein's gassing of innocent civilians – or perhaps Nasser's earlier use of such terror weapons against Yemeni villages.

In particular, Hanson takes issue with the comparison made by Arafat between the events in Bethlehem in spring 2002 and the battle for Stalingrad in the Second World War. He writes:

> During the months-long ordeal [in Stalingrad], there were perhaps a million casualties – 120,000 Germans were captured, only 5,000 of whom were ever repatriated, and then not until the mid-1950s. In turn, Russian total casualties probably exceeded the Germans losses – in all, quite a different scene from the high-fiving Palestinians who emerged from their takeover of the Church of the Nativity ...

William Baker, writing in *The Iranian*, also takes issue with the ill-conceived historical comparisons of Israel to Nazi Germany made by those who attack Israel in, among other places, *The Iranian*. Apparently he is writing for a public that accepts many of these baseless correlations. So Baker's method is to systematically debunk the internal logic of such analogies. He writes:

> If the comparison is designed to draw attention to Israeli aggression, now or in the past, why limit oneself to analogies with the Nazis? One could add Stalin or Afghanistan etc. ... If the goal is to draw a comparison between Israel's de facto attempt to colonize the West Bank and Golan, then why utilize such a poor example

as that of Nazi Germany? Better examples might be drawn from British colonialism, French in Vietnam, Assad against the Kurds etc.[49]

Baker adds that Israel has not perpetrated genocide. If Israel is really a Nazi-like state, he says, negotiations with them would be silly, but the Palestinians have negotiated with Israel.

Some pundits point out that Israelis also misuse the Holocaust in their writings about the Israeli–Palestinian conflict. Yaron London, writing in *Yediot Achronot*, an Israeli daily, condemns the parallels made in the Israeli press between the second Intifada and the Holocaust.[50] In London's opinion, the viewing of enemies through the lens of the Holocaust warps reality. It shows that many Israelis have not made a transition in their minds from Holocaust victims to a strong nation capable of defending itself. Moreover, London believes that if Israelis see events through the prism of the Holocaust, they cannot rightly censure their opponents for assailing them with Holocaust imagery. He writes:

> We engage in glorification of our victimization and see all our ene-
> mies, Sadam [Hussein]), Arafat as Hitlers. We see [Marwan]
> Barguti as [Adolf] Eichmann. How can we complain about the
> author José Saramago, a great writer and not a small fool, for
> falling into the trap set him by the Palestinians when we ourselves
> do not spurn analogies between the Holocaust and other historical
> phenomena far from it, especially when they sully the image of
> our enemies …

One of the most frequent topics of discussion is the intertwinement of the Israeli–Palestinian conflict and antisemitism in Europe at the start of the twenty-first century.[51] Many authors, seeking the root cause of twenty-first-century European antipathy to Israel, write about guilt for the Holocaust as an important factor in shaping European bias.

David I. Kertzer, a professor of anthropology at Brown University and author of *The Popes Against the Jews: The Vatican's Role in the Rise of Modern Anti-Semitism*,[52] suggests that the use by Israel's Muslim opponents of the kinds of antisemitic stereotypes that the Nazis employed, and that played a role in paving the way to the Holocaust, has barely caused eyebrows to be raised in Europe or the Americas. In Kertzer's words: 'the tepid response of the Christian world has also been disturbing, because what is going on in the Muslim world today has its roots in the Christian past'.[53]

An editorial in the *New York Times* also posits that the explanation for contemporary antisemitism in Europe is tightly bound to Europe's antisemitic past and, more specifically, to the Holocaust. Given their background, according to the *Times*, Europeans should be more sensitive to twenty-first-century antisemitism. The editor writes: 'But much of Europe has a special responsibility to be cautious. Its cultures are drenched in a history of antisemitism. The mixing of historic European anti-Semitism with the more modern version in the Muslim world is a dangerous cocktail.'[54] The editorial offers an additional explanation for European anti-Israel bias. Casting Jews as villains apparently soothes the consciences of many in Europe for their role in the Holocaust.

The *Times* editor is not alone in articulating the idea that many Europeans are relieved by the image of Jews ostensibly acting immorally. Ariel Sharon made a similar statement that was reported in *Yediot Achronot*.[55] In unsparing language, Yitzhak Matatyahu Tenenbaum, writing in the right-wing Israeli newspaper *Hamodia*, makes a sweeping generalization about European antisemitism. He accuses all Europe of unparalleled antisemitism and offers an analysis based on his contention:

> Why is Europe so anti-Semitic and not the other continents of the world? Why do the French and Belgians, the Germans and Spaniards, the Italians and the Swiss accuse Israel of Nazism and not the Indians and the Chinese, the Australians and the Koreans? … Because the hoard of Nazi insects lies upon their heads and makes them psychologically justify their aggressiveness … It is the way of the violent aggressor to attack his victim …[56]

In the way of many who make sweeping generalizations, Tenenbaum concedes nothing positive at all to those he attacks, although there is much to be said about the positive aspects of Jewish life in the countries he assails.

In much more sober vein, François Géraud, an author and a columnist at *Le Nouvel Observateur,* also believes Europeans are availing themselves of the opportunity of easing their guilt by transforming 'the image of the Jew as martyr into the Jew as executioner.'[57] According to Géraud, this is an escape from their confrontation with the Holocaust. He writes:

> the Christian nations as a whole have never really grasped the Holocaust. I believe that the relatively tardy discovery of the Holocaust, its hallucinatory extent and precision and, above all, its systematic and gratuitous slaughter of an entire people caused a shock far more profound than is generally believed …

A corollary of this discussion is the question of when does criticism of Israel become antisemitism? Tim Wise, who presents himself as an anti-racist essayist, lecturer and activist, addresses this question from a very clear position of anti-Israel bias. Writing in the online publication *ZNET*, he says that in his opinion Zionism is just another form of White Supremacy. He continues to draw a misshapen parallel between Zionism and Nazism, declaring: 'To attempt to decouple the concepts of Zionism and Judaism, or anti-Zionism and antisemitism, are seen as lost or ignoble causes by both group.'[58] In pseudo-objective tones, he goes on to declare that nonetheless:

> it is indeed necessary to decouple these concepts: to demonstrate that one can oppose Zionism without prejudice towards Jews as Jews, and also to show that one's support for Israel doesn't necessarily insulate oneself from the charge of anti-Semitism.

A *Washington Post* columnist, Richard Cohen, also believes that those who call criticism of Israel antisemitism are wrong. For him, this is a type of mystification. He writes:

> To equate anti-Zionists or critics of Israel in general with anti-Semites is to liken them to the Nazis or the rampaging mobs of the pogroms. It says that their hatred is unreasonable, unfathomable, based on some crackpot racial theory or some misguided religious zealotry. It dismisses all criticism, no matter how legitimate, as rooted in prejudice and therefore without any validity.

A more balanced position, that concedes that some criticism of Israel is antisemitic, is expressed in a *New York Times* editorial.[59] On the one hand, the editor writes, 'Israelis have been too quick, over the years, to view criticism of their government as motivated by anti-Semitism.' Nevertheless, the editorial continues, it is hard to see much of the criticism as anything else since,

> the dark shadow of Europe's past seemed to be reappearing when the liberal Italian daily *La Stampa* depicted a baby Jesus looking up from the manger at an Israeli tank, saying, 'Don't tell me they want to kill me again.' Or when a Lutheran bishop in Denmark delivered a sermon in the Copenhagen Cathedral comparing Ariel Sharon's policies toward the Palestinians to those of King Herod, who ordered the slaughter of all male children under the age of 2 in Bethlehem.

Here, too, the editor asserts that European guilt for past antisemitism, and especially the Holocaust, is a factor in this kind of biased presentation in the press.

The American syndicated columnist Charles Krauthammer thinks that because Europe was so deeply affected by the Holocaust for over 50 years, the scourge of deeply rooted antisemitism was kept at bay. 'But now the atonement is passed. The genie is out again,' he writes.[60] And what has led to its liberation? Krauthammer, too, believes it is Europe's inability to accept Jews who defend themselves. He writes:

> What so offends Europeans is the armed Jew, the Jew who refuses to sustain seven suicide bombings in the seven days of Passover and strikes back ... Just when Europe had reconciled itself to tolerance for the passive Jew – the Holocaust survivor who could be pitied, lionized, perhaps awarded the occasional literary prize – along comes the Jewish state, crude and vital and above all unwilling to apologize for its own existence ...

If some writers believe that Europe has been traumatized by the Holocaust, the editor of the *St Louis Post-Dispatch* thinks an additional force is also at work. He terms Europe 'a continent with amnesia'.[61] He asks: 'Has Europe forgotten the lesson of the Holocaust so soon – or did it never learn it?' For him the problem is perhaps less the violent outbursts of anti-Israel rhetoric and antisemitic deeds during the second Intifada, than the anti-Jewish attitudes in the social élites. He writes: 'In the long run, though, it is the polite prejudice of large portions of the intelligentsia, including the press, that is the most ominous sign of a continent with amnesia.'

The European left in particular bears the most responsibility for the deep anti-Israel feeling that has engulfed much of Europe, according to some authors. Sever Plotzger, an Israeli journalist, declares this clearly in an article in *Yediot Achronot*.[62] An editor of the American Jewish magazine *Commentary*, Gabriel Schoenfeld, makes a similar point in a wide-ranging article that explores the connections between the Holocaust, the Israeli–Palestinian conflict and twenty-first-century antisemitism in Europe.[63] First, he paints a graphic picture of the inversion of the Holocaust throughout Europe, showing it is not a phenomenon confined to a specific locality. He offers a litany of inverted hate in the streets of Europe:

> In Tuzla, a town in Bosnia, some 1,500 demonstrators carried placards reading 'sharon and Hitler, Two Eyes in the Same Head' and 'Israel – the Real Face of Terrorism.' In Dublin, Ireland, the banners, several featuring Nazi swastikas superimposed over stars of David, read 'Stop the Palestinian Holocaust' and

'Jerusalem: Forever Beloved, Forever Palestinian.' In Barcelona, Spain, demonstrators carried placards inscribed 'Israel Murderer; USA Accomplice,' and 'No to Genocide.' In Paris, the posters read 'Hitler Has a Son: Sharon'; in Belgium, 'Hitler Had Two Sons: Bush and Sharon.' In Salonika, a solidarity concert was staged under the slogan: 'Stop the Genocide Now – We Are All Palestinians.' In Bilbao, Spain, thousands marched through the streets chanting 'No to Zionist terrorism.' In Berlin, the placards read 'Stop the Genocide in Palestine' and 'Sharon is a Child Murderer.' In cities and towns across France, 'Death to Jews' and 'Jews – murderers' were refrains heard at a multitude of rallies.

Schoenfeld then sets forth his view about the origins of this flood of hatred, portraying how the far left's embrace of the Palestinian cause, antisemitism, anti-Americanism and anti-globalization are intertwined. He writes:

But one salient fact about the picture I have been painting is this: there is a clear fit between anti-Israel or anti-Jewish hatred and the general ideological predispositions of the contemporary European Left ... Today, a new chapter is being written. There are, to be sure, neo-Nazis to be found among those burning the Star of David and chanting obscene slogans against the Jewish state in the streets of Europe; but the ranks are more heavily composed of environmentalists, pacifists, anarchists, anti-globalists, and socialists.

Schoenfeld also tries to maintain an historical perspective, citing precedents for this groundswell of hatred and trying to avoid sensationalism. Nevertheless, he believes that in the twenty-first century, antisemitism has taken on a new twist and its own momentum. He writes:

One does not wish to exaggerate. Today's virulent anti-Semitism is, in part, an epiphenomenon of the Israel–Arab conflict – or, more accurately, of Israel's effort to withstand the Arab determination to destroy it ... But there is also no denying that the new anti-Semitism has taken on a life of its own, gathering strength from long-repressed theological hatreds suddenly given license to emerge, from all sorts of misplaced social resentments that have nothing to do with the Jews, and (to judge from the Left–Arab coalition) from broader ideological agendas in which Israel is a mere stand-in, a conveniently vulnerable target for those not yet willing or able to take on the mighty United States.

In a series of articles that were first published in the weekly *New York*

Observer and then republished in slightly different form in a number of places, Ron Rosenbaum, the author of *Explaining Hitler: The Search for the Origins of His Evil*, engendered a fascinating discussion about where the 'new' antisemitism seems to be heading. Like Schoenfeld, he also believes that Israel is the target of this 'new' hatred. The version of his article published in the *San Francisco Chronicle* is entitled 'The Second Holocaust – and European Complicity'.[64] The title encapsulates his two main ideas: Israel is on the verge of destruction by a nuclear attack, i.e. the Second Holocaust, and Europeans will have a certain responsibility for it when it happens.

Like other writers on the subject, Rosenbaum sees guilt for the Holocaust as a stepping-stone to the anti-Israeli and antisemitic posture that many Europeans have assumed. He writes:

> The memory of the Holocaust is precisely what explains the one-sided anti-Israel stance of the European press ... there is a need to blame someone else for the shame of 'European civilization.' To blame the victim. To blame the Jews.

In Rosenbaum's vision of the future, widespread European anti-Israel attitudes and concomitant support of the Palestinians will combine with two other factors to allow the destruction of Israel to happen. The first is the deeply entrenched hatred of Israel and Jews among Muslim fundamentalists. This hatred, in Rosenbaum's estimation, will lead them to attack Israel by nuclear means the moment they are able. The second is Israeli restraint in its war on terrorism. Based on ethical considerations, this restraint will inhibit the destruction of the looming threat before it is out of control. Rosenbaum writes:

> So the time has come to think about the second Holocaust. It's coming sooner or later; it's not whether, but when. I hope I don't live to see it. It will be unbearable for those who do. That is, for all but the Europeans – whose consciences, as always, will be clear and untroubled.

To Rosenbaum's gloomy voice were added those of Nat Hentoff and George F. Will in other articles published around the same time.[65]

In an extremely articulate piece entitled 'Hitler Is Dead', Leon Wieseltier, the literary editor of the *New Republic*, suggests that Rosenbaum and those who agree with him have lost their perspective.[66] Wieseltier concedes that American Jewry has been shocked by the 'new' antisemitism, but he does not see why they should be, since antisemitism never disappeared from Europe.

More importantly, perhaps, Wieseltier terms the kind of thinking employed by Rosenbaum mythical or typological. He calls it an a historical view of events – the kind of thinking that regards all who threaten the Jews as *Amalek*. It is this kind of assessment he asserts, that automatically turns the horrible massacre in Netanya on the eve of Passover 2002 into the Night of the Broken Glass, *Kristallnacht*, of November 1938. Wieseltier writes:

> The murder of 28 Jews in Netanya was a crime that fully war-
> ranted the Israeli destruction of the terrorist base in the refugee
> camp at Jenin, but it was not in any deep way like Kristallnacht.
> Solidarity must not come at the cost of clarity. Only a fool could
> believe that the Passover massacre was a prelude to the extermi-
> nation of the Jews of Israel; a fool, or a person with a particular
> point of view about the Israeli–Palestinian conflict. So the analogy
> between the Passover massacre and Kristallnacht is not really
> a historical argument. It is a political argument disguised as a
> historical argument.

If we want to understand the 'new' antisemitism, Wieseltier asserts, we must acknowledge that most Jews overthrew typological thinking in the modern period. They came to understand that the world and historical processes are complex. Modern Jews came to see

> that their myths would not ameliorate their misery; that there
> was not only one question and only one answer; that the entire
> universe was not their enemy and their enemy was not the entire
> universe; that the historical differences mattered as much as the
> historical similarities, because a change in history, progress, nor-
> mality, tranquility, was possible; that historical agency required
> historical thinking, that is, concrete thinking, empirical thinking,
> practical thinking, secular thinking ...

He implies that reverting to a historical perceptions of the world breeds panic, not understanding.

Other writers, among them Leonard Fine in *The Forward*[67] and Richard Goldstein in *The Village Voice*,[68] fundamentally concur with Wieseltier's analysis. Goldstein adds that a nuclear attack on Israel is unlikely because the state exists in the midst of large Arab populations. So on a very practical level, the question is not if a second Holocaust is inevitable, but how to combat antisemitism and anti-Israel prejudice.

Wieseltier brings a cool head to the discussion about the implications of the convergence of anti-Zionism, antisemitism, anti-Americanism and anti-globalization. He reminds his readers that, although the present is always connected to the past, history does not repeat itself and that, despite all the problems we face, mankind has progressed and continues to do so. Yet one is left wondering if his assessment is not a bit too blasé – after all, who in the street would have expected Osama Bin Laden's men to attack New York City on 11 September 2001?

This is what troubles Jonathan Rosen. In his essay 'The Uncomfortable Question of Anti-Semitism', written before those of Rosenbaum and Wieseltier, Rosen adopts a tone that in retrospect sits between the two.[69] He does not believe there is cause for panic, but he does believe that something fundamental has changed in the wake of the attack on the Twin Towers in New York City and the interlacing of Arab and Muslim anti-Israeli propaganda with European antisemitism. In particular, he is deeply troubled by the allegation levelled against the Jews: that they were responsible for the attack in New York City – an allegation that is accepted as fact in much of the Muslim world. These changes, he believes, directly affect American Jews, and shake their complacency.

Rosen's is a thoughtful essay in which he explores, as an American Jew, why he feels things are becoming dangerous for Israel. He uses the Holocaust as the anchor of his understanding of current events and the 'change of mood' regarding Jews. He writes:

> Jews were not the cause of World War II, but they were at the metaphysical center of that conflict nonetheless, since the Holocaust was part of Hitler's agenda and a key motivation of his campaign. Jews are not the cause of World War III, if that's what we are facing, but they have been placed at the center of it in mysterious and disturbing ways.

For Rosen, the catalyst for his unease is the shattering of a long- held conviction that the Holocaust led not only to the destruction of six million Jews, but to the displacement of the so-called Jewish Question as well. He writes:

> I had somehow believed that the Jewish Question, which so obsessed both Jews and anti-Semites in the 19th and 20th centuries, had been solved – most horribly by Hitler's 'final solution,' most hopefully by Zionism. But more and more I feel Jews being turned into a question mark once again. How is it, the world still asks – about Israel, about Jews, about me – that you are still here? I have always known that much of the world wanted Jews simply to disappear, but there are degrees of knowledge, and after Sept. 11 my imagination seems more terribly able to imagine a world of rhetoric fulfilled … What happened on Sept. 11 is proof, as if we

needed it, that people who threaten evil intend evil … I grew up thinking I was living in the post-Holocaust world and find itsounds more and more like a pre-Holocaust world as well.

Yehudah Mirsky, who served in the United States State Department's Human Rights Bureau and is currently a Javits Fellow at Harvard, offers a more academic analysis of the constellation of events explored by Rosen. In the *New Republic*, in an article entitled 'From Fascism to Jihadism', Mirsky lays out the profound similarities he sees between the most aggressive form of Muslim fundamentalism ('Jihadism') and the fascist ideologies that swept Europe after the First World War.[70] Among the motifs that are common to both: they are the consequence of great societal change and of the deflection of legitimate grievances by contemptuous leaders; they have taken liberal ideas – nationalism in the case of fascism, and criticisms of globalization and colonialism in the case of Jihadism – and have harnessed them to their disreputable goals; they have charismatic demagogic leaders; they blame much of their troubles on America; they believe in 'redemptive millennial violence'; they threaten the 'fabric of civilization'; and, last, they are intensely antisemitic. (Of course this is true of Nazism, but not necessarily of early Italian fascism).

In Mirsky's analysis, the only way to neutralize the threat Jihadism poses is to vanquish it, like Nazism and Soviet communism, and to make its former adherents undergo a process similar to denazification. The underlying problem, Mirsky stresses, is one of deeply entrenched, but frighteningly distorted, beliefs about the western World and Jews in particular. Until a climate is created in which these beliefs can be quashed, they will persist.

Among the more thoughtful writers, there is a wide range of ideas about the origins and meanings of Muslim/Arab anti-Semitism, twenty-first-century European antisemitism and what to do about both. It will take a future historian to assess who among them was most correct in his or her analysis. Their discussion, however, unlike the writings of those who instrumentalize the Holocaust, is certainly legitimate. These articles provide a rich and necessary diet for the exchange of ideas.

CONCLUSIONS

The linking of the Holocaust to the Israeli–Palestinian conflict in the press illustrates several important and related concepts. The tremendous impact of the Holocaust on our society is evident in the many articles discussed in this chapter. Whether used to attack Israel or to defend it, whether used for rhetoric alone or to truly try to understand events better, citing the Holocaust and the terms associated with it, as employed by the writers, signifies that they have become powerfully loaded symbols, used by a broad stratum of mankind. The Holocaust has assumed such a central place in our world that some, among them many Palestinians, want their history to be seen as a Holocaust too. Many Palestinians, and those who defend them, imply that only by calling their suffering a Holocaust will it be seen as commensurate to the suffering of the Jews and will be considered legitimate. It would seem that it is less important for them to see the uniqueness of the Palestinian situation than to try to equate it with the Holocaust, no matter to what extent history must be bent to do so.

In a related but yet quite different way, many Jews interpret the situation in Israel during the second Intifada and the related outbreak of European antisemitism through the lens of the Holocaust. This too is indicative of the great power the Holocaust unleashed and of its continuing ripple effects on Jews throughout the world. It is one of several illustrations of the fact that the Holocaust has become a central and deeply entrenched part of contemporary Jewish consciousness. Even for those who seek to prove that Israel and Jews throughout the world are in position quite different to that of the Holocaust era, the Holocaust remains a touchstone for their analysis. For those Jews who have assumed the role of iconoclast, and who viciously attack Israel or Jews in general, the Holocaust also is integral to their viewpoint. In this they are similar to Jews in the late nineteenth and early twentieth century who rebelled against traditional Jewish practice; for them Judaism always remained a central issue in their lives, even if it was from the vantage point of dissent or rejection.

It is clear that the impact of the Holocaust upon us is still so great that we cannot divorce it from issues that touch on the killing of Jews, or attacks on the Jewish state, or the threat of either. Similarly, the role of Europeans in the Holocaust binds them tightly to any discussion of these, especially at a time when antisemitism has gained ground in their backyard. Seeing events through the prism of the Holocaust is not always detrimental to our vision. Sometime, as in the articles of Mirsky, Rosen, Schoenfeld and Wieseltier, it provides us with ideas worth pondering as we struggle to find clarity.

NOTES

1. R. S. Wistrich, *Muslim Anti-Semitism: A Clear and Present Danger* (New York: American Jewish Committee, 2002).
2. For example, see B. Lewis, *Semites and Antisemites: An Inquiry into Conflict and Prejudice* (London: Weidenfeld and Nicolson, 1986); R. Wistrich, *Hitler's Apocalypse, Jews and the Nazi*

Legacy (London: Weidenfeld and Nicolson, 1985); and (ed.), *Anti-Zionism and Antisemitism in the Contemporary World* (Houndmills, Hampshire: Macmillan, 1990).

3. Towards the end of 2001. Egyptian television produced a 30-part series, 'Horseman Without a Horse', reported by Matthew Kalman in the *National Post Online*, 7 December 2001 and broadcast in the autumn of 2002 during Ramadan in 22 countries. It was based on the *Protocols of the Elders of Zion*, a pamphlet first published at the end of the nineteenth century and based on a forged document that claims to reveal a Jewish plot to take over the world. Invoked by the Nazis, the *Protocols* continues to be published and read throughout the world although courts of law have twice determined them to be a forgery (in Port Elizabeth, South Africa, 1934 and Berne, Switzerland, 1934–35). See Hadassa Ben-Itto, *The Lie That Wouldn't Die: The Protocols of the Elders of Zion* (London: Vallentine Mitchell, 2005) and N. Cohen, *Warrant for Genocide: The Myth of the Jewish World Conspiracy and the Protocols of the Elders of Zion* (London: Serif, 1996).

4. *CNSNews.com* (8 May 2002).

5. Among the works by Faurisson published in English are: R. Faurisson, *Maurice Papon and Yves Jouffa: A Double Standard* (Paris: Le Temps Irreparable, 1997) and *Witness to the Gas Chambers of Auschwitz* (San Diego, CA: CODOH, 1999). Paul Rassinier is one of the 'fathers' of Holocaust denial. Among his works published in English are P. Rassinier, *Drama of the European Jews* (Silver Springs, MD: Steppingstone Publications, 1975); *The Holocaust Story and the Lies of Ulysses: A Study of the German Concentration Camps and the Alleged Extermination of European Jewry* (Costa Mesa, CA: Institute for Historical Review, 1978); and *The Real Eichmann Trial, or The Incorrigible Victors* (Torrance, CA: Institute for Historical Review, 1983). Garaudy's major work of Holocaust denial is: R. Garaudy, *The Founding Myths of Modern Israel* (Newport Beach, CA: Institute of Historical Review, 2000).

6. *Daily Star* (27 April 2002).

7. *Dawn* (11 May 2002).

8. For a clear discussion of how the rumours in Jenin came about, see Zeev Schiff, 'Back to Jenin', *Haaretz* (17 July 2002).

9. *CNSNews.com* (30 April 2002).

10. *Paknews.com* (6 April 2002).

11. For an example of the writings against Saramago's statement see G. Schoenfeld, 'Israel and the Anti-Semites', *Commentary* (June 2002).

12. *Arab News* (5 May 2002).

13. *WAFA*, (30 April 2002).

14. *WAFA*, (15 June 2002).

15. *Arab News* (30 June 2002).

16. *Arab News* (24 June 2002).

17. *The Australian* (20 April 2002).

18. I was their guide.

19. *Independent* (7 April 2002).

20. *Guardian* (30 April 2002).

21. *Sunday Nation* (28 April 2002).

22. *Maariv* (24 April 2002).

23. *American Diplomacy* (30 March 2002).

24. *Arab News* (21 May 2002).

25. *London Review of Books*, 4, 9 (23 May 2002).

26. *Daily Nation* (9 May 2002).

27. *Arab News* (1 May 2002).

28. *Sun Sentinal* (21 June 2002).

29. *Daily Telegraph* (10 April 2002).

30. *Washington Times* (10 December 2001).

31. O. Kraus and E. Kulka, *The Death Factory: Document on Auschwitz* (Oxford: Pergamon Press, 1966).

32. *National Review Online* (21 June 2002).

33. *DEBKA.com* (22 June 2002).

34. *Haaretz* (19 April 2002).

35. *The Age* (10 April 2002).

36. *Jerusalem Post* (7 April 2002).

37. There is an immense bibliography that discusses these issues. Among the most important books are I. Abella and H. Troper, *None is Too Many: Canada and the Jews of Europe, 1933–1948* (New York: Random House, 1983); R. Breitman and A. Kraut, *American Refugee Policy and European Jewry, 1933–1945* (Bloomington, IN: Indiana University Press, 1987); R. Breitman, *Official Secrets: What the Nazis Planned, What the British and Americans Knew* (New York: Hill and Wang, 1998); J. Favez, *The Red Cross and the Holocaust* (Cambridge: Cambridge University Press, 1998); H. Feingold, *The Politics of Rescue: The Roosevelt Administration and the Holocaust* (New Brunswick: Rutgers University Press, 1970); M. Gilbert, *Auschwitz and the Allies* (New York: Holt, Rinehart and Winston, 1981); T. Kushner, *The Holocaust and the Liberal Imagination: A Social and Cultural History* (Oxford: Blackwell, 1994); W. Laqueur, *The Terrible Secret: An Investigation in the Suppression of Information about Hitler's 'Final Solution'* (London: (Weidenfeld and Nicolson, 1980); B. Wasserstein, *Britain and the Jews of Europe, 1939–1945* (London: Institute of Jewish Affairs, 1979); D. Wyman, *Paper Walls: America and the Refugee Crisis, 1938–1941* (Massachusetts: University of Massachusetts Press, 1968); and *The Abandonment of the Jews: America and the Holocaust* (New York: Pantheon Books, 1984).
38. *Hatsofe*, (16 April 2002).
39. There is a very important bibliography that discusses the role of the Catholic Church and especially Pope Pius II in the Holocaust. Among the most important titles are R. Braham (ed.), *The Vatican and the Holocaust: The Catholic Church and the Jews during the Nazi Era* (New York: Rosenthal Institute for Holocaust Studies, 2000); J. Cornwell, *Hitler's Pope: The Secret History of Pius XII* (New York: Viking, 1999); S. Friedlander, *Pius XII and the Third Reich, A Documentation* (New York: A.A. Knopf, 1966); D. I. Kertzer, *The Popes Against the Jews: The Vatican's Role in the Rise of Modern Anti-Semitism* (New York: Knopf, 2001); J. Morley, *Vatican Diplomacy and the Jews during the Holocaust, 1939–1943* (New York: Ktav, 1980); M. Phayer, *The Catholic Church and the Holocaust, 1930–1965* (Bloomington, IN: University of Indiana Press, 2000); S. Zuccotti, *Under His Very Windows: The Vatican and the Holocaust in Italy*, (New Haven, CT: Yale University Press, 2000).
40. *Maariv* (9 April 2002).
41. *Corriere della Sera* (12 April 2002). An English translation is available on the website of the American Jewish Committee, *www.ajc.org/default.asp*.
42. The extermination camps are Auschwitz-Birkenau, Belzec, Chelmno, Majdanek, Sobibor and Treblinka. I. Gutman (ed)., *The Encyclopedia of the Holocaust* (New York: Macmillan, 1990), pp. 461–3.
43. *New York Times* (8 May 2002).
44. *Daily News Tribune* (9 April 2002).
45. *Hatsofe* (23 April 2002).
46. *Sun Times* (7 April 2002).
47. *Time* (22 April 2002).
48. *National Review Online* (21 May 2002).
49. *The Iranian* (10 May 2002).
50. *Yediot Achronot* (21 April 2002).
51. Avi Beker, Secretary-General of the World Jewish Congress, was quoted in several sources as saying 'We haven't had this level of anti-Semitism since World War II.' *Washington Times* (2 May 2002).
52. Kertzer, *The Popes*.
53. *New York Times*, (9 May 2002).
54. *New York Times* (20 April 2002).
55. *Yediot Achronot* (15 April 2002).
56. *Hamodia* (24 June 2002).
57. *Haaretz* (23 June 2002).
58. *ZNET* (29 April 2002).
59. *New York Times* (20 April 2002).
60. *Seattle Times* (29 April 2002).
61. *St Louis Post-Dispatch* (1 May 2002).
62. *Yediot Achronot* (9 April 2002).
63. G. Schoenfeld, 'Israel and the Anti-Semites'.
64. *San Francisco Chronicle* (28 April 2002).
65. *New Republic* (27 May 2002) (the article was posted on the Internet on 16 May 2002).

66. Nat Hentoff, 'Who's an Anti-Semite?' *Village Voice*, posted on the Internet on 2 May 2002; George F. Will, 'Final Solution Phase 2' , *Washington Post* (2 May 2002).
67. *The Forward* (31 May 2002).
68. *The Village Voice* (25 May 2002).
69. *New York Times* Magazine (4 November 2001).
70. *New Republic* (9 April 2002).

7
The Inscription:
A Case Study in Historical Evidence, Memory and Commemoration

In the summer of 2000 a book reached Yad Vashem from the Law Library of the University of Tel Aviv. It was not the kind of book that usually finds its way to Yad Vashem, because it was a book of questions and answers regarding various aspects of Jewish religious law and its content had nothing to do with the Holocaust, its antecedents or its repercussions. Entitled *Chut Hasheni* (either referring to the passage in the Bible that tells about the spies sent out by Moses to discover what the Land of Israel was like before the children of Israel entered it or to the passage in the Song of Songs that uses this term), the book was published in 1833 and written by Rabbi Yair Chaim Bacharach. The importance of the book for Yad Vashem was that the back flap, along with many handwritten items regarding the contents of the book, contained a very enigmatic inscription about the fate of several people during the Holocaust. It is not known who wrote the inscription or where it was written. From its form and content it is quite plausible that it was written at the time of the events it describes, but that is far from a certainty.

The original Hebrew inscription reads:

בערך 5-4 לע ע פרייטאג תש'ב – 9/5
ח' ימים לפני ר ה
כשהיו כבר מלובשים בגדי-שבת באו הארורים
הגסטפוי י מ ש

3 משה בצלאל
1 ישראל יוסף הוא יצא ראשונה מן הבית
2 רבי אחריו יצא האדמו' לראות מה קרה לישראל
4: בורנשטיין רב מקוטנא בן אמ הר ד מסוכטשוב

ג' שבועות אח כ
והי המעשה בכ'ב באלול
בע ש ק
ובשבת קודש נצ-וי 6/9
כ'ג אלול תש'ב – 1942

נורו יחד כ מ בצ אלתר עם האדמו'ר הי ד
אברהם חיים נלקח שבועות אחדים קודם
הרבנית חנה עם ז' בנותי ג כ לפניהם

After filling in the words for the abbreviations the inscription reads:[1]

בערך [בשעה] 5-4 לע[ת] ע[רב] פרייטאג [=יום שישי] תש'ב – 5/9
ח' ימים לפני ר[אש] ה[שנה]
כשהיו כבר מלובשים בגדי-שבת באו הארורים
הגסטפו ימ[ח] ש[מם]

3 משה בצלאל
1 ישראל יוסף הוא יצא ראשונה מן הבית
2 אחריו יצא האדמו'ר [=מנהיג החסידות] לראות מה קרה לישראל [יוסף הנ'ל]
4: רבי בורנשטיין רב מקוטנא בן א[דוננו] מ[ורנו] הר[ב] ד[?] מסוכטשוב

ג' [=שלושה] שבועות אח[ר] כ[ך]
והי[ה] המעשה בכ'ב באלול
בע[רב] ש[בת] ק[ודש]
= ובשבת קודש [פרשת] נצ[בים]-וי[לך] 6/9
= כ'ג אלול תש'ב – 1942

נורו יחד כ[בוד] מ[שה] בצ[לאל] אלתר עם האדמו'ר ה[שם י]קום] ד[מו]
אברהם חיים נלקח שבועות אחדים קודם
הרבנית חנה עם ז' [=שבע] בנותי[ה] ג[ם] כ[ן] לפניהם.

A translation of the inscription reads:

At about 4 or 5 o'clock in the evening Friday, 5 September 1942, eight days before Rosh Hashanah [the Jewish New Year], when we were already dressed in our Sabbath clothes, the damned Gestapo, may their names be erased, came.

3 Moshe Bezalel
1 Yisrael Yosef left the house first
2 After him went the *Admor* [Hasidic Rabbinic leader] to see what had happened to Yisrael
4 Rabbi Bornstein the Rabbi of Kutno, son of the *Admor* D from Sochaczew.

Three weeks later. And this act was on the 22nd of the month of Elul, on the holy Sabbath Eve and on the Holy Sabbath of the chapter Nitzavim-Veylech, 6 September, 23 of Elul 1942, they shot his honour Moshe Bezalel Alter with the *Admor*, Hashem [G-d] will avenge his blood.

Avraham Chaim was taken weeks earlier.

The *Rabbanit* Chanah with her seven daughters was also [taken] before them.

From the inscription itself a few 'facts' emerge fairly clearly: several events and different people are being discussed. First, the Gestapo entered a place where there were Jews getting ready for the Sabbath, on a Friday late in the afternoon, eight days before Rosh Hashanah, 1942. The date given is 5 September. The next section seems to have been written down not in the order of the events, but the numbers given seem to present the proper sequence of events. Yisrael Yosef went out of the house first, followed by an *Admor* who went to see what happened to him. Next something happened to Moshe Bezalel and finally something happened to Rabbi Bornstein from Kutno.

The next part of the inscription is about another event that may have happened that day or happened three weeks later.[2] This depends on whether the phrase 'three weeks later' is the date the inscription was written, or is meant to say that the next event happened three weeks later: Moshe Bezalel was shot along with 'the *Admor*'. Either before the Gestapo raid, or between the raid and the later murder of Moshe Bezalel, Avraham Chaim was taken, as were the *Rabbanit* Chanah and her seven daughters.

How can one go about trying to identify the people mentioned in the inscription and placing the events described in some sort of historical context? One must first try to check the hard facts mentioned, such as dates and names of people. The first event described in the inscription actually took place on 4 September 1942. The slight discrepancy probably arises from the differences in counting days in the Jewish calendar versus the civil calendar. According to the Jewish calendar, a day begins and ends at sunset and, of course, according to the civil calendar, days begin and end at midnight. It is conceivable that the person who wrote the inscription did not have both a Jewish and secular calendar at hand, and was trying to figure out the secular dates by the Jewish dates.

The two people mentioned who are most easily traced are Rabbi Bornstein, the Rabbi of Kutno, and *Admor* D of Sochaczew, since both men were associated with a specific place. There is a fairly large literature about prominent rabbis, and there is much pertinent information about them in the many memorial books published about Jewish communities after the Holocaust. Most of this information has yet to be organized into lexicons or other such easily accessible reference material,[3] but with a surprisingly little bit of digging, the first ends of the threads of the story may be revealed.

Rabbi Avraham Bornstein became Rabbi of Kutno in 1939. He was the brother-in-law of the former Rabbi of Kutno, Yitzhak Yehuda Trunk, who died in 1939. His wife's name was Reiza-Mindel, the daughter of Rabbi Yaacov Bunam Danziger, the son of the late *Admor* of Aleksandrow, Rabbi Shmuel Zvi Danziger. Rabbi Avraham Bornstein had two children, Shmuel, born in 1941, and Sarah, born afterwards. According to several sources – including a Page of Testimony[4] filled out by Avraham's brother, Aharon Bornstein – Avraham, his wife and children died in the Holocaust, probably in Otwock in 1942.[5]

Admor D of Sochaczew is Rabbi David Bornstein, the *Admor* of Sochaczew. A number of sources provide fairly detailed information about him and his fate during the Holocaust. Rabbi David Bornstein was the third Rabbi of the Sochaczew Chasiddic dynasty. He was the son of Shmuel Bornstein, known for his work *Hashem Mi-Shmuel.* David Bornstein served as the Rabbi of Wyszogrod until the outbreak of the First World War, and then as the Rabbi of Tomaszow Mazowiecki. He assumed the head of the Sochaczew dynasty in 1926 when his father died. At the outbreak of the Second World War he was in Lodz.[6]

After the Germans entered Lodz, they entered Rabbi David Bornstein's house and attacked him, sometime just before Chanukah. They beat him and cut off his white beard. Fearing for his safety, his disciples supplied him with false papers and dispatched him to Warsaw. At one point he left Warsaw for Otwock, but then returned to Warsaw. Rabbi David Bornstein encouraged Jews in the ghetto to keep up their Torah learning, and in the Warsaw ghetto he established several *Yeshivot* along with Rabbi Arie Zvi Fromer of Koziegłowy and Rabbi Avraham Weinberg of Strykow. The *Yeshivot* were located on Nalaboki Street and Grzysbow Street. He also tried to help the needy and urged Jews to do their best to bring their dead to a proper burial. Around Purim (14 March) 1940, Rabbi David Bornstein's disciples arranged all the papers necessary for him to leave Poland for Italy. But he refused to leave. Before the outbreak of the war, Rabbi David Bornstein visited Palestine, and even bought land there. He had tried to arrange his own immigration and had encouraged members of his flock to go to the Land of Israel. Before learning of the possibility of going to Italy, he had tried to find out if the authorization for his immigration to Palestine had reached his Lodz address, but he was informed that it had not. Around the time that flight to Italy became an option, the Rabbi came to believe that G-d did not want him to go to Palestine or abandon his flock.[7]

Before the start of the deportations from Warsaw, Tammuz (22 July) 1942, Rabbi David Bornstein warned other Rabbinic and lay leaders about what they could expect. Rabbi David Bornstein told them that the soldiers with the *Totenkopf* (death's head) insignia, that is to say SS men, from Lublin would carry out the 'evil decree'. According to one source, this pronouncement brought Adam Czerniakow, the head of the Warsaw Jewish Council, to ask the Germans with whom he worked what was in store for the ghetto.[8]

Could other sources corroborate or shed light on the words and deeds of Rabbi David Bornstein in the Warsaw Ghetto? Was his warning about the upcoming deportations correct in whole or in part? Can his warning be clearly linked to Adam Czerniakow?

The main deportation drive in Warsaw of course happened in the summer of 1942. It was carried out by troops under the command of Hermann Hoefle, a senior SS officer, who wore the death's head insignia. His troops included Polish 'Blue' Police, Ukrainian, Lithuanian and Latvian support troops, and SS men.[9] Hoefle was the deputy of Odilo Globocnik, the SS and Ppolice leader based in Lublin. Globocnik was responsible for the implementation of Aktion Reinhard, the drive to murder the Jews of the Generalgouvernement. So David Bornstein's information about the evil decree emanating from Lublin was correct.

In Czerniakow's diary, there is no direct reference to a meeting with various religious leaders during the month of Tammuz. Nevertheless, he does write of many rumours in the ghetto about looming deportations, and on 18 July 1942 he asked the ghetto commissioner, Heinz Auerswald, if deportations were impending. Over the next few days he continued to try to clarify what would happen.[10] In the diary of Hillel Seidman, the meeting between the various leaders is noted. It took place at 27 Nowolipki Street and included many religious and secular leaders, amongst which was Rabbi Joseph Koenigsberg, who had just reached Warsaw from Lublin, where he was the director of a *Yeshiva*, and who told of the murder drive that had happened there. Rabbi Bornstein of Sochaczew, along with Rabbi Danziger of Aleksandrow and Rabbi Alter, is cited specifically as having attended the meeting, but Czerniakow is not mentioned.[11]

Returning to the story of Rabbi David Bornstein, during the deportations from Warsaw he hid first in the shop of Kahan and Heller. When he was warned the shop was soon to be raided, the *Admor* moved to the Fritz Schultz shoe-making shop. Along with other rabbis in the Schultz shop, he worked and studied Torah.[12]

According to one source, Rabbi David Bornstein was in the Schultz shop until Succoth (26 September) 1942 and from there went to 67 Gesia Street – the address of the Yosef Fastag factory, which had 500 Jewish workers.[13] According to another source, he left the Schultz shop when the Germans began raiding it and from there he went to the Yosef Fastag factory, where he remained until after Yom Kippur (21 September). From there he went to live on 29 Muranowska Street.[14] Both sources place him in the Schultz shop in early September 1942.

Around Succoth, Rabbi David Bornstein became sick with dysentery. After six weeks, on 8 Kislev (17 November) 1942, he had a heart attack and died. Rabbi Kolonymous Kalmish Shapiro, the *Admor* from Piasnice, and Rabbi Menahem Ziemba purified his body for burial. His funeral procession was said to have been the last such procession in the ghetto. Rabbi David Bornstein was buried in the main cemetery on Gesia Street.[15]

According to the inscription in *Chut Hasheni*, Rabbi David Bornstein was the father of Rabbi Avraham Bornstein. Actually he was his older brother, born in 1876, some 34 years older than Avraham, who was born in 1910.[16] The great gap between their ages suggests why the person who wrote the inscription might have thought they were father and son.

So far, given the information at hand, it would seem that the events described might have happened in Otwock, since it was in Otwock that Rabbi Avraham Bornstein apparently died. But if we look at some of the other people mentioned and their trail, such a scenario is not very plausible.

It is far more likely that the events being discussed took place in the Warsaw ghetto. Both Rabbi David Bornstein and Rabbi Avraham Bornstein were in the ghetto. Early in September 1942, Rabbi David Bornstein found refuge in the Schultz shoe shop. According to several sources, among the residents of the shop were the *Admorim* from Kromolow (Nahum Hacohen Rabinowicz), Piasnice (Rabbi Kolonymous Kalmish Shapira), Strykow (Rabbi Avraham Weinberg) and Aleksandrow (Rabbi Menahem Danziger), the *Gaon* from Kozieglowy (Rabbi Arie Zvi Fromer), *Harav Hatzaddik* Moshe Bezalel Alter and the *Gaon* Rabbi Menachem Ziemba.[17]

As this list shows, Moshe Bezalel Alter, who is mentioned in the inscription, also found refuge in the Schultz shop. Moshe Bezalel Alter was the brother of the then Rabbi of Gur, Avraham Mordechai Alter, and the son of the former Rabbi of Gur, Yehudah Leib Alter. He was born either in 1861 or 1868, so he was between 74 and 81 years old at the time.[18] Before arriving in the Warsaw ghetto, he was a rabbi in Kalisz-Pawianicz and he served as the president of the Union of Polish Rabbis.[19] Rabbi Moshe Bezalel Alter was very concerned with the spiritual life of young Hasidic Jews in the Warsaw ghetto. A letter he wrote in December 1940, shortly after the closing of the Warsaw ghetto, urged young people to continue to study the Torah, at least eight hours a day, and to make great efforts to honour their parents despite the deteriorating situation.[20]

There is good reason to suggest that part of the inscription describes a Gestapo raid on the shop. The Gestapo is clearly mentioned in the inscription and such raids were going on at the time. According to the diarist Abraham Lewin, from Wednesday 2 September through Shabbat 5 September 1942, the Schultz and Toebbens shops and the HG Zimmerman factory in the Warsaw ghetto were being raided and many of their workers were deported.[21]

This brings us to the question: who was Yisrael Yosef, who 'left the house first'? There is a man named Yisrael Yosef who is mentioned in the Sochaczew memorial book and who was associated with the Admor of Sochaczew. He was one of the *Parnasim* (wealthy benefactors or officials) of the Warsaw Jewish community. After Bornstein returned to Warsaw from Otwock, Yisrael Yosef provided a place for the Sochaczew Rabbi to live in the Warsaw ghetto, at 24 Muranowska Street.[22] It is quite plausible that this Yisrael Yosef accompanied the Sochaczew Rabbi as he moved from one hiding place to another.

More clearly present in the Schultz shop was Yerachamiel Yisrael Yosef, the son of the Aleksandrow Rabbi Yitzhak Menahem Danziger. The arrest and deportation of the Aleksandrow Rabbi and his son is described at some length in a book written by one of the Rabbi's disciples after the Holocaust. According to that account, in the middle of Elul (early September) 1942, the Gestapo entered the Schultz shoe shop where the Rabbi was working. They made all the workers get out, and then carried out a *selektion*. The Aleksandrow Rabbi was selected for deportation. His son Yerachmiel Yisrael Yosef joined him voluntarily for the deportation. The manager of the shop, Avraham Handel, tried to have the Rabbi released on the grounds that he was his 'best worker'. But the Nazis refused to accept that statement and they beat Handel. The son and the *Admor* were sent to Treblinka, where they were murdered.[23] The inscription may very well be describing the fate of the *Admor* of Aleksandrow and his son: 'the *Admor*' who went out to see what happened to Yisrael Yosef, was the *Admor* of Aleksandrow. It would appear that the following scene occurred. The *Admor* of Aleksandrow heard the commotion outside and rushed out to investigate, especially worried about his son Yerachmiel Yisrael Yosef. As soon as he was outside the Gestapo ordered him to remain, and he was subjected to a *selektion* along with his son. The Admor was chosen for deportation and the son was not, but he decided to join his father. There are many such stories, described in the testimonies and memoirs of Holocaust survivors, about family members who willingly joined other family members about to be deported.

The meaning of the next section of the inscription is harder to pin down. Although it is clear who the Bornsteins are, it is not clear exactly to what the inscription is alluding when it states: 'Avraham

Chaim was taken weeks earlier.' It could be about Avraham Bornstein
or about Avraham Weinberg, or some other Avraham Chaim who was
in the Schultz shop. However, the simple fact that Avraham Bornstein
is mentioned in the inscription suggests that it might be about him. If
the sources available about Avraham Bornstein are correct, he died in
Otwock. If he died in Otwock, he was not taken to Treblinka from the
Schultz shop. It is possible that he was taken from the building and
subjected to a selection process that left him in the shop. If he was
indeed in the shop in early September, and if he indeed died in Otwock
with the rest of his family, how did they get there? From where and to
where was he 'taken'? Perhaps he was taken from the shop, somehow
managed to escape and joined his family in Otwock, where he ultimately met his death. Or maybe, if the document itself was written
three weeks after the events it described, Rabbi Avraham Bornstein and
his family left the Warsaw ghetto before the raid on the Schultz shop,
made it to Otwock, but there met their grim fate sometime in late
August 1942. Both of these scenarios, of course, are only conjectures.

The other events that may have happened at the time of the raid on
the shop or three weeks later also remain unclear. There is no reason to
doubt that Moshe Bezalel Alter was shot either during or after the raid
on the Schultz shop. We have no record of his ultimate fate during the
Holocaust that would contradict this. But who was the *Admor* shot with
him?

It is possible to rule out several of the *Admorim* who were present in
the Schultz shop. The *Admor* mentioned was not Rabbi David
Bornstein, since he died of a heart attack in November 1942. Neither
was it Rabbi Yitzhak Menaham Danziger of Aleksandrow, because he
died in Treblinka soon after he arrived there. It was not Rabbi
Kolonymus Kalmish Shapiro, who was also mentioned as having
been in the shop – he died on 4 Heshvan 2 November 1943.[24] We also
know that he took care of Rabbi David Bornstein's body after the
Admor from Sochaczew died in November 1942. The *Admor* from
Kromolow, Rabbi Nahum Hacohen Rabinowicz, apparently was
murdered in Auschwitz, after having worked with other *Admorim* in
the ghetto.[25] If he was murdered in Auschwitz, he may have been
deported from Warsaw in the spring of 1943, since at that time Warsaw
Jews were generally sent to that camp. Or he may have reached
Auschwitz by way of Majdanek, like some others taken at the time of
the Warsaw Ghetto Uprising. There is a Page of Testimony for him that
was submitted by his grandson. It gives his date of birth in 1867, his
profession as a rabbi and his residence before the war as in Zawierce,
but it gives no details about his death. There is a Page of Testimony for
Menahem Ziemba who was also in the Schultz shop. He was born in
1890 and, according to the information provided by his niece, he died

in Treblinka in 1943. Moreover, because he was involved in purifying the body of the Sochaczew Rabbi on 8 Cislev, it could not have been Ziemba who was shot three weeks after the raid. We have a Page of Testimony for Arie Zvi Fromer, born in 1892 in Pilica in Poland. According to that page, he was the head of the *Yishivah*, Chochmai Lublin, and a *Parshan* (explicator) of the Talmud. He lived in Sosnowiec before the war and was in Warsaw during the Holocaust years. According to his cousin, who submitted the Page of Testimony in 1956, the Rabbi died in an underground bunker with 15 of his students. No date is given for his death. No information is available for Avraham Weinberg of Strykow. Given what we know, 'the *Admor*' murdered along with Bezalel Moshe Alter could have been either Arie Zvi Fromer or Avraham Weinberg.

As to the last line, there is not even the slightest thread of information available. It is totally unclear who the *Rabbanit* Chanah and her seven daughters were. As far as can be determined, she was not the wife of either of the Bornstein rabbis, nor the wife of the Rabbi of Aleksandrow, Rabbi Fromer, nor of Menahem Ziemba. None of their wives was named Chanah. All we can know about her is from the inscription: she and her daughters were murdered in the Holocaust.

No less absorbing than the inscription itself and its possible meanings are issues that became apparent while trying to decipher it. First are the issues around the sources and their reliability.

Is the inscription itself a historical source? The answer depends on when it was written and by whom. The enigmatic style of the inscription, its lack of order and lack of clear information, all suggest it may have been written in some haste at the time of the events it describes. If the words 'three weeks later' really indicate the date it was written, that would squarely place the inscription as a contemporary account. Moreover, if it was written in the Schultz shop or by someone who had been in the shop, it makes a great deal of sense why it was written in a book of Jewish religious law, since that is what the rabbis and their disciples studied in the shop. Even were it written by a witness well afterwards, it would still be similar to other kinds of post-war written testimony we have about the Holocaust. However, despite the distinct possibility that the inscription was written in the Warsaw ghetto in September 1942, it is impossible to determine with certainty that it was written at the time, and it is even less clear who might have written it. So, if it cannot be treated like a normative historical document, then what is the value of the inscription? At the very minimum, its value is commemorative. If the inscription does nothing else, it commemorates, however cryptically, the events and people it describes.

The many sources used to decipher the inscription also are problematic. None of the sources, except for Lewin's and Czerniakow's diaries, are really contemporary accounts. All the others are post-war accounts. Many of these, however, are neither scholarly accounts nor eyewitness testimonies in the classic sense. Much of the information about the various people mentioned in the inscription was culled from memorial books about communities and hagiographic writings about the various rabbis. Generally the information in these sources was taken from the testimonies of the disciples of the rabbis. But, unlike the oral testimony usually used in writing history, the testimonies in their entirety were not taken down and placed in an archive. They are not available to others to study and determine if they were used accurately.

Unlike the writings of professional historians who strive to compare many kinds of sources with oral testimony, and compare the oral testimonies themselves for their internal integrity, the authors of these books apparently simply took the testimonies at face value. That is not to say that they may not accurately reflect events, but the reliability of the books containing them is severely reduced by the non-scholarly approach of the authors. Still, these sources have great value to scholars and the general public alike. Often they are our only published sources available about the fate of the ultra-Orthodox leaders and their disciples, and often they are the only published works on the Holocaust read by the ultra-Orthodox segment of Jewish society.

Another well of information for some of the people mentioned directly in the inscription or indirectly in other sources, are Pages of Testimony. Over two million Pages of Testimony have been submitted to Yad Vashem since 1955. Usually, family members, friends or neighbours of murdered Jews fill out these forms and submit them. The initial goal of the project was not to provide historical source material for scholars, but to gather the names of the victims of the Holocaust in order to commemorate them. With the computerization of this huge source of data, however, the data and cross-sections thereof are now also available to scholars to be used with care. In the case of the inscription, all the relevant Pages of Testimony were filled out during the first years of the collection project by relatives of the victims. The reliability of the information contained in the Pages of Testimony varies, depending on just how much the person filling them out knew and just how close a witness to events he or she was. Sometimes a Page of Testimony, however incomplete, is the only source available about the fate of an individual. In the case of their use here, some of the Pages of Testimony corroborate other available information or add to it without contradicting it.

On an entirely different level, the fact that the inscription was written in a book of Jewish religious law is significant. Such books, with the great value of their content, were often passed from generation to generation. These books, which are considered holy, are never just thrown away by Jews, but when they can no longer be used they are stored in *Genizah*. This means that Jews never wilfully destroy these books. The fact that the book was important enough as a publication to place it in the Law Library of the University of Tel Aviv also attests to its value.

Whoever wrote in the book, even if it was the only one available to him or her to write in, probably knew that it was valuable and would be preserved if possible. He or she might well have guessed that in all likelihood somebody sometime would see the inscription and pay attention to it. This is exactly what happened.

The nearly 170-year-old book, which had started out its life as something to be read by the Orthodox Jewish learned public and somehow survived the period of the Holocaust, made its way to the secular bastion of learning, Tel Aviv University. There, students interested in Hebrew law could study it. A reader in the Law Library at Tel Aviv University noticed the inscription and told a relative working at Yad Vashem about it. The director of the Yad Vashem Archives, Dr Yaacov Lozowick, upon learning of the inscription, made contact with the library. Suddenly the book was seen to have significance beyond its original contents. The dean of the Law School, Professor Menahem Mautner, clearly realized this significance. Despite the value of the book for his own library, Dean Mautner transferred it to Yad Vashem, where it would be preserved and made available to researchers of the Holocaust.

The tremendous explosive force of the Holocaust eviscerated Jewish life wherever it hit. It reduced the evidence of former Jewish life to a myriad tiny fragments. Some fragments disintegrated or became lost. Others may be present, but are broken and only barely recognizable; and yet others are broken beyond recognition. Sometimes it is not even clear if the pieces at hand actually belong to the puzzle or, if they do, where they should be placed. But those fragments that can be used are employed to reconstruct parts of the large picture we call the Holocaust.

There is a difference between the kind of picture needed to understand history and the kind needed to commemorate events. For our historical understanding, the clearer and more detailed the picture reconstructed, the better our ability to interpret it. But for the purpose of commemoration, even the smallest fragment that gives us pause to reflect, and strikes a chord within us, may suffice.

Of the people mentioned in the inscription, it is the *Rabbanit* Chanah and her seven daughters about whom we know almost nothing. Indeed, it could be that this is a variation of the story of Chanah and her seven sons, a tale of Jewish martyrdom set in the period of the Hasmonean (Maccabbi) revolt, told in the apocryphal work *Second Maccabbees*. Perhaps it is not meant to be a historical presentation of an event in the Holocaust at all, but an allegory for the murder of the Jews of Warsaw. Like Chanah's sons during the Hasmonean revolt, the Jews of Warsaw were murdered one after the other, because they were Jews. Chanah's sons went proudly to their deaths, encouraged by their mother not to waver one iota from their beliefs, despite the cruel punishment meted out by the Greek rulers of the Land of Israel. The writer of the inscription may be trying to tell us that the Jews of Warsaw went to their death in a similar manner – unbowed and proud of being Jews.

Chanah and her seven daughters, if we take them literally, are not the only Holocaust victims for whom we have only the most fractional information. Among the many Pages of Testimony deposited at Yad Vashem is one that recalls a widow in Kavala, Macedonia, who had a small icecream stand outside a school.[26] She worked hard to raise her children, made wonderful icecream, and was killed in the Holocaust. The Holocaust survivor who submitted the Page of Testimony was a student in the school. He did not know her name or those of her children, but obviously did not want them to be forgotten.

So even if we do not know exactly who they were, in an inscription in a book in Yad Vashem, it is written that there once was a *Rabbanit* named Chanah in the Warsaw ghetto and that she was murdered with her seven daughters. We need not know exactly who Chanah and her seven daughters were, we need not know if they were real people or a symbol of mothers and daughters in the Warsaw ghetto, to grieve for them, to feel their pain and to remember the many mothers and daughters, fathers and sons, murdered in the Holocaust.

NOTES

1. My thanks to Professor Dan Michman, the Chief Historian of Yad Vashem, for supplying the full text.
2. My thanks to Nadia Kahan, the Director of the Information Unit at Yad Vashem, for bringing this interpretation to my attention.
3. Dr Pnina Meisels, of Bar Ilan University, is currently compiling such a lexicon, and I thank her for her help regarding the identity of several *Admorim*.
4. Pages of Testimony are forms that are filled out by Holocaust survivors or family members of victims and are deposited in Yad Vashem, the Martyrs' and Heroes' Remembrance Authority, in Jerusalem.
5. Y. U. Zilberberg, *Malkut, Malkut Beit David* [The Kingdom of the House of David] (B'nai B'rak [self-published], 1991) [in Hebrew], p. 427; Page of Testimony for Avraham Bornstein, submitted by his brother Aharon Bornstein in 1955.
6. Y. M. Aharonson, '*Admor* Rabbi David ZAL', in A. S. Stein and G. Weisman (eds), *Pinkas Sochaczew* [Sochaczew Community Book] (Jerusalem: Irgun Yotzei Sochaczew, 1962) [in Hebrew], pp. 632–8; and B. Zemach, 'Rabbi David Bornstein, Admur Mi-Sochaczew', in A. S. Stein and G. Weisman (eds), *Pinkas Sochaczew* [Sochaczew Community Book] (Jerusalem: Irgun Yotzei Sochaczew, 1962) [in Hebrew], pp. 639–44.
7. Zilberberg, *Malkut*, pp. 359–66.
8. Ibid., pp. 367–8.
9. I. Gutman, *The Jews of Warsaw, 1939–1943, Ghetto, Underground, Revolt* (Bloomington, IN: University of Indiana Press, 1982), p. 203.

10. R. Hilberg, S. Staron and J. Kermisz (eds), *The Warsaw Diary of Adam Czerniakow*, (Chicago, IL: Ivan Dee, 1999), pp. 381–5.
11. H. Seidman, *Diary of the Warsaw Ghetto* (New York: The Jewish Week, 1957), pp. 21–4.
12. Zilberberg, *Malkut*, pp. 373–
13. Y. Erlich, *Abirai Roim* [Knights of the Shepherds] (Tel Aviv: Morasha, 1985) [in Hebrew], p. 664.
14. Zilberberg, *Malkut*, pp. 373–5.
15. Aharonson, '*Admor*', p. 638; and Zilberberg, *Malkut*, pp. 381–2.
16. Erlich, *Abirai Roim*, pp. 622 and 664.
17. A. Surski, 'Metoldot Ha*Admor* Hakadosh Maran Rabbi Kolonymous Kalmish Shapira ZAL, Me-Piasnice' [From the History of the Holy Rabbi Kolonymous Kalmish Shapira of Blessed Memory, from Piasnice], in K. K. Shapira, *Sefer Esh Kodesh* [The Book of Holy Fire] (Jerusalem: Vaad Hasidai Piasnice, 1960) [in Hebrew], pp. 1–28; and Zilberberg, *Malkut*, p. 373 .
18. Pninah Meisles, Lexicon of Rabbis, draft database.
19. Seidman, *Diary of the Warsaw Ghetto*, p. 22.
20. S. Huberband, *Kiddush Hashem: Jewish Religious and Cultural Life in Poland During the Holocaust* (Hoboken, NJ: Ktav, 1987), pp. 182–4.
21. A. Polonsky (ed.), *A Cup of Tears: A Diary of the Warsaw Ghetto by Abraham Lewin* (Oxford: Basil Blackwell, 1989), pp. 175–6.
22. Aharonson, '*Admor*', p. 638.
23. Y. Makover, *Sefer Roeh Neeman, Rabenu Hakadosh Mialeksander* [The Book of the Faithful Shepherd, Our Holy Rabbi from Aleksandrow] (Jerusalem: Machon Zecher Naftali, 1990), [in Hebrew], pp. 467–9.
24. Y. Alfasi, *Hahasidot* [Chasidism] (Tel Aviv: Maariv, 1972) [in Hebrew], p. 102.
25. S. Spiwak (ed.), *Sefer Sicharon Zawiercie Vehasviva* [Memorial Book for Zawiercie and its Surroundings] (Tel Aviv: Irgun Yotzei Zawiercie, 1968) [in Hebrew], pp. 468–70.
26. My thanks to Dr Yaacov Lozowick, Director of the Yad Vashem Archives, for bringing this Page of Testimony to my attention.

Select Bibliography

Adelson, A. (ed.), *The Diary of Dawid Sierakowia: Five Notebooks from the Lodz Ghetto* (New York: Oxford University Press, 1996).

Arad, Y., *Ghetto in Flames: The Struggle and Destruction of the Jews in Vilna During the Holocaust* (Jerusalem: Yad Vashem, 1980) (reprinted New York: Holocaust Library, 1982).

—— *Belzec, Sobibor, Treblinka: The Operation Reinhard Death Camps* (Bloomington: University of Indiana Press, 1987).

Azrieli, D. J., *One Step Ahead, David J. Azrieli (Azrylewicz), Memoirs: 1939–1950* (Jerusalem: Yad Vashem, 2001).

Bankier, D., *The Germans and the Final Solution: Public Opinion Under Nazism* (Oxford: Blackwell, 1992).

Barnavi E. (ed.), *A Historical Atlas of the Jewish People from the Time of the Patriarchs to the Present* (New York: Alfred A. Knopf, 1992).

Bauer, Y., *Jews for Sale: Nazi-Jewish Negotiations, 1933–1945* (New Haven, CT: Yale University Press, 1994).

Berkovits, E., *Faith After the Holocaust* (New York: Ktav, 1973).

—— *With God in Hell, Judaism in the Ghettos and the Death Camps* (New York: Sanhedrin Press, 1979).

Braham, R. *The Hungarian Labor Service System, 1939–1945* (Boulder, CO: East European Quarterly, 1977).

—— *The Wartime System of Labor Service in Hungary: Varieties of Experiences* (New York: Columbia University Press, 1995).

—— *The Politics of Genocide: The Holocaust in Hungary*, revised and enlarged edn, 2 vols (New York: Rosenthal Institute for Holocaust Studies Graduate Center, City University of New York, 1994) (originally published by Columbia University Press, 1981).

—— (ed.), *The Vatican and the Holocaust: The Catholic Church and the Jews during the Nazi Era* (New York: Rosenthal Institute for Holocaust Studies, 2000).

—— and S. Miller (eds), *The Nazis' Last Victims: The Holocaust in Hungary*

(Detroit, IL: Wayne State University Press, 1998), pp. 117–36.

Breitman, R., *The Architect of Genocide: Himmler and the Final Solution* (London: The Bodley Head, 1991).

Browning, C. R. *Ordinary Men: Reserve Police Battalion 101 and the Final Solution* (New York: HarperCollins 1992).

—— *Nazi Policy, Jewish Workers, German Killers* Cambridge: Cambridge University Press, 2000), pp. 58–88.

Bulliet, R. W. (ed.), *The Columbia History of the 20th Century* (New York: Columbia University Press, 1998).

Cohen, A., *The Hehalutz Resistance in Hungary, 1942–1944* (Boulder, CO: Social Science Monographs, 1986).

Cohen, A. A., *The Tremendum: A Theological Interpretation of the Holocaust* (New York: Crossroad, 1981).

Cohen, Y. R. *The Burden of Conscience, French Jewish Leadership During the Holocaust* (Bloomington: Indiana University Press, 1987).

Cornwell, J., *Hitler's Pope: The Secret History of Pius XII* (New York: Viking, 1999).

Crampton, R. and B. Crampton, *Atlas of Eastern Europe in the Twentieth Century* (London: Routledge, 1996).

Dekoven Ezrahi, S., *By Words Alone: The Holocaust in Literature* (Chicago, IL: University of Chicago Press, 1980).

Fackenheim, E., *To Mend the World, Foundations of Post-Holocaust Jewish Thought* (Bloomington: Indiana University Press, 1994).

—— *God's Presence in History: Jewish Affirmations and Philosophical Reflections* (New York: New York University Press, 1970)

Fatran, G., *Haim Maavak Al Hisadrut, Hanhaga Yehudit Beslovakia, 1938–1944* [A Struggle for Survival? Jewish Leadership in Slovakia 1938–944] (Tel Aviv: Moreshet, 1992).

Friedlander, S., *Piux XII and the Third Reich, A Documentation* (New York: A. A. Knopf, 1966).

—— *When Memory Comes* (New York: Farrar, Straus and Giroux, 1979).

—— *Nazi Germany and the Jews* (New York: HarperCollins, 1997).

Fuchs, A., *The Unheeded Cry: the Gripping Story of Rabbi Weismandl* (Brooklyn, NY: Messorah Publications, 1984)

Gerlach, C., *Kalkulierte Morde: Die deutsche Wirtschafts- und Vernichtungspolitik in Weissrussland 1941 bis 1944* (Hamburg: Hamburger Edition, 1999).

Greenspan, H., *On Listening to Holocaust Survivors: Recounting and Life History* (Westport, CT: Praeger, 1998).

Grenville, J. A. S., *A History of the World in the Twentieth Century*, enlarged edn, (Cambridge, MA: The Belknap Press of Harvard University Press, 2000.

Gutman, I., *The Jews of Warsaw, 1939–1943: Ghetto, Underground, Revolt* (Bloomington: University of Indiana Press, 1982)

Herbert, U. (ed), *National Socialist Extermination Policies: Contemporary German Perspectives and Controversies* (New York: Berghahn Books, 2000).

Hilberg, R., *The Destruction of the European Jews,* revised and definitive edn (New York: Holmes and Meier, 1985).

Howard M. and W. R. Louis (eds), *The Oxford History of the Twentieth Century* Oxford: Oxford University Press, 1998).

Huberband, S., *Kiddush Hashem: Jewish Religious and Cultural Life in Poland During the Holocaust* (Hoboken, NJ: Ktav, 1987).

Hupchick D. P. and H. E. Cox, *A Concise Historical Atlas of Eastern Europe* (New York: St. Martin's Press, 1996).

Kaplan, M., *Between Dignity and Despair: Jewish Life in Nazi Germany* (New York: Oxford University Press, 1998).

Katz, S., *Post-Holocaust Dialogues: Critical Studies in Modern Jewish Thought* (New York: New York University Press, 1985).

Kershaw, I., *Hitler, 1889–1936: Hubris* (London: Allen Lane, 1998).

—— *Hitler, 1936–1945, Nemesis* (London: Allen Lane, 2000).

Kertzer, D. I., *The Popes Against the Jews: The Vatican's Role in the Rise of Modern Anti-Semitism* (New York: Knopf, 2001).

Kushner, T., *The Holocaust and the Liberal Imagination: A Social and Cultural History* (Oxford: Blackwell, 1994)

Langer, L., *The Holocaust and the Literary Imagination* (New Haven, CT: Yale University Press, 1975).

—— *Versions of Survival, The Holocaust and the Human Spirit* (Albany: State University of New York Press, 1982).

—— *Preempting the Holocaust* (New Haven, CT: Yale University Press, 1998).

—— *Holocaust Testimonies: The Ruins of Memory* (New Haven, CT: Yale University Press, 1991).

Levi, P., *Survival in Auschwitz: The Nazi Assault on Humanity* (New York: Collier Books, 1971).

Levin, D., *Fighting Back: Lithuanian Jewry's Armed Resistance to the Nazis* (New York: Holmes and Meier, 1985).

—— *Baltic Jews under the Soviets, 1940–1946* (Jerusalem: The Hebrew University, 1994).

Lozowick, Y., *Hitler's Evil Bureaucrats: The Nazi Security Police and the Banality of Evil* (London: Continuum, 2002)

Marrus M. and R. Paxton, *Vichy France and the Jews* (New York: Basic Books, 1981).

Matzner, D., *The Muselmann: The Diary of a Jewish Slave Laborer* (Hoboken, NJ: KTAV, 1994.

Morley, J., *Vatican Diplomacy and the Jews During the Holocaust, 1939–1943* (New York: Ktav, 1980).

Morse, A. *While Six Million Died: A Chronicle of American Apathy* (New

York: Random House, 1968).

Muhlfelder, L., *Because I Survived, An Autobiography* (Rockville, MD: Shengold, 2000).

Overy, R., *The Penguin Historical Atlas of the Third Reich* (London: Penguin Books, 1996).

Patterson, D. *Sun Turned to Darkness: Memory and Recovery in the Holocaust Memoir* (Syracuse, NY: Syracuse University Press, 1998).

Perel, S., *Europa, Europa* (New York : John Wiley, 1997).

Peukert, D., *Inside Nazi Germany: Conformity, Opposition and Racism in Everyday Life* (New Haven, CT: Yale University Press, 1987).

Phayer, M., *The Catholic Church and the Holocaust, 1930–1965* (Bloomington: University of Indiana Press, 2000).

Poliakov, L., *Harvest of Hate* (London: Best Seller Library, 1954).

Polonsky, A. (ed.) *A Cup of Tears: A Diary of the Warsaw Ghetto by Abraham Lewin*, (Oxford: Basil Blackwell, 1989).

Ponting, C., *The Twentieth Century: A World History* (New York: Henry Holt, 1998).

Poznanski, R., *Jews in France During World War II* (Hanover, NH: Brandeis University Press, 2001).

Roberts, J. M., *Twentieth Century, The History of the World, 1901 to 2000* (London: Penguin, 1999).

Roseman, M., *A Past in Hiding: Memory and Survival in Nazi Germany* (New York: Metropolitan Books, 2001).

Rosenfeld, A. *A Double Dying: Reflections on Holocaust Literature* (Bloomington: Indiana University Press, 1980).

Roskies, D., *Against the Apocalypse, Responses to Catastrophe in Modern Jewish Culture* (Cambridge, MA: Harvard University Press, 1984).

Rubenstein, R., *After Auschwitz, Radical Theology and Contemporary Judaism* (New York: Bobbs-Merril, 1966).

Schweid, E., *Wrestling Until Day-break: Searching for Meaning in the Thinking of the Holocaust* (Lanham, MD: University Press of America, 1994).

Shapiro, R. M. (ed.), *Holocaust Chronicles: Individualizing the Holocaust through Diaries and Other Contemporaneous Personal Accounts* (Hoboken, NJ: Ktav, 1996).

Sofsky, W., *The Order of Terror: The Concentration Camp* (Princeton, NJ: Princeton University Press, 1997).

Starkopf, A., *Will to Live: One Family's Story of Surviving the Holocaust* (Albany: State University of New York Press, 1995).

The Times Atlas of European History (London: Times Books, 1994).

Trunk, I., *Judenrat: The Jewish Councils in Eastern Europe Under Nazi Occupation* (New York: Macmillan, 1972).

United States Holocaust Memorial Museum, *Historical Atlas of the Holocaust* (New York: Macmillan, 1996).

Werber, J., *Saving Children: Diary of a Buchenwald Survivor and Rescuer* (New Brunswick, NJ: Transaction Books, 1996).

Wiesel, E., *Night* (New York: Hill and Wang, 1960).

—— *All Rivers Run to the Sea: Memoirs* (New York: Knopf, 1995).

Wistrich, R., *Hitler and the Holocaust* (New York: Modern Library, 2001).

Wygoda, H., *In the Shadow of the Swastika* (Urbana: University of Illinois Press, 1998).

Wyman, D., *The Abandonment of the Jews: America and the Holocaust* (New York: Pantheon Books, 1984).

Wyszogrod, M., *A Brush With Death: An Artist in the Death Camps* (Albany: State University of New York Press, 1999).

Yahil, L., *The Holocaust: The Fate of European Jewry, 1932–1945* (New York: Oxford University Press, 1990).

Young, J., *Writing and Re-Writing the Holocaust: Narrative and the Consequences of Interpretation* (Bloomington: Indiana University Press, 1990).

—— *The Texture of Memory: Holocaust Memorials and Their Meaning* (New Haven, CT: Yale University Press, 1993).

Zuccotti, S., *Under His Very Windows: The Vatican and the Holocaust in Italy* (New Haven, CT: Yale University Press, 2000).

Zuckerman, Y., *A Surplus of Memory: Chronicle of the Warsaw Ghetto Uprising* (Berkeley: University of California Press, 1993).

Index

Agha, Yusef, 131
Aharonson, Y. M., 103
AIPAC (American Israel Public Affairs Committee), 135
Aktion Reinhard, 76, 163
Al-Maeena, Tariq A., 129
Alam, M. Shahid, 128
Aleksandrow, 162–7
Allied responses to the Holocaust, 16, 20, 140, 143
Alter, Avraham Mordechai, 164
Alter, Moshe Bezalel, 161, 163–4, 166–7
Alter, Yehuda Leib, 164
Amalek, 152
American diplomacy, 134
American Jewish Congress, 24
American Jewish Joint Distribution Committee, 24, 78
Ancel, Jan, 120
Anielewicz, Mordechai, 34, 71
anti-Americanism, 150, 152
anti-globalization, *see* globalization
antisemitism, 16, 20, 35, 39, 43, 51, 105, 142, 144, 147; Arab and Muslim, 126–31, 137–41, 146, 151, 153–4; Catholic, 141; criticism of Israel as, 148–9; Italy, 142; using Holocaust imagery, 125–37, 146; using Holocaust imagery, China, 131; using Holocaust imagery: Ariel Sharon equated to Hitler, 128–30, 133, 150
Arab News, 129-31, 134, 136–7
Arad, Yitzhak, 19
Arendt, Hannah, 21
Arras, Christian, 115–16
Arrow Cross, 90
aryanization, 52
Ascher, Avraham, 72
Association of Belgian Jews, 77
Auerswald, Heinz, 81, 163
Auschwitz, 36, 41–2, 65, 87, 95, 110–11, 115–18, 129, 137–8, 166

Austria, 90

Bacharach, Yair Chaim, 159
Baeck, Leo, 79–80
Baker, William, 145
Banat, 60
Bankier, David, 15
Barcelona, 150
Barguti, Marwan, 146
Barnavi, Eli, 58, 63–5
Bauer, Yehuda, 19, 87
BBC, 110–11
Bedzin-Sosnowiec, 89
Belzec, 53, 116
Ben Gurion, David, 34
Benz, Wolfgang, 43
Bergen Belsen, 120, 138, 142
Berkovits, Eliezer, 26, 37
Bethlehem, 141, 145, 148
Bettelheim, Bruno, 25
Bin Laden, Osama, 153
Bingel, Erwin, 53
Born, Friedrich, 24
Bornstein, Aharon, 162
Bornstein, Avraham, 161, 164, 166
Bornstein, David, 160–4, 166
Bornstein, Sarah, 162
Bornstein, Shmuel, 162
Braham, Randolph, 19
Brandeis, Louis, 34
Browning, Christopher, 13–14, 84
Brzecz, 113
Buchenwald, 117, 120, 142
Bulliet, Richard W., 32–4, 36, 52
Burleigh, Michael, 15
Burzio, Giuseppe, 85
Bush, George W., 130

Caplan, Betty, 136
Caruba, Alan, 126
Cesarani, David, 46

Chelmno, 66
Cholavski, Shalom, 19
CNSNews.com, 126, 128
Cohen, Arthur, 26, 37
Cohen, David, 72
Cohen, Richard, 148
Cold War, 35–6, 43
colonialization, 56n53, 154
comic books, 36
Commentary, 149
Commissariat Général aux Questions Juives, 75
communism, 51, 154
Corriere della Sera, 142
Cox, Harold E., 58, 60–3, 66
Crampton, Ben, 58, 62–3
Crampton, Richard, 58, 6–3
Croatia, 60
Czerniakow, Adam, 34, 80–3, 163, 168
Czortkow, 53

Dachau, 25, 114, 129, 142
Daily Star, 127
Daily Telegraph, 137
Danziger, Menahem, 164, 166
Danziger, Yaacov Bunam, 162
Danziger, Yerachamiel Yisrael Yosef, 165
Dawidowicz, Lucy, 17
Dawn, 128
de Sousa Mendes, Arista, 141
death's head *see Totenkopf*
DEBKAfile, 139
defending Israel: Holocaust imagery, 137–54;
    Holocaust imagery, Palestinians equated to
    Nazis, 137–9; Holocaust imagery, Yasser
    Arafat equated to Hitler, 137–8, 143, 146
dehumanization of Jews, 96–7
Deir Yassin, 131–2
denazification, 154
Denmark, Jews, Rescue of, 20, 49
Desberg, Yehudit, 143–4
diaries, 18, 93, 101, 108–10, 121, 163, 168
Drancy, 116
Drogobych ghetto, 77
Dublin, 149
Dubnow, Simon, 51
Dvinsk (Duenaburg), 67

Edelheit, Hershel, 24
Eichmann, Adolf, 21–2, 71, 76, 86, 145
Eicke, Theodore, 97
Einsatzgruppen, 4–5, 41, 53, 63-5
El-Affendi, Abdelwahab, 127
Elenbogen, Marianne *née* Strauss, 103–4,
    107, 110–11, 114–16, 118
Elliot, Mark, 144
Engel, David, 107–8, 110
Essen, 115
ethnic cleansing, 35
Europa Plan, 86

Euthanasia Progamme, 3
extermination camps, 36, 53, 63, 66, 123n83,
    142; *see also* individual camps

Fackenheim, Emile, 26, 37, 94, 96–97, 111;
    614th commandment, 94
Fallaci, Oriana, 142
Farbstein, Esther, 103
fascism, 38, 154
Fastag factory, 163–4
Fatani, Afnan Hussein, 130–1
Faurisson, Robert, 126
Fein, Helen, 25
Fields, Suzanna, 137–38, 142
Final Solution and development of, 2, 4, 40–1;
    42, 48–9, 52–3, 84, 90, 96, 109, 153;
    Belorussia, 39, 76–7; explanations for, 38–9,
    44–6, 51–2; Germany, 72, 79; Hitler's role,
    53; Hungary, 73–4, 76, 88–9; Jewish per
    ceptions of, 82, 84, 88–9, 101, 107–10;
    Poland, 73, 80–1; Slovakia, 73, 88; Soviet
    Union, 73
Fine, Leonard, 152
Fisk, Robert, 131–2
Fleischmann, Gisi, 78, 84, 87
forced labour, 52, 73, 81
France: Italian zone of occupation, 75;
    southern zone, 75; Vichy, 75–6
Frank, Anne, 34, 106, 131
Frank, Hans, 76, 81
Frei, Norbert, 15
Frieder, Armin, 84
Friedlander, Henry, 15
Frielander, Saul, 17–18, 24
Friesel, Evyatar, 64–5
Fromer, Arie Zvi, 162, 164, 167

Garudy, Roger, 126
Generalgouvernement, 76, 81, 163 ; *see also*
    Poland
Generalplan Ost, 2
genocide, 35–6, 38, 50–1, 129, 136, 146, 150;
    Armenians, 51; Rwanda, 51
Gens, Jacob, 82–4
Géraud, François, 147
Gerlach, Christian, 39
Germany, deportations from, 110
Gestapo, 79, 114, 116, 119, 165
ghettos, 73
Gilbert, Martin, 24, 67
Ginat, Gonen, 141
globalization, 150, 152, 154
Globocnic, Odilo, 76, 163
Goldberg, Jonah, 138
Goldhagen, Daniel Jonah, 15, 20, 46
Goldstein, Richard, 152
Greenspan, Henry, 97–9, 101, 104, 121
Grenville, J. A. S., 36, 46–50
Grunwald, Malchiel, 71

Guardian, 132
Gur, 164
Gutman, Israel, 15, 19
gypsies, *see* Romanies

Haffner, Sebastian, 15
Hahn, Lili, 116
Hamas, 138
Hamodia, 147
Handel, Avraham, 165
Hanson, Victor Davis, 144–5
Hashem Mi-Shmuel, 162
Hatsofe, 141, 143
Hebrew Committee for National Liberation, 24
Hecht, Ben, 21, 29n39
Heichler, Lucien, 134–5
Heller, Fanya Gottesfeld, 106–7, 118–20
Hentoff, Nat, 151
Herzl, Theodore, 34
Heydrich, Reinhard, 76
Hilberg, Raul, 13, 19, 71
Himmler, Heinrich, 73, 87
historical atlases, 23–24
Hoefle, Hermann, 163
Holocaust: imagery *see* antsemitism:
Holocaust imagery and defending Israel:
   Holocaust imagery; and Zionism, 37;
   Christian responses to, 37; definition of,
   1–8; denial of, 127; European responsibility
   for, 141–2, 144, 147–9, 151, 155; impact on
   society, 154–5; literature of, 26, 29n57;
   Palestinian analogies to, *see* Holocaust:
   uniqueness of; psychological studies of
   25; relative place in popular histories of
   the twentieth century, 34–6, 66; sociological
   studies of, 25; survivors, 134; survivors,
   children of, 134–5; theological and philosophical responses to, 25, 29n56, 37;
   uniqueness of, 45–6, 51–2, 136, 145; victim
   of, 5–7, 47, 62; victim of, statistics, 1, 43,
Hungary and Romania, 64, 66–7, 74
Horthy, Miklos, 89–90
Howard, Michael, 33, 36, 39–41
Hungary: deportations from, 89–90; Jews, 14;
   labor service, 6–7, 73; maps of, 62; *see also*
   Jewish response: Hungary; Rescue of Jews:
   Hungary
Hupchick, Dennis P., 58, 60–3, 66
Hussein, Saddam, 145
Huttenbach, Henry, 97

illegal immigration, 41
Independent, 131
International Red Cross, 24, 89
Israeli–Palestinian conflict, 9, 31, 125–55
Izbica, 104, 115–16

Jabotinsky, Vladimir, 34

Jehovah's Witnesses, 1, 3
Jenin, 129, 135, 145
Jerusalem Post, 140
Jewish Agency, 78
Jewish Defense League, 135
Jewish leadership: images of, 71–2
Jewish police, 83
Jewish response, 41, 50, 52
Jewish response: Germany, 49–50, 52, 66, 79,
   103–4, 114–16; Hungary, 88–90; power
   lessness, 88, 90; passivity, 21, 140; personal
   decision making, 111–18; Poland, flight to
   Soviet territory, 112–14; religious obser-
   vance, 105–106, 120; Slovakia, 84-8; Vilna,
   82–4
Jihadism, 154
Johnson, Jeff, 128
Joodse Raad, 72
Judenrat (Jewish council), 72, 77; *see also*
   Association of Belgian Jews, Joodse Raad,
   Union Générale des Israélites de France,
   Ustredna Zidov, Zsido Tanacs
Judenrat: Vilna, 82-4

Kahan and Heller shop, 163–4
Kalisz-Pawianicz, 164
Kaments Poldosk, 73
Karabell, Zachary, 37
Kasztner, Reszo (Israel), 22, 28n38, 71–2, 78,
   88, 90; train, 120
Katz, Steven, 26
Kavala, 170
Kershaw, Ian, 15
Kertzer, David I., 146
Kindertransports, 114
Koenigsberg, Joseph, 163
Komoly, Otto, 78, 89–90
Konin, 103
Kossow, 112
Kovner, Abba, 34, 82, 84
Kozieglowy, 162, 164
Kraus, Ota, 138
Krauthammer, Charles, 149
Kristallnacht, 5–6, 10n12, 43, 49, 52, 66, 79–80,
   114, 152
Krombach, Ernst, 104, 115–16
Kromolow, 164, 166
Kube, Wilhelm, 76–7
Kuka, Erich, 138
Kushner, Tony, 16
Kutno, 161-7

La Guardia, Anton, 137
La Stampa, 148
Langer, Lawrence, 26, 95, 99–100, 106
Laor, Yitzhak, 135–6
Le Benet, 116
Le Nouvel Observateur, 147
Levi, Primo, 18, 24

Levin, Dov, 19
Levin, Nora, 17
Lewin, Abraham, 165, 168
Lewis, Bernard, 126
Lichtenbaum, Manek, 81
Lifton, Robert Jay, 25
Lodz ghetto, 52, 77, 100, 106, 108–10, 112,
    115–16, 162
London Review of Books, 135
London, Yaron, 146
Louis, W. Roger, 33, 36, 39–40
Lozowick, Yaacov, 21, 169
Lublin, 41, 163
Lutz, Charles, 23, 89
Lwow ghetto, 77

Maariv, 134, 141
Madagascar, 49
Mahmoud, Fatma Abdallah, 126–7
Majdanek, 41, 166
Martin, J. Paul, 37
Matzner, David, 116, 118, 120
Mauthausen, 142
Mautner, Menahem, 169
Mayall, James, 38
Mazower, Mark, 43
Mein Kampf, 42, 139
memoirs, 11, 18, 93–7, 101–5, 117, 121, 165
memorial books *see Yizkor* books
Mirsky, Yehuda, 154–5
Morse, Arthur, 16
Mosse, George, 20
Muselmanner, 96, 111, 118
Mussolini, Benito, 75

Nachman of Braslav, 97
National Committee for Rescue (Britain), 20
National Review Online, 138, 144
Nazi administration: Belgium, 74; France,
    75–6; Germany, 74; Netherlands, 74;
    Poland, 74
Nazi anti-Jewish policies, *see* Final Solution
Nazi ideology, development of, *see* Nazism
Nazism, 34–5, 37–8, 40, 43–8, 51, 65, 96–7, 119,
    127, 154
neo-Nazis, 150
Netanya, 152
Netanyahu, Benyamin, 137
Neumann, Oskar, 78, 84
New Republic, 151, 154
New York Observer, 150–1
New York Times, 146, 148
Nitra Yeshiva, 84
Niznansky, Eduard, 87
Novaky, 86
Nuremberg laws, 79, 136
Nuremberg trial, 15, 42

O'Connell, Robert, 38

Operation Defensive Shield, 125, 128–30
oral testimony, 13–14, 18, 54, 93, 98–102, 105,
    121, 134, 165, 168
Organization Todt, 107
Oswiecim *see* Auschwitz
Oszmiana, deportation from, 83
Otwock, 162, 164, 166
Overy, Richard, 58, 65—6

Pabiance, 110
Page of Testimony, 162, 166, 168, 170
Paknews.com, 129
Pale of Settlement, 63, 82
Paris, 150
Patai, Raphael, 14
Patterson, David, 94–8
Perl, Saloman, 107
Perlasca, George, 89
personal accounts *see* diaries, memoirs and
    oral testimony
Persson, Göran, 31
Pétain, Philippe, 75
Peukart, Detlev, 15
Piasnice, 164
Pilica, 167
Piux XII, Pope, 85
place names, spelling of, 61
Plotzger, Sever, 149
Pohl, Dieter, 4
Poland, 48; represented in atlases, 58, 62, 65,
    68
Polesia, 57, 65, 67
Poliakov, Leon, 15, 17 Pollack, Zonka, 53
Ponting, Clive, 33–4, 36, 50–4, 55n6, 56n53
Pripet Marshes, 57
prisoners of war, Soviet, 1, 6
Protocols of the Elders of Zion, 139, 156n3
Prywes, Moshe, 105

Rabinowicz, Nahum Hacohen, 164, 166
racism, 37–8, 47, 51, 65; eugenics, 51
Radom, 103, 105, 112
Rahman, Hasan Abdel, 128
Ramallah, 129
Rapke, Jeremy, 140
Rassinier, Paul, 126
reference works, problems in, 22–5
Reich, Walter, 143
Reichsvereinigung *see* Reichsvertretung der
    Deutschen Juden
Reichsvertretung der Deutschen Juden, 76,
    79–80
Reinhart, Tanya, 135
Reitlinger, Gerald, 17
Relief and Rescue Committee, Budapest, 22,
    29n40, 71, 78
Rescue of Jews, 20, 49, 53, 140–1; Hungary,
    2–3, 53, 64, 78, 88–0, 120; Romania, 120;
    Slovakia, 78, 84–8

Rich, Norman, 42
Righteous Among the Nations, 49, 140–1
Roberts, J. M., 32, 36, 42–6
Romanies (Gypsies), 1–2, 40, 48, 62, 67
Roosevelt, Franklin D., 16
Roseman, Mark, 103–4, 111, 114, 121
Rosen, Jonathan, 153–5
Rosenbaum, Ron, 151–2
Rosenfeld, Alvin, 26
Roskies, David, 26
Rotta, Angelo, 23
Rovno ghetto, 77
Rubenstein, Richard, 26, 37
Rubenstein, William, 20
Ruck, Michael, 15

Sabra and Shatila massacre, 129
Sadowne, 107, 120
Safran, Alexandre, 120
Salonika, 150
San Francisco Chronicle, 151
Saramago, José, 129, 146
Schoenfeld, Gabriel, 149–50, 155
Schultz shoe shop, 163–7
Schweid, Eliezer, 26
SD, 118
Second World War, 3, 4, 11, 17, 34, 42–3, 50–1,
    145; maps of, 60, 62–3
Seidman, Hillel, 163
September 11, 2001, 153–4
Sered, 86
sexual abuse of Jewish women by Germans,
    119–20
Shamir, Israel, 136–7
Shanghai, 103
Shapiro, Kolonymous Kalmish, 164, 166
Shappel, Nathan, 96
Sharon, Ariel, 140, 147–8; *see also* antisemitism:
    using Holocaust imagery: Ariel Sharon,
    equated to Hitler
Shirer, William, 15
Sierakowiak, David (diary of), 100, 106,
    108–10, 112
Six Day War, 126
Skala, 106, 119
Slavs, 1, 2, 48, 62
Slovakia: national uprising, 75, 86–7; depor
    tations from, 84–5, 87–8
soap made from Jewish fat, myth, 97, 120
Sobibor, 116
Sochaczew, 160–7
Sofsky, Wolfgang, 25
Soloveitchik, Joseph, 37
Sosnowiec, 167
South Africa: apartheid, 37, 133
Soviet Union: German occupation of, 60
Speer, Albert, 28n30, 39
SS, 4, 74, 76–7, 89, 107, 118, 120, 163
St Louis Post-Dispatch, 149

Stalingrad, 145
Starkopf, Adam, 107, 113–14, 119
Starkopf, Pela, 107
Stein, André, 111
Steyn, Mark, 144
Strauss, Richard, 114
Strauss, Siegfried, 114
Stroop report, 134
Strykow, 162, 164, 167
Sun Times, 144
Sunday Nation, 133
survivors, 19, 44, 98–101
Switzerland, 120; dormant bank accounts, 31
Szalasi, Ferenc, 90
Szenes, Hannah, 34

T4 see Euthanasia Programme
Tamir, Shmuel, 22
Tec, Nechama, 101, 104, 107, 120–1
Teitelbaum, Joel (Satmar Rebbe), 120–1
Tenenbaum, Yitzhak Matatyahu, 147
The Age, 140
The Forward, 152
The Iranian, 145
The Village Voice, 152
Theresienstadt, 87, 110–11, 116
Third Reich, 35, 137
Time, 144
Tiso, Jozef, 75, 85, 87
Tomaszow Mazowiecki, 162
Totenkopf, 163
Treblinka, 107, 115–16, 120, 134, 165–7
Trieste, 76
Trunk, Isaiah, 72
Trunk, Yitzhak Yehuda, 162
Tuczyn ghetto, 57, 65, 77-8
Tutu, Desmond, 132–133, 137
Tuzla, 149

Uman, 53
Unger, Shmuel David Halevi, 84
Union Générale des Israélites de France (UGIF),
    75
United Nations (UN), 129
Unites States Holocaust Memorial Museum,
    58, 66–6, 8, 143
University of Tel Aviv Law Library, 159, 169
Ustredna Zidov, 76, 78

Vatican, 87
Vhyne, 86
Vienna, 76
Vilna (Vilnius) ghetto, 51, 82–4, 103, 109;
    underground and uprising, 83–4
Volhynia, 57, 65, 67

WAFA, 130
Wallenberg, Raoul, 23–4, 64, 89
Wansee Conference, 67

War Refugee Board, 16
Warsaw ghetto, 4–6, 15, 68, 78, 80–2, 90, 105, 107–8, 113–14, 134, 162–7, 170; Jews, 102, 113; *Judenrat*, 78, 80–2; uprising, 50, 66–7, 89, 134, 166
Washington Post, 148
Washington Times, 137, 142
Weinberg, Avraham, 162, 164, 167
Weinberg, Gerhard, 42
Weismandl, Ber (Dov), 84, 86–8
Weismann, Chaim, 34
Weitz, Yehiam, 72
Werber, Jack, 102–3, 105, 112, 117–18, 120
Wiesel, Eli, 18, 101
Wieseltier, Leon, 151–3, 155
Wiesenthal, Simon, 111
Wilkomirski, Binjamin, 120
Will, George F., 151
Wise, Tim, 148
Wisliceny, Dieter, 73, 86–8
Wisse, Ruth, 121
Wistrich, Robert, 16, 24, 126
WIZO (Women's Zionist Organization), 84
Wolfsburg, 120
Working Group, 78, 84–8
Wygoda, Herman, 102, 107, 111–12

Wyman, David, 16
Wyszogrod, 162
Wyszogrod, Morris, 105–6, 112

Yad Vashem, 8, 13, 93, 120, 131, 134, 140, 159, 170
Yad Vashem: Archives, 13, 22, 169
Yad Vashem: Library, 11, 13, 49, 121n2n3
Yahil, Leni, 17
Yediot Archronot, 146–7, 149
Yishivat Chochmai Lublin, 167
Yizkor books, 19, 161
Yom Hashoah (Holocaust Remembrance Day), 125, 131, 137
Young, James, 26

Zartal, Idith, 63–4
Zawierce, 166
Zemin, Jiang, 131
Ziemba, Menahem, 164, 166–7
Zionist Youth: Hungary, 88–9; Slovakia, 85
ZNET, 148
ZOB, 78
Zsido Tanacs, 76, 88
ZTOS, 78
Zuckerman, Yitzhak, 28n30